# A REPORTER LOOKS
# AT THE VATICAN

# A REPORTER LOOKS

*New York*

# AT THE VATICAN

## By Barrett McGurn

*COWARD-McCANN, INC.*

# Contents

# 1. A Pope Dies

Our "tipsters"—news sources jointly employed by the foreign correspondents in Rome—told us that the Holy Father was suffering from his peculiarly incongruous, almost humiliating ailment of hiccoughs. Yet Pope Pius XII had been seriously ill four times before. I decided not to "cover" the story. It seemed to me, as correspondent for one of the larger New York newspapers, that a slight routine sickness would not rate much space. If a really dangerous affliction showed itself I could then report it. With some of the others in the corps of thirty-odd American newspapermen permanently stationed in the Eternal City I flew North with the American Air Force on a one-day junket to report maneuvers by United States fighter planes based in an Alpine valley not far from Communism's Iron Curtain.

Those who stayed behind in Rome telegraphed the story of the Pope's condition. For a week the eighty-three-year-old leader of the world's 500,000,000 Roman Catholics had been hiccoughing again in a disturbing recurrence of an ailment which had tormented him four years earlier. Three days before, on October 1, 1958, Pope Pius had sat mute through a general audience. As hundreds of pilgrims, tourists—devout and curious—looked up to him for the speeches in six languages which had made his receptions one of Europe's wonders, the gaunt Bishop of Rome had merely moved his hand in the sign of the cross as he gave the blessing of the Apostle Peter.

That had been unusual indeed, but Pius had often experienced slight ill health before and had continued to carry the uniquely heavy burden of one acclaimed not only as the primate of Italy's

3

50,000,000 Roman Catholics, but also as patriarch of the whole West, and far more, as the very Vicar of Christ on earth—God's representative in the world.

One tipster at the Vatican, who often typed out bulletins on "slight indispositions" of the Pope, had it right on October 1st when he advised me and his score of other clients in the press club and in the diplomatic corps that "some alarm" was felt. But even he helped to kill his own story by adding cautiously, "There is no real sign of worry in the Vatican, however, for the pontifical physician is away in Brussels." Surely if anything were seriously wrong the Pope's private physician, Dr. Riccardo Galeazzi-Lisi, an eye specialist who had somehow won the Pope's confidence, would be back in Rome at the side of his august patient.

So it seemed to those of us who went off that Sunday morning to bounce through storm clouds in a small air-force plane to the Alps. But within four days of that journey and eight days of the tipster's sanguine note Pius XII was to die and a new epoch for the world's largest religion was to begin.

The signs of illness during the first four days of that fateful Roman October were so few that correspondents could feel justified in leaving the Holy Father's slight difficulty to him in his own private distress, to Dr. Galeazzi-Lisi's substitute, to the Pope's few aides at his Castel Gandolfo warm-weather residence on the hills outside Rome, and to the members of Pius XII's family whom he saw rarely. Within hours, however, every painful detail of a Pope's last illness, death and burial were to be part of the "file" of all of us as we chronicled for millions the story of how a twentieth-century pope dies as he lives—on stage.

Those of us who went North with the Air Force had to stay overnight in the Alps because of bad flying weather, but we were back in Rome at noon the next day.

"Have you sent much on the Pope?" a friend asked me at the foreign press club. It was something far worse than hiccoughs now. There was talk of a stroke. I radioed my office in New York—WILL SEND NINE HUNDRED WORDS ON POPE'S ILLNESS—and set to work to find out as much as I could about what had happened.

There is an old saying in Rome that "A pope is never ill until he's dead." The Vatican is taciturn on all news stories, but on the question of the Pope's health there is a special reticence. I knew that it would not be easy to get the full story, but I also realized that this time there was news that had to be covered and that whatever I learned would be worth using at length.

Formal relations between the Vatican and the press were almost nonexistent. There was a kind of Vatican press office, but it was not even called that; it was known as the press office of *L'Osservatore Romano*, the daily newspaper which is published in the Vatican but which has only "semiofficial" status. Its spokesman, Luciano Casimirri, was friendly and willing but often "uninformed," and the information we got from his office did not rank as official; it could always be denied by higher sources.

So we depended to a large extent on tipsters—Vatican hangers-on, some of them intimate with high-ranking members of the Church hierarchy, others Vatican employees who were in a position to hear rumors of an impending story. I recalled that during the fatal illness of Pius XI in 1939, Aldo Forte, the United Press correspondent, got the first flash of the Pope's death by persuading an old friend, the man in charge of the Vatican fire department, to let him back into the Vatican firehouse late at night after the doors were closed.

So I began calling friends, some of whom I had known for twenty years, priests in or near the Vatican; and gradually the anguishing account of a great pope's final agony was pieced together. Covering such a story is a climactic event in the work of a Vatican reporter; the way in which it was made known to the world tells so much of a human institution that has no parallel, and of the great and noble man who was Pius XII, that it is worth recording in detail.

For weeks before his illness, Pius XII had been working with mounting intensity. He had always astounded those who knew him by the concentration with which he applied himself from early morning until well after midnight every day, even Sundays, to his tasks as the teacher and director of the Roman Catholic one-fifth of the world; but the tempo lately had increased. His extraordinary speeches, each designed to highlight the latest technical advances in some field and to go on from there to point a moral, were getting longer and were being prepared weeks in advance.

"It was almost as if he felt death coming and tried to meet it by working harder," an aide of the Pope later remarked.

Cardinal Francis Spellman of New York, Pope Pius's closest American friend and one of the most intimate of his acquaintances, saw the Pope on October 3rd and thought he was "a little weak." Those in the Cardinal's confidence reported that he was far more concerned than his words indicated, and that he was also convinced that the Holy Father himself believed that a critical moment was at hand.

The Pope received a group of pilgrims who had accompanied Cardinal Spellman to Rome. He talked to them of "guardian angels," spirits given to each person to counsel and protect. He urged his visitors to "know them now" as a first step toward the "eternity of joy" in Heaven which is the Catholic expectation. This insistence on a doctrine taught to children and not often mentioned among adults was all the more striking addressed as it was to the many jeweled and fur-clad wealthy persons who had come to Rome with the New York Cardinal. They represented material success as no other recent visiting group had done. A spiritual word to those who have all that is material is always apt in the Vatican view, but somehow it seemed clear that in those hours the sophisticated modern mind of Pius XII was concentrating on the most elementary supernatural concepts of the Catholic otherworldly creed.

The men who run railroad news kiosks also had an audience. For them, too, the Pope had a well-prepared word. Their tiny stands, he told them, were eyes through which many looked on the world. Let it be a wholesome vision that their patrons received, the Pope appealed. By that, he said, he meant that they as Christians shared in the responsibility of writers, editors and publishers not to distribute material that would corrupt the morals of the buyers.

Others called. To one group the Pope read only the last third of what he had written. He looked tired, worn, hollow cheeked. He paused between sentences to hiccough.

"A pope is never ill until he is dead."

I drove to the Vatican to ask Luciano Casimirri what had happened. My friend's eyes were troubled. His instructions, I learned later, were to emphasize the positive. Doctors' bulletins were doing the same. Dr. Galeazzi-Lisi had returned from Belgium, and three specialists better able than he to diagnose and treat the Pope's condition were working with him.

"This morning the Pope suffered from dizziness, a blurring of vision and general illness," Casimirri told me. "He was still able to walk but he was carried to his bed. It isn't true that he was paralyzed. He said his Mass as usual in his private chapel. His footman, Paolo Stoppa, who is the only one with him at night at Castel Gandolfo, was at the Mass. The Pope went to his desk at 8:30 A.M. That's when it happened."

The Pope had suffered a stroke and sunk into a coma. He seemed dead. The doctors, too, however, had issued a bulletin phrased as consolingly as the truth would permit:

> The Holy Father had a tranquil night. The hiccoughs which bothered him for several days have stopped. This morning at 8:30 o'clock the Holy Father was struck by disturbances in the blood circulation of the brain. The progress of the situation is under study.

The language may not have been designed to confuse reporters. It was surely intended to combat alarm among the Pope's well-wishers around the earth. But as the next three days wore on the truth behind the taut words seeped out. Pius XII fought for life with vigor and calm; the vigor of a man who had never neglected methodical daily exercise; the calm of a priest whose conscience was clear and whose faith was strong. Consciousness came and went. Sometimes the dying pontiff was delirious. At one point he began the recitation of the Rosary, the series of prayers dedicated to the Virgin Mary. He fell unconscious during the prayers, regained himself, began again and a second time slipped off. In a lucid moment he asked to hear Beethoven's First Symphony and listened with pleasure. Classical music and the works of the ancient authors such as Cicero in Latin were among the few diversions the world's number one priest permitted himself. Within minutes after the music ended the second and eventually fatal stroke occurred.

Well into the forty-eight hours between the two strokes the dying Pope attempted to carry on with the work he considered his continual responsibility. He asked to be carried to his desk and said that he had speeches and audiences to which he had to attend. Assistants who had never dared to oppose the Pope's will refused him, insisting that everything could wait and that the doctors were adamant in demanding an interruption of the pontiff's efforts. In delirium the Pope started up and gave what seemed to be a speech at an audience. Those beside him heard his words change from Italian to French to English to German to Spanish to Portuguese as the Pope used the six languages which were the just pride of his pontificate; tongues whose command had made it possible for this Father of Catholics to talk to all but a small minority of his following directly in their own idioms.

A diplomat was allowed in to see the Pope briefly on the day between the two strokes.

"Why," the Pope asked him, "have the other audiences been suspended?"

He had lost all memory of the first dread day.

"They say he is a little better today," an eminent churchman told me, "but it is true only in the sense that yesterday he was almost dead."

"Humanly speaking," another said, "I think we're coming to the end. I see where the chief justice of the Japanese supreme court says that the Pope has got over illnesses that were just as bad. It isn't so. He never had a stroke before."

There is a "habit of looking for miracles" in the Church, but there was no other good reason for hope, another priest said candidly.

One friend of mine had a view of the honey-colored walls of the Vatican Palace.

"I see they're back at the Secretariate of State," he told me on the telephone. "The windows are open."

That too was significant. When the Pope went to Castel Gandolfo for the warmest four or five months of the year the key section of the Vatican, the Secretariate of State, closed down. No important decision could be taken in the Pope's absence, and the Vatican's general directorate marked time. But now the State Secretariate had resumed activity. That meant that major matters were being treated again. The business, it was clear, was that of warning the 50 cardinals and the 100 papal diplomats of the world that the Pope was critically ill. Governments in formal contact with the Church of the bulk of the world's Christians would want official knowledge. Cardinals, many of them very old and ill, would need to prepare for sudden trips to Rome to elect a successor for Peter.

In the days just before the first stroke when it was already apparent that Pius was dangerously feeble, the Vatican had rather pointedly made it known that applications for audiences were welcome. The Pope himself, dogged in his determination not to abate what he considered his duty, had wanted it that way, and the monsignors and simple priests on his staff had not felt strong enough to resist. Slowly, as the truth became plainer both to those beside the Pope's bed and to the rest of us outside, the attitude changed. There was still some brave show of confidence as I drove into the medieval village square of Castel Gandolfo to doze through the night of October 6th to 7th behind the wheel of my car. The heavy wooden doors of the pontiff's residence were closed as they always were at night, while life inside the villa was going on as usual. At 6 A.M. when they reopened, those within said that there was no news as far as they knew; the Pope was still recovering from his stroke of the morning before. Photographers and television cameramen who had mounted guard all night beside their lamps and tangled wires washed up and shaved at the Renaissance fountain in the square.

Next night I slept at home, taking a call every two or three hours from a "stringer," an assistant reporter, at the Vatican press office. There were rumors that the Pope was dead but the

Vatican spokesman kept insisting from dusk to dawn that there was nothing to add, the reporter on watch told me at intervals. I telephoned a brief insert to the recording machine at my paper's relay station in Paris and went back to sleep. If the Pope were indeed dying I would have to have some rest in order to handle the big story when it came. Not everyone reasoned that way. One reporter told me he had not slept for the whole seventy-two final hours of Pope Pius XII's agony.

Vatican Radio, the official mouthpiece of the Holy See during the crisis, had begun by emphasizing the cheerful and optimistic, just as Casimirri and the doctors had. It put great emphasis on the end of the hiccoughing and on the repose the Pope sometimes had at night. Then for a day or so the Vatican broadcasts had become dry indeed. There was little information and even less opinion on what the medical announcements meant. With the second stroke, Father Francesco Pellegrino, a short dark Italian Jesuit, director of the Vatican news broadcasts, took a new line. Artificially sustained hope was over. From then on Catholics of the world were prepared for the thought that another pontificate in a chain of more than 250 going back to the birth of the Christian era was nearing its end. An hour after the second stroke, as the Pope lay again in coma, Father Pellegrino gently broke the news in a broadcast. There was "a new factor," he said. The doctors were now "most reserved" in their predictions. The "gravity" of the Pope's condition could not be hidden. The reason for the announcement was "not to cause excessive alarm" but also not to "feed excessive hope." Within two hours four Rome newspapers published special editions, some of them with front pages bordered in black, announcing falsely that the Pope was dead. The Vatican daily newspaper *L'Osservatore Romano* reprimanded them for slipshod journalism a few hours later. The story spread that one of the Vatican tipsters had arranged a signal, the opening of a certain window, as the sign that the Pope had died. The window had been thrust open, not by the functionary who was to be rewarded for the news but by another who wanted to let air into the overheated rooms. A news agency flashed the mistaken bulletin, and papers were on sale with it in central

Rome within ten minutes. I had no sympathy for such a blunder in a situation that called for prayerful respect, but I did understand the anguish of editors faced with the need to get the facts through the screen of vague words such as those of Father Pellegrino.

The fiasco of the false announcement was the last important error in the reporting of this grim drama. At 11 o'clock on the morning of the third day of the Pope's torment the Vatican announced the second 8:30 A.M. stroke. At 11:15 A.M. Vatican Radio began playing music of a slow and mournful type. At noon Father Pellegrino announced that the pontiff had been unconscious most of the morning, "perhaps due to the drugs he has received." He added significantly that the Pope's sister, in a room near the stricken pontiff, showed "perfect resignation to the will of God."

From then on it was merely a question of newspaper readers, radio listeners and television watchers waiting while Pius XII, in the words of Antonio Gasbarrini, the chief physician at his bedside, "burned out every wisp of vitality." Decades of daily hourlong walks had given the once-ailing young Eugene Pacelli, Pius XII, a sturdy heart and fiber. As the Pope struggled and sank, the Vatican Radio switched from its early false optimism and reticence to painfully explicit detail. Hour by hour Father Pellegrino reported the rising temperature, the struggling heartbeat, the fevered pulse, the increasingly noisy difficulty with breathing, the significant acidity of the dying pontiff's breath.

The Pope's condition was "grave" but there was still "a ray of hope," the Jesuit reported at 1:30 P.M. October 8th. "The feeble hopes are not increasing," the priest said at 3:55 P.M. "The weak hopes are almost entirely gone," he added at 5:30 P.M. The alert and enterprising manner the doctors had shown until then had given way to "a resigned and calm trepidation," Father Pellegrino told his radio audience and the world at 7:30 P.M.

By late evening the priest went further: "It can now be said with certainty that the prognosis is fatal." Lungs, heart, bladder —all were involved. The Pope burned with a fever of 106 degrees. Pilgrims in the murk of the Castel Gandolfo square watched the blank windows of the papal residence and prayed the Rosary. With others I waited in the foreign press club, following the news ticker which would carry the flash. A long-distance operator was with us, ready to get our distant newspaper offices.

As midnight passed, Monsignor Domenico Tardini, the Pope's acting secretary of state, his chief assistant, celebrated a mass for the dying in the room beside the pontiff. The Monsignor sobbed, we were told, as he consecrated the host.

For the next two hours Vatican Radio broadcast nothing but doleful music. At 4 A.M. we had the flash. The nineteen-year reign of Pius XII was over. The man who had heard millions raise the cry of "Long live the Pope" was dead.

# 2. A Pope Interred

Christ's Vicar had expired as he had lived, in view of the world. Early inept efforts to give him the privacy which seems the right of every dying man had been replaced by a fullness of publication that few events in history have ever received. This was partly the result of the peculiarly intrusive quality of journalism in the era of instant telegraphic and radio hookups and of television. Part of it, though, was due to the unique character of the Papacy; that most ancient of human institutions, adorned or encumbered—whichever you choose—by traditions that go back to the tumult of the Middle Ages and beyond. It was important, in other days, that there be no doubt when the Father of Christendom died and a successor was called to replace him. Full, even pitiless, publicity was required. Now in another era when the intrigues of a thousand years before seemed no longer credible, safeguards against chicanery lingered on in rigid new formulas. If a Pope died the cardinals had to make sure of it personally, and as the Pope was placed in his coffin and immured in his tomb official witnesses had to look on. The screen which is pulled around the deathbed of others was to be held wide ajar for the world to see—in print in our dispatches, in photographs (some of them smuggled more or less scrupulously from the pontiff's very bedside) and in television. The spectacle was so ghoulish that some of the press reacted. A Rome newspaper published a cartoon of a dying man's request. "No television!" the man begged.

It was shocking, but more was to come. In the most bizarre episode of all, Dr. Galeazzi-Lisi offered candid pictures he had snapped of the dying Pope and clinical details so gruesomely frank that the Italian editor who acquired them suppressed a part. The reaction was swift. The College of Cardinals, which had taken over as the supreme authority of the Catholic Church, dropped the doctor as the Vatican's physician and the medical profession of Rome took action to expel him.

There was a moment's revulsion but soon the penetrating publicity resumed. From the first hours after the original stroke the papal bedchamber had been busy with the more or less obtrusive coming and going of dignitaries. There was an occasional diplomat. There were many Italian Government officials. Most important there was the Dean of the College of Cardinals, seventy-four-year-old full-bearded Eugene Tisserant, a former French staff officer in the Middle East during World War I. If the ailment proved fatal it was he who was to say the old words in Latin meaning "He is dead."

As officials came and went, one detail caught some eyes. The bed toward which the gaze of so many governments and peoples was turned was of cheap brass, its poverty emphasized by the electric cords twisted at the head of it. As Pius XII had once told officers of the American Catholic Veterans' Association who had recounted their lack of official expense accounts and salaries, "If it's Catholic, it's poor."

In the moments just before dawn on October 9, 1958, when Pius died, it was Cardinal Alfredo Ottaviani, Acting Director of the Holy Office, the heir of the ill-remembered Inquisition, the guardian of the Catholic faith, who took the cardinals' first note of the Pope's passing. In an indication of the change that works slowly in what the Vatican considers unessentials, the cardinal looked on as a doctor placed a stethoscope over the dead man's heart and then listened through it himself. The extraordinary custom of certifying death by tapping the Pope's forehead with a silver hammer and calling him by his Christian name was abandoned.

Outside in the village plaza the atmosphere changed. In place of the churchlike mood of prayerful anguish there was now a

strange, rather harder one of expectation, deprivation and un-
reality; a far less personal and humane state of mind. The Holy
Father was gone. By common Catholic belief, the dead pontiff's
soul was in Heaven, for surely Pius's virtues—in the general view
—had been heroic. Soon there would be another pope. There
would be changes, shifts of Church officials, and perhaps even
of secondary policies. Enough of the memory of the central
Italian temporal kingdom of the popes lingered among the
Castel Gandolfo's villagers to make them wonder what the succession in the Papacy would mean for them. In the confusion
of emotions the villagers read a proclamation by their young
mayor, a Catholic physician, asking them to go in a body to pay
respects to Pius's remains. By late afternoon a crowd of 5,000
surged in a suffocating crush at the still-closed main entrance of
the pontiff's residence.

All of them wanted to see the dead prelate, the man whose
blessings in the residence courtyard had so often been sought
during his life. How much was piety, how much was the Roman
taste for spectacle that moved them, few could probably judge
inside their own mixed feelings. For almost all it was surely some
of each.

The black-cassocked village pastor, Monsignor Dino Sella,
talked to us about the great priest's passing. He wondered what
would become of Mother Pasqualina (the former Josephine
Lehnert), the sixty-three-year-old Bavarian nun who had kept
house for Pius XII for forty-one years—from the time when he
was a papal diplomat in Germany during World War I. In recent
years three other nuns had helped Mother Pasqualina. The Pope's
six pet birds, including a goldfinch Gretel, were something else
over which Monsignor Sella puzzled.

Mother Pasqualina might stay as supervisor of the new Pope's
kitchen and household, but "they generally change their staffs,"
the veteran of several pontificates told us. And as for the birds,
they would certainly be "a gift to somebody." As it turned out,
the warblers were taken away and then returned to the apartment
of the new Pope. Aging Mother Pasqualina stayed in Rome as
her order's representative. Few knew Rome and its people better.

Italian-fashion there was no queue in front of the Papal villa; just a mass fifty persons wide pushing up the ramp to the entrance. Some turned pale in the hot crowd. Father Pellegrino, who had restored confidence in the Vatican announcements by his frank telling of the story of the Pope's last hours, took control and described what was happening within over an amplifying system. Dr. Galeazzi-Lisi needed another hour or so for a new embalming technique which would preserve the dead pontiff's remains "for at least one hundred years"; a system requiring no breaking of the skin. Everyone in the plaza would be allowed in and there would be "no privilege" in determining who should first file past the pontiff's bier.

"If there is any it should be for the good people outside."

The soothing words represented a rather empty wish. Officials, beginning with the President of Italy, Giovanni Gronchi, were shown into the funerary room so frequently during the afternoon that Dr. Galeazzi-Lisi complained that the traffic was at least partially responsible for such failures of the embalming as occurred. The doctor denied that there were many, but later on the throngs that poured past the Pope's body saw a discoloration suggesting a grievous miscarriage of the experimental process. Democratic feelings against privilege were understandable to Vatican officers, but it was also clear to them that there are hierarchies of people and of values and that exceptions and distinctions need to be made.

The Communist 20 per cent of Castel Gandolfo was mixed with the rest. Monsignor Sella was not scandalized. I asked him about it when I noticed that the village's Number One Communist, Marino Bernardino, had closed his small, boxlike cobbler's shop for the afternoon. It is opposite the Swiss-guarded door of the papal villa. It was there that Bernardino sat for years after World War II under a shrine to Stalin, like the lamplit ones to the Sacred Heart of Jesus which many another Italian shoemaker and shopkeeper maintains. It was from there that Bernardino had watched the procession of limousines bearing papal visitors; a rich parade, which he said confirmed him in his Communism.

Bernardino let no one peep in at his Moscow memorial that day. Monsignor Sella, the cobbler's next-door neighbor, was not surprised by any of the Communist good behavior.

"They're Communists in their own way," he said. "They all feel Catholic."

It was not the kind of orthodoxy Cardinal Ottaviani's Holy Office prescribed, but the pastor accepted it as a parish reality.

"Have faith in me and in the authorities," Father Pellegrino called down to us through the amplifiers, and obediently and quietly we waited.

An hour later the priest's voice was back.

"I'm here," he said, "you see I kept the appointment. . . ."

The priest announced that the "venerated remains" had been re-clothed. The Pope was dressed in a floor-length cassock of white, his shoulders covered by a short ermine-edged red cape. On his head was a snug red ermine-bordered rimless cap such as popes wore in the sixteenth century. It was a headpiece used in modern times as part of the Pope's funeral dress, but no longer worn in life.

"Trust me a little longer," the priest asked. "At this moment the Pope's remains are moving in a small procession through the apartment here. Now I can see them. Noble guards on either side are slowly coming forward. Prayers are being chanted. The Holy Father's remains are encased in cellophane. . . ."

The cellophane was part of the scheme for preserving bodies which Dr. Galeazzi-Lisi and an associate had decided, almost wholly on their own authority, to try on the illustrious deceased. "Aromas" such as the early Christians had used were at work inside the transparent envelope.

"Be careful crossing the television cables at the entrance," Father Pellegrino went on. "Don't touch them. The current is very high."

After a wait of nearly two hours it was time to go in.

The doors opened and we flooded past a knot of a half-dozen Swiss Guards and papal police who struggled with indifferent success to slow down and channel the surge. We climbed a circling staircase, and on the second floor entered a throne room where the body of the Pope lay in state. The dead pontiff lay on a pillow on the flat surface of a bier at the eye level of the spectators, a rosary entwined in his folded hands. He was no longer recognizable as the man to whom millions had prayerfully come for a blessing. Beside him, silent and erect, stood two Noble Guardsmen—expressionless helmeted Rome aristocrats in flamboyant and archaic military uniforms. A few monsignors and priests of lesser rank stood beside them. The crowd pressed from behind and we filed on.

The unparalleled final salute to a pontiff was under way, but already, almost invisibly, the foundations of a new pontificate had been laid. That morning—within eight hours of Pius's death —thirteen cardinals had met to assume temporary command of the unique and vast Catholic Church organization.

For a third of a day a Frenchman, Cardinal Tisserant, had been Catholicism's supreme officer, but at noon the Cardinals in Rome—almost all of them Italians—chose seventy-nine-year-old Benedetto Aloisi Masella, a native of Pontecorvo, near Rome, to be Chamberlain of the Church until a new pope was elected. Cardinal Aloisi Masella became Catholicism's chief, and Swiss Guards were assigned to protect him as they had guarded Pius during the latter's long reign.

Pius was the first pope in generations to die away from the Vatican. Old books of ceremonies prescribed to the smallest detail the custom in the case of death at the Vatican, but the cardinals had only a three-line note left by Pius XII to advise them what to do in the event of his death somewhere else. The note was part of an Apostolic Constitution Pius had drawn up in 1945, six years after his election to the Papacy. The document summed up traditions governing the funerals and elections of popes and made a few small changes.

Provision Thirty-one of Pius's Constitution said simply:

"If it should happen that a Roman Pontiff die away from Rome it is up to the Sacred College of Cardinals to do what is necessary for a dignified and decorous transfer to St. Peter's Basilica."

Accordingly, next afternoon, October 10th, a city hearse rolled out of the papal villa for the drive to the Eternal City. The vehicle at once became the subject of comment. As one Roman paper said later, it was more than merely "modest." It was grotesquely out of place amid the rarely equaled pomp with which it was surrounded. It was an old and tired small car, the sort to which the humblest Roman could aspire. Glass walls exposed the casket, but every eye was caught by what was on top. A two-foot-tall gilded model of a papal tiara surmounted by a cross was surrounded by four barearmed, barewaisted and barelegged four-foot gilded cherubs holding dangling cords and tassels. Poor in material and poor in inspiration, the baroque display saddened many who saw it. Yet perhaps in spite of itself the shabby, tastelessly pretentious hearse may have been appropriate. Poverty, as Pius had told the American veterans, was no stranger to the Church.

In Rome the triumph of an ancient emperor awaited the churchman's procession. A throng of half a million packed either side of the street as the parade, joined by thousands of clergy on foot, wound along the same route the returning conquerors of antiquity had once followed. It curved past the hulk of the Colosseum where youths looked down from the top tier a hundred feet overhead. It twisted through the ancient Forum at the foot of the gently sloping original hills—the Esquiline, the Caelian, the Palatine, the Capitoline, the Viminal, the Quirinal. Out of sight behind the Palatine was the seventh hill, the Aventine. Nuns stared with rapt expressions. A few eyes were tear-reddened. The entire crowd was soundless and attentive. Businessmen, Communists, anticlerical Liberals and Socialists, ladies of light virtue and swindlers, all looked on the dead Bishop of Rome as at the least an unusual man who had labored nobly for what he saw as right.

Diplomats and, in private, churchmen were already busy with speculations about the man the half-a-hundred cardinals of the world would choose to succeed Pius in this most influential spiritual position; but for the next nine days the largest of all churches bustled with the incomparable funeral rites of a pope. From early on the morning of October 11th, two days after Pius's death, throngs of tens of thousands poured through St. Peter's Square, the huge enclosure before the church; a space big enough —as Europeans used to say—to drill a small army. Police made use of a dozen trucks to form bottlenecks that pinched the invasion into a safer, smaller size. Many people fainted. Some of the old and ill provoked pity and were lifted over fences which had been put up to supplement the wall of trucks. At least one old man died in the excitement. At the edge of the crowd were peddlers, alert to the opportunity, who sold sandwiches from pushcarts. They were not the only profiteers. Thirty pickpockets, a perpetual plague at St. Peter's, were arrested.

Inside, Pius lay on a catafalque seven feet high—a lonely small figure in full bishop's array, held up toward heaven at the spot where he had so often received multitudes in audience. Police at the bier urged us to move on.

The bizarre kept pace with the magnificent and the awesome as the final rites continued. Dr. Galeazzi-Lisi, along with all the rest of us, saw the darkening of the Pope's exposed face, and night after night he climbed a ladder in the empty immense basilica to resume the fumigation. The doctor complained that the corrosive heat from television lights and from the human river beside the catafalque created unusual difficulties for his new process. The doctor's aides, it was known, were thinking of sales for the process in the rich and reputedly funeral-conscious United States. A clamorous failure in a test like this would not help.

While men such as the embalmer made their private calculations, the long procedure of consigning a pope to his tomb approached its two climaxes. The first one came five days after Pius's death. In a three-hour ceremony—the like of which is never otherwise seen—before an audience of 3,000 and amid the sweet and uncomprehending chanting of a boys' choir, the Pope's body was lowered by red ropes into a 1,000-pound lead, elm and cyprus triple casket. It was incensed and sprinkled with holy water by twenty cardinals including two Americans (Cardinals Spellman of New York and McIntyre of Los Angeles), was covered by a white face veil and a red blanket, and received for identification a bag of the annual coins struck off during the dead prelate's pontificate. It was finally sealed amid the clatter of carpenters' drills, twisting screwdrivers, hissing acetylene torches, and rattling hammer blows. The cardinals gathered around the well in front of the papal altar under Michelangelo's 400-foot-tall dome to see the casket lowered by rope and pulley to the floor beneath the basilica hall where most popes are buried. Pius was indeed in his coffin. A pontificate was over, and amid all the pomp the lesson of death could not have been spelled out more clearly to the aged cardinals who would meet a fortnight later to choose the man they felt best equipped to ascend Catholicism's throne. When I asked a churchman later about the considerations which would go into the cardinals' choice, it was death he mentioned first.

"You can be sure of one thing," he said. "They are all old men who know one fact for certain. They will all soon meet their Maker for an accounting. You can be certain that it is that above all which will guide them."

Such selfish interests as motivated some humbler functionaries on the margins of the climactic Church event would not dominate the cardinals.

The ultimate event in the earthly story of the Catholic Church's Pope of World War II was the brilliant final Mass; the last of nine successive daily services of the kind. Present were 40 cardinals and delegates of 53 countries, including the secretaries of state and foreign ministers of the United States, France and West Germany. Royalty, nobility, diplomats and newspapermen crowded into the apse of St. Peter's as 5 cardinals, including Archbishop Spellman, gave the final blessing to a 20-foot-tall bier symbolizing the interred pontiff. The presence of so many national representatives, and especially those of the United States, was a triumph for which the deceased Pius—a devotee of diplomacy—had worked with special effort.

After the Mass, all was over except for a stream of the faithful pouring past the uninscribed white marble tomb of Pius in the crypt below. Many asked the guards if they might touch their rosaries to the stone coffin. The bodies of saints are revered by Catholics as relics—a tangible indirect contact with the mystery of life after death. A cult of Pius as a saint was forming.

# 3. ... Long Live the Pope

In the days after Pius's entombment Peter Van Lierde, a tall, fifty-two-year-old Netherlander, was busy as Acting Bishop of Vatican City, gathering evidence that the buried Pope deserved to be inscribed in Church rolls as St. Pius XII, the second pope so honored in the twentieth century and only the third since the Middle Ages. Pius X, who died in 1914, had been raised to the Catholic altars by Pius XII, but in the preceding 600 years only Pius V of the sixteenth century had been so acclaimed.

With Bishop Van Lierde, many in that moment looked past the tomb to Pius in glory, but cardinals, diplomats and journalists were, to a great extent, already immersed in other considerations. However difficult it seemed to be to replace one who had been hailed for nineteen critical years of this century as Christ's Very Vicar, a new pope in the endless line had to be chosen. Newspapermen promptly found themselves the target of a scolding in *L'Osservatore Romano*. They were charged with treating the sacred elevation as being on a par with any other competition at the polls. At least some publishers shared *Osservatore*'s reaction. On the day Pius fell critically ill one editor held back a Vatican correspondent's story listing the most prominent *papabili*—potential candidates for the Papacy. It was offensive, the editor decided, to run such speculation in the same issue that carried the news of Pius's illness. The story was published later, when even feeble hope had vanished.

Since Catholics of the world and many non-Catholics look to the Pope for spiritual and moral guidance, they see him as one chosen and sustained not only by men and by his own efforts but by God, by the Holy Spirit. The view is the same that the sometimes controversial New York Archbishop Francis Spellman expressed in 1939 when I saw him drive in from Boston to take up government of the New York archdiocese. A few of us, including Frank Leahy, coach of the then all-conquering Notre Dame football team, met the future cardinal at the city's edge.

"I will pray," the prelate said, "as if everything depended on God; I will work as if everything depended on me."

A reporter asked one of the three American cardinals his opinion of prospects in the papal election in which he was about to take part.

The Holy Spirit, the cardinal answered, would indicate the man best adapted to meet the problems of the times.

The answer was different indeed from those that many ambassadors and ministers plenipotentiary accredited to the Holy See were giving in reply to the same question. The diplomats were deep in mundane speculations. Would the cardinals consider it wise to break the uninterrupted six-century tradition in favor of choosing one of their own number? Would they select the first non-Italian in four centuries? Would the churchmen select an old man for an "interim" pontificate devoted largely to the naming of new young cardinals? Would the Senate of Catholicism choose a relatively liberal pope dedicated to a search for a formula of coexistence with the Communists?

The two points of view were not as contradictory as they seemed, a well-informed old priest told us. He pointed out what happened in elections of Jesuit generals. The delegates of the world's largest and best-educated order meet for a three or four day *informatio*—gathering of information. No one asks point-blank:"Do you think Father X would make a good general?" But acquaintances of the potential leader are questioned repeatedly: "Does he have administrative experience?" "Is he prayerful?" Then for an hour before the election delegates are instructed to wipe their minds clean of the pros and cons of the individuals' qualifications and to pray and meditate. The election follows.

The spirit in the papal election, the priest said, was the same. There was faith in the inspiration of the Holy Spirit but there was also a recognition that men, with their abilities and weaknesses, were involved. Just as there should be a spirit of prayerful appeal for divine guidance, so should there be as shrewd as possible an appraisal of the men through whom the Holy Spirit would be expected to act.

"Our American Catholics should understand that," the priest said.

The cardinals met once each day, deciding election details and handling a few items of urgent Church business. Dr. Galeazzi-Lisi's resignation as Vatican Health Officer was "accepted." The election date was set: two weeks from the end of Pius XII's nine-day funeral service. Rooms in the election area were assigned, mostly by lot. As decreed by a six-century tradition, the cardinals would vote in "conclave" or *"cum clave"*—with a key or under key as the word signifies. Until a new pope was chosen all would be locked in and none but the Grand Penitentiary, the cardinal with the power of absolving the gravest sins, would have free communication with the outside world. All others, even Monsignor Alberto di Jorio, the Conclave Supervisor, would have their mail examined, and most of them would eschew any outer contact.

Who would be chosen? The question was so momentous that some people reacted frivolously. It would be a short conclave, one of those on the margins of the event said with a smile, because "the good sisters of St. Martha [who run the hospice for retired priests inside the Vatican] will do the cooking; they don't know how to use oil and they never use butter!" The informant had dined at the sisters' unassuming table and was sure that the Church princes would not want to eat there for long. It was his little joke.

It was only the fourth time that citizens of the United States would cast ballots. Were any of them *papabile?* Any male Catholic who had reached the age of reason—seven—was technically eligible, but any American (a North European diplomat told reporters privately) would be "a disaster." Communists would have an easy time of it in Asia and Africa, shrugging off the Vatican as an American tool. Even in Europe the voice of the Church would fade beneath the shout that it was an agent of Wall Street and of the State Department.

Short, round-cheeked Cardinal Spellman, the best known of the world's cardinals, was the lightning rod for attacks against the idea of an American Pope. A Rome Communist daily, *Paese Sera*—the Country's Evening Paper—summed up the opposition with an ironic comment from Red Zingaro, a comedian.

"Considering the present world situation," the actor said, tongue in cheek, "I feel that what is needed is a political pope, and I feel the one best adapted is Cardinal Spellman."

All the arguments against an American were summed up in the comedian's comment in reverse. It is the tradition in papal elections, at least it was so in the two I have watched as a reporter (in 1939 and in 1958), to say that the choice lies between "a religious pope or a political pope." The speaker in such cases always ended by saying that a "religious" rather than a "diplomatic" pope was what was needed. In Communist circles it was taken as axiomatic that a pope "in present world circumstances" should stay away from politics and confine himself to religious services. That seemed to the Communists a comfortable long step toward eliminating the massive barrier of Church opposition in Europe. Finally, no prelate seemed so "American," so much identified with the political, military and economic power of the West and thus so far removed from the impartial spiritual role of a pope, as the New York Archbishop. To mention the idea of Cardinal Spellman as *papabile* was to explode it.

*Paese Sera* had its chuckle but there were others in Rome who thought the suggestion not so preposterous. The old worlds of Rome and of Europe had already heaped so many of the burdens of the free nations on American shoulders that it was conceivable that a coming conclave, if not the one of the moment, would thrust even Peter's heavy crown and keys into American hands, one Church thinker told me. The Americans who had armed Greece against Communists after World War II, who had given most of the soldiers to the defense of Korea in 1950, who had financed European recovery and organized the Atlantic Protective Alliance of the fifties, were the same to whom Catholicism's cardinals might yet look for a future Bishop of Rome.

This was still speculative, however, and the ponderings of diplomats, journalists, and even privately of churchmen, moved elsewhere. *Osservatore* frowned at some of these efforts, but later it was a satisfaction to many of us in the Rome press corps to read tributes from official American Catholic sources conceding that our analyses had often been shrewd.

On most lists a high place was reserved for the heavy-set, even corpulent, patriarch of Venice. Cardinal Angelo Giuseppe Roncalli, a seventy-seven-year-old native of the piously Catholic Italian Alps, fulfilled many of the requisites most often mentioned: he had some experience of the world, had passed a half decade as a bishop in charge of a diocese, and had spent a few years getting to know the special little community of the Vatican. In addition he knew several languages. For thirty years he had been a papal diplomat in the Balkans, Turkey and, most important of all, France. For the past five years he had ruled the influential Venice Archdiocese, tempering his theoretical knowledge of men and their problems with a more immediate contact with their virtues and failings.

Listed as a drawback was the age of the Venice patriarch. No cardinal over seventy had been chosen in two centuries, and few over seventy-five had ever mounted Peter's throne. Pius XII was elected on his sixty-third birthday. Pius IX, the last pope to rule the large central Italian papal kingdom—a domain absorbed in 1870 by modern Italy—was fifty-four when he took the throne. Leo XIII, the pope of the social encyclicals, and the sainted Pius X were each sixty-eight at their elections. Benedict XV of World War I was sixty. Pius XI, the blunt-spoken mountain climber of the two decades between the two world wars, was sixty-five. Should the cardinals decide on an "interim" pontificate —a pause after Pius XII's lonely and authoritarian reign—the patriarch's age would be no handicap. Finally, as an Italian cardinal the Venice prelate was favored by two strong traditions. What was going on among the cardinals was hard to tell, but everyone else in Rome, including many of those in constant communication with the elderly Church princes, buzzed with discussion of the Italian and cardinal traditions.

"If they ever want to choose a foreigner now is the time," a priest on duty with a Church information service told me. There were several eminent "foreign" candidates, although as some Romans pointed out, no one is a "foreigner" inside a church which believes in a divine mission to all men.

At the head of every "foreign" list was Cardinal Gregory Agagianian, patriarch of Armenia, a member of the small Oriental (as opposed to Latin) wing of the Catholic Church. The bearded prelate was sixty-three, just as Pius XII had been at the time of his election. He was a polyglot such as even the multilingual Romans had rarely known. In addition to English learned in Boston, he spoke ten other languages including his native Russian. Born in Tiflis in what is now the Soviet Union, the town from which Stalin came, he had been in Rome almost fifty years. He had come there at the age of nine as a seminarian and had rarely journeyed elsewhere. The Cardinal spoke Italian with a Roman twang; in all but his origin he was Italian. To Cardinal Spellman he had a special bond: the two had been classmates in the Rome Seminary at the time of World War I.

A gentle, kindly man, the Armenian cardinal charmed everyone he met.

Another "foreigner" was Cardinal Tisserant, Dean of the College of Cardinals, and one of the most brilliant of Catholic churchmen. He directed the Vatican's congregation, or department, for Oriental affairs, and had become one of the prime experts on religious conditions behind the Iron Curtain and on Soviet intrigue. He was seventy-four, already elderly even for a cardinal, but still in impressively sturdy health only slightly impaired by a wound received during World War I while a French staff officer in the Middle East. Like Cardinal Agagianian he was multilingual. He began a conversation with me once with the demand: "What will it be: English, French, Italian?" They were the only languages I spoke, as he knew. He commanded another ten.

The cardinal dean had also been in Rome nearly half a century. No one could contest that, although a non-Italian, he knew the Vatican well. An outspoken man however, he had never feared incurring disagreement and even resentment. In the common view that might hurt his candidacy, and his nationality was a handicap. A "French pope" was something dreaded by many in Rome, even by those with little knowledge of the Church. Many conceded the genius of the French, possibly the most gifted people of the world, but felt that the Parisian taste for carrying ideas to what seemed their logical, drastic conclusions might prove ruinous to a church fated to live among so many cultures and under so many political systems.

No one of a great nation—whether it be France, the United States, Germany, Britain, and perhaps even Spain—should be Pope, these Romans argued. Inevitably such a pope would be suspect of serving his native country. The Netherlands and Belgium—almost alone among Europe's largely Catholic "foreign" nations—could be considered, the same persons went on. Far better, they concluded, to carry on with the tradition of Italian Popes; that at least avoided drawing the issue of nationality into the elections.

"Otherwise," one authority said, "should there be a Brazilian, let us say, this time, the French—for example—would be likely to insist that it was their turn next time. It would be to the advantage of no one that such a situation should arise."

The mention of Belgium and the Netherlands as countries of possible *papabili* was little help; there was only one cardinal in the two of them and he was eighty-four. At that age, in the general judgment, Archbishop Joseph van Roey was ineligible, even for interim service.

A few other non-Italians were cited. Emanuel Goncalves Cerejeira, seventy, the patriarch of Lisbon, was one. He had been a cardinal twenty-nine years. He had been *papabile* even in 1939.

"I have known Cardinal Cerejeira many years and very favorably," one of the most important members of the Holy See diplomatic corps told me. "But I can't see the College of Cardinals choosing a Portuguese at a time when Portugal, more than any other nation, is clinging to its colonies in Africa."

The considerations, certainly as far as perceptive diplomats were concerned, were endless in complexity.

Attention was concentrated on the Italians. Might the cardinals go against the custom of choosing one of their own number? The very ballots on which the cardinals would vote specified that the vote was for "the most reverend and most eminent Lord Cardinal . . ." And in the oath the College members would take it was specified that the Holy See's rights and liberty would be defended by "whomever among us" was chosen. The cardinals were free to look outside their own body but it was plain that the machinery of centuries invited them to turn their eyes toward their own senate. One churchman with a rather earthy taste for American slang and an opportunity to detect the trend of influential thinking told me with a smile that, "My left elbow tells me it will be a cardinal." His judgment was correct.

Not all were so sure, however. Some Vatican officials, whose task it was to keep the world informed of all that was not secret, advised me to watch for signs of an outsider as soon as the conclave began. The cardinals would vote four times each day; twice in the morning, twice in the late afternoon. After each unsuccessful pair of ballots the voting papers and scratch sheets would be burned with damp brush to advise the world by the traditional black smoke that there was still no pope. The burning would be done without brush when a pontiff was elected. The thin, gray fumes would be the signal that a new pontificate had begun. If the smoke did not come on time—at about noon in the morning and 5:30 in the afternoon—it would be an indication that a noncardinal had been called, my friend emphasized. The noncardinal would not be summoned until he had received the votes required for election. The signal of either failure or success would be withheld until the outsider had joined the cardinals inside Michelangelo's Sistine Chapel, and had accepted or refused. Even if the noncardinal were instructed secretly to wait in Rome there would be at least an hour's significant delay, my informant pointed out.

In the judgment of all only one noncardinal was likely. He was sixty-three-year-old Archbishop Giovanni Battista Montini, of Milan, former Acting Secretary of State of Pius XII, an acute student of international politics and a reformer. Son of a Christian Democratic (Catholic) party deputy who had been hounded by the Fascist dictator Mussolini, the archbishop had been one of the best Vatican friends of the late Italian Premier Alcide De Gasperi, the Catholic democrat who headed off both Communism and a Fascist revival in postwar Italy by allying with Socialists against extreme conservatives.

In the opinion of some, the Milan archbishop was too much dedicated to experiment and change, too "Leftist." He was not, of course, "soft on Communism"; no Catholic archbishop was that. In any case he was not a cardinal. Both he and the other Acting Director of the Secretariate of State, Monsignor Domenico Tardini, had asked Pope Pius not to make them cardinals at the time of the last nominations, five years earlier. Each knew how hard it was for Pius to distribute the seventy red hats among the many racial, national and organizational leaders, and Vatican diplomats and staff officials who had reason to hope for the Church's high honor. It was known that the appointment was offered to both and refused, but the fact remained that Archbishop Montini was not a cardinal at the moment of the conclave.

If he had been, he would certainly have attracted the center of the College's attention. As it was he was an "outsider." Even so, one diplomat with an intimate acquaintance of the Vatican was convinced that it was "the shadow of Montini" that would stand before the cardinals as they looked for Pius's successor.

As the cardinals met day by day, men of twenty-four nations, few of whom knew one another well, the *informatio* of the papal electors went on unobtrusively. Some governments saw to it that the cardinals learned their wishes. From the start the Italians had shown their interest by arranging a funeral mass for Pius XII attended by the president, almost the whole of the cabinet, and nearly every main official of the civil organization and the armed forces. The reminder that the Vatican was inside Italy, and that Italians prided themselves on offering their sons to the Papacy, was clear. France saw to it that its six cardinals knew what the government of the devout Charles De Gaulle would like: a pope at least vaguely familiar with the ideal of a united Europe and friendly to it; a pontiff who would help Catholics and Protestants to live peacefully together in countries like France where the tiny Protestant minority of 1,000,000 is an important elite. The French made arrangements to spell out this message after as well as before the election. They chose as De Gaulle's delegate to the Papal coronation, the Protestant who was then Foreign Minister of largely Catholic France, Maurice Couve de Murville.

Was it to be an Italian cardinal? If so, the choice narrowed. Half the seventeen cardinals of Italy were over eighty. In many speculations the old-age line was drawn arbitrarily at the end of the eighth decade. Should it be a young cardinal? Archbishop Giuseppe Siri of Genoa, a stern, unsmiling and active foe of the Communists, was fifty-two. The cardinal was known as a scholar although he was not skilled in languages. A friend of private enterprise, he had been criticized as too far removed from the workers' aspirations in an old continent rent by decades of class struggle. Most difficult in the eyes of almost everyone was the fact that he was much "too young." Popes have great power. The same human considerations that dictated a close scrutiny of *papabili* pointed the wisdom of some degree of alternation in office. There is a wry and not intentionally irreverent Roman expression: "What is wanted is a *Padre Santo* [Holy Father] not a *Padre Eterno* [Eternal Father—God]."

The speculation narrowed, but at least some of those who weighed and wondered finally gave up.

"Who will it be?" an ambassador of one Latin country repeated my question. "I don't know. The Holy Spirit inspires them, not I."

Whoever it was his wholly Catholic country would accept, he said.

After three days and eleven ballots we had our answer. As we crowded together, nearly a quarter of a million of us in St. Peter's Square, so tightly packed that it was hard to squeeze to our knees to receive the new Pope's blessing, we heard from the balcony of the great church the confident, masculine voice of the first Pope John in six centuries. The seventy-seven-year-old ex-patriarch of Venice read the old words of the Apostolic Benediction with a fatherly assurance. The crowd shouted a cry of welcome to the unfamiliar portly figure: "Long Live the Pope!" "Long Live Papa Giovanni!" Another era in the old Catholic and Christian history had begun.

# 4. Two Popes

All pontificates have much in common, one of Pius XII's most intimate collaborators pointed out after John's coronation. A pope, through his diplomatic corps, negotiates with governments about their own citizens. The situation is unique, and much of the "style"—much of the policy and comportment of every pontificate—is dictated by that fact regardless of the background and personality of the pontiff. Acting as the "Universal Father" and as "Servant of the Servants of God" imposes duties and sets limits.

Even so, the difference between the two occupants of St. Peter's throne could scarcely have been more pronounced.

From the moment the little-known Venetian patriarch appeared on St. Peter's balcony, there were exclamations of astonishment and admiration that the new spiritual sovereign acted *veramente da Papa*—"really like a Pope!"

A functionary fussed at the elbow of the white-clad pontiff. Evidently he was whispering final recommendations. The ritual for papal blessings is detailed and precise, established by tradition.

"I know, I know . . ." we heard the Pope murmur.

Too much can be read into a phrase and a tone, but many of us thought we detected the strong, calm confidence of a leader already psychologically adjusted to a bewildering and profound responsibility.

In nineteen years in the Papacy Pius had impressed a generation with the idea that a pope of modern Catholicism is an austere, physically tenuous man—aloof, grave, even humorless. He was a priest with a Pentecostal gift of tongues; a scholar who gave daily evidence that he was abreast of advances in a score of fields of modern research from nuclear physics to professional sports. He seemed without peer and irreplaceable.

Yet the peasant-born cardinal had accepted the succession, and was facing its tasks with no hesitation. Even in that there was contrast. As a reporter, I remembered the change I had seen in Cardinal Eugene Pacelli from the moment I saw him enter the 1939 conclave, and a fortnight later watched him carried on the pontifical litter in the coronation ceremony at St Peter's. With a fixed, unseeing glance and stiff, expressionless cheeks he had become a pope of gaunt and one might say horrified appearance. Cardinal Pacelli had known for years that he was virtually Pius XI's designate for the succession, but the change from the relative lack of responsibility of Secretary of State of a notably self-reliant pope to the position of final Church authority bore down on his frail shoulders.

Pope John granted an audience to several hundred of us of the temporarily expanded Rome press corps. Several times he slipped into the first person singular, forgetting the papal, royal—and editorial—plural. He had to be forgiven, he smiled, for he was not yet used to "the universal paternity." Astonished reporters, unaccustomed to such pontifical familiarity, stared back, grinned, and applauded. The new "Father" was already winning goodwill and affection.

John received us in the frescoed Clementine Hall, a room whose walls and ceiling are covered with flamboyant seventeenth-century paintings. Sturdy blond Swiss guards in their yellow-blue-red-striped Renaissance costumes stood rigidly at his side. The Pope answered our grins with one of his own, charged us pleasantly but firmly with not having got "two lines right" about what had gone on inside the conclave during the election, and appealed to us to take as a motto the words of Italy's great novelist, Alessandro Manzoni, *Il santo vero non mai tradir!*—"Truth is holy; never betray it!"

The pontiff's left knee jiggled from side to side as he spoke. Once in awhile the old man's pudgy, ring-adorned hand rose to the back of his head to lift and replace the papal white skullcap.

With every motion there was another smile. The ex-ambassador, ex-cardinal was still unsure in his high new role, but as we had sensed in St. Peter's Square, was embracing it without qualms. Just as Pius had been awed, so John was trusting. Just as one was appalled, so did his successor show both the faith of a child and the assurance of a goodwilled, extroverted, and not easily daunted man. Each faced the same task with a like appraisal of its intensity and gravity, but with the contrasting emphasis of nearly opposite personalities.

Following Pius XII would not be easy, one of the veterans in the corps of accredited diplomats commented during the preparations for the conclave. Pius, he said, was assuredly great.

Even before he left Venice, however, the future pope provided much of the answer of how the gifted and dedicated Pius could and should be followed. He wrote to the director of his diocesan seminary that there should be prayers, not for the "continuance" of what Pius represented, but for "progress along the line of the eternal youthfulness of the Church." Pius had been a stout and leafy branch on a nineteenth-century tree; new life must spring from the trunk.

Within days after taking the vacant throne, John said the same thing in another way. He asked that the picture of Pius XII be placed beside his desk. But with it he requested others; that of Pius XI whom he had known when they had both worked for awhile as young priests in the Milan Catholic library; that of tiny aristocratic Benedict XV, the pontiff of World War I, remembered as a man of no wasted words; and those of St. Pius, who had also been a patriarch of the lovely canal city and of Leo XIII, the nonagenarian whom John remembered from an audience on his first visit to Rome.

"They were all saints," the new pontiff said of the popes he had known. He was successor to each and to 250 before them. Each had his own ways. He would have his.

For John the problem of succeeding the Pope of the forties and fifties was resolved. For us who watched as journalists, however, the change was not that easily made. We looked on with fascination as the difference between the two popes became plain.

For awhile there seemed nothing but differences; some to the advantage of one personality, some to that of the other.

Pius's superior command of languages was an immediate obvious contrast. He had been fluent in over a half dozen, including all the leading ones of his intercontinental spiritual following. It was a staggering accomplishment, even in the Old World where linguistic talent is widespread. Besides his native Italian he spoke Latin with ease. His German was excellent, polished during two decades as a papal nuncio, or ambassador, in Bavaria and Berlin. His French was fine, showing much study of Bossuet, Bourdaloue and other French preachers and classical writers. His English, learned in his sixties, was clouded by an Italian accent but his understanding of it, even from the mouth of an American, was good. I heard it in a twenty-minute talk a year before his death. He perceived instantly not only the main points but also the subtler variations in word choices. He had spoken Spanish and Portuguese, too, and it was said that a Russian grammar sat on his desk in his later years.

By contrast, John told us in the press audience—in a French sprinkled with occasional phrases of Italian—that he only knew French, the European's traditional second language, *comme ci, comme ça*—merely "so-so." There was a popular twang to it; not quite the French of the academicians. *Bistro* French—wineshop French—one reporter judged it. But it was far more than merely adequate. One Italian newspaperman used the Pope's own deprecatory appraisal of it next morning as one of the main points of his article. This, he said, is a pope so humble that he is "the only Italian who will say he can't speak French." The two languages, with a common Latin mother, are close. And what's more, the reporter added, the Pontiff's admission was not true. His French, he said, was fine. The new Pope's modest manner was a quality that many noticed.

Pius was the son of an upper-middle-class family which had been a pillar of the papal court and intimate with Rome's "black" nobility for generations. (Rome alone in the world has two titled societies: one tracing its family origins to the black-robed world of the Church, to the brothers and sisters of Popes; the other identified with the much younger and now exiled royal family of Italy.) Pius, through his three nephews, had been linked to both noble worlds, for the Italian King made his brother's children princes. All three were prominent members of Pius's court: one of them the Vatican's foremost legal advisor; one a member of the diplomatic corps as "Envoy Extraordinary and Minister Plenipotentiary" of minute Costa Rica; and two—the diplomat and one other—officers of the Pope's corps of Noble Guards. A family that had organized the Vatican paper *L'Osservatore Romano* a century earlier and had directed the negotiations with Italy creating the minuscule independent State of Vatican City in 1929, had continued in the highest levels of Vatican work and honor. Part of the withdrawn manner of Pius XII was certainly the result of his conception of the demands of his elevated role. Another part was no doubt the result of a shyness millions of visitors never suspected. But without doubt some of it was the fruit of an aristocratic indoctrination which had become instinct.

John, by contrast, told protocol officers, in one of his first acts, that his callous-handed peasant brothers were not to be called "their excellencies" as the aides had proposed. The title of "relative of Pope John" was enough, he decreed. It was from no lack of affection. He had spent every summer vacation in the Alpine village with his little-schooled, farm-laborer brothers. It was the sense of fitness of a man of no pretense, born to poverty but self-respecting.

In his first speeches John often said that he marveled that one of such humble origin and merits could be lifted so high. This was the sort of remark that would have been inconceivable from the delicately reared Pius, an aide of both remarked. And of course in his case it would not have been true. He was, as he knew and accepted, one of those favored by family history on a continent where the past is much of the present.

From his first hours the new Pope not only accepted the idea of differences but emphasized them. He returned to traditions which Pius and other popes of the modern era had permitted to lapse. He revived an article of papal dress which his own generation knew only from Renaissance paintings or from the special

18876908

funeral wardrobe of a pontiff. It was the *camauro*—a warm velvet cap like an oversized beret pulled tightly around the ears. News photographers got a Page One picture one day as John, on the balcony of St. Peter's, waved good-bye to an enormous crowd and then tugged on the *camauro*, twisting it until he had it right. I watched with opera glasses, seeing what few others below could observe, but gigantic telescopic lenses on cameras in the plaza got a fine close-up. Perhaps it was a matter of confusing the man with the ermine-edged maroon head covering but it seemed a hearty, jolly garment. The *camauro* alternated for John with the white skullcap of recent generations, a slight and pure but cold article of attire. Whether the psychological as well as physical warmth of the *camauro* and the chill of the *zucchetto* influenced the new Pope's choice was a matter of speculation, but his self-assured refusal to be prisoner of the casual decisions of his predecessors was clear.

Pope John's very choice of a name had been a declaration of independence for his pontificate. Popes are free to choose any appellation they wish, but there is a tendency to repeat the names of a strong predecessor. Cardinal Pacelli, for instance, in a sign that he would not reverse the policy of the anti-Communist and anti-Nazi Pius XI, had himself called by the same name. John did think of Pius XIII, he revealed one day in a typically chatty audience. He had thought of Benedict XVI and Clement XV, too. They were all, he said, "peaceful" names.

If he were to stay within the narrowest lines of the even older and heavier papal tradition, John might have felt himself limited to one of 9 names—or even of 7. All 30 popes since the end of the sixteenth century had stayed within a choice of 9: Clement and Pius, each used by 7; Innocent, the name of 4; Benedict and Leo, the names of 3 each; Alexander and Gregory, the names of 2 each; and Paul and Urban, each used once. For two centuries only 7 of the names had been worn; none had called themselves Paul or Alexander.

In all papal history only 81 names had been taken and no one in more than 1,000 years, since Landon of 913 to 914, had called himself by a name not used before. Despite this, the independent-

minded John thought of breaking even that unwritten rule. He
thought of being Papa Giuseppe—Pope Joseph—the first to use
that name. He decided, however, as others may have too, that
"Joseph" should be left sacred in the Church's highest annals to
the saint who was Christ's foster father. At one audience John
reportedly said that he had even considered "Pope Peter II."
There is a lively old Roman superstition traceable to the spurious
"Prophecy of St. Malachy" of the sixteenth century that the
world will end when Pope Peter II reigns. John did not put it
to the test.

He chose to revive the most popular and controversial of all
papal names. No "pope" had borne it since 1415 and the pontiff
of that time was later ruled a false claimant to the throne. It was
a period of the worst chaos the Papacy had known. Three men,
Gregory XII, a Venetian who is counted now as the true Pope,
Benedict XIII, a Spaniard, and John XXIII, a Neapolitan, laid
claim to the Papacy simultaneously for five years. Just as Benedict XIII (1724 to 1730) reused the name of a fifteenth century
antipope, so did Cardinal Roncalli determine to place in history
a second John XXIII. Fascinated news photographers hurried to
Florence to take a picture of the already occupied and ancient
tomb of "John XXIII."

Whatever else could be said the name was the one most popes
had cherished, the new Pope explained. It had been the name
of his pious and fondly remembered peasant father. It was that
of the little church of his Alpine village where his admiration
for the bent old parish priest had aroused his vocation. It was the
name of the cathedral of the Pope as Bishop of Rome. "St. John
Lateran," not St. Peter's, is the Pope's church. It was the name,
too, of great Biblical saints—John the Baptist, the forerunner of
Christ, and John the Evangelist, the beloved Apostle. To all those
many and holy associations the new pontiff felt an attraction.
Due to an error in papal records for the tumultuous years of the
end of the tenth century, Pope John XIV (983 to 984) had been
listed for awhile as two successive pontiffs—John XIV and John
XV—while an antipope, John XVI (997 to 998), was also for a
time mistakenly admitted into the line. The result, according to

the Vatican's official yearbook, the *Annuario Pontificio*, was that the numerals following the names of the Popes John of the first years of the second Christian millennium were higher by two than they should have been. A quixotic effort to straighten out the situation was made by skipping the name "Pope John XX," but according to the Vatican list the fact is that Pius XII's successor should have been Pope John XXI. This complicated historical problem may have deterred others from using the name of John, but it did not stop the doughty new pontiff. However rightly or wrongly John XXII was called by that name in 1316, he had used it. Eliminating the antipope, John picked up from there.

The choice of a name was one the new Pope had to make at the moment of election. It was one of many decisions in which he had to cast the die of his pontificate with little time for pondering. He had also to decide whether to honor the conclave's able director, Alberto di Jorio, by lifting him to the College of Cardinals. In earlier pontificates it had been the practice for the new Pope at the moment of doffing his red cardinal's skullcap to place it on the head of one of the conclave's most prominent noncardinal leaders. The act, in the presence of the other college members, made the new appointee at once a part of that body. Pius XII and other recent Popes had folded their old skullcaps and put them away. Appointments to the Church's Senate need careful weighing. In a church of 500,000,000 many have a claim to an honor which is second only to that of the Papacy. There were few places. For four centuries membership had been held to seventy.

John felt that he had considered the question enough. Monsignor di Jorio, although not even a bishop, had long been the Cardinal College's secretary. John accepted the *zucchetto* of papal white and put his old one on the monsignor's white hair.

The octogenarian Pius, worn by two decades of preaching on the most complicated modern ethical problems, had seemed too weary to make the appointments and promotions the Vatican needed. John made clear that nominations, whether or not always exhaustively pondered, would be made. His philosophy was apparent. Honors and responsibilities would be shared. If some of those who deserved them were passed over they would have to believe, as religious men, that other and better rewards awaited them.

The Pius of the later years, hesitant over appointments, was replaced by a John who made them swiftly, even at the head of the State Secretariate, the post of key influence which is the number two place of authority in the Catholic Church. Domenico Tardini, seventy, a mere monsignor, occupied it on a "substitute" basis as he had for a generation. Pope John made him Cardinal Secretary of State and soon began telling callers that many of the matters on which they wished decisions were to be submitted to Cardinal Tardini for action at his discretion. In Pius's time all major matters were for no one but him to decide, as diplomats accredited to the Holy See recognized.

Pius, like all his predecessors for a century, had rarely taken part in functions outside the Vatican. Except for trips to the summer residence at Castel Gandolfo and the audiences which flourished there during Pius XII's time, the Pope of the forties and fifties went to a church dedication or other function away from the Vatican little more than once a year. Starting with a Christmas visit to a jail—which reduced many prisoners to sobs —the new Pope of the ancient Christian "works of mercy" ducked in and out of the Vatican with and without the customary police escorts and with or without taking chances with Rome traffic lights and jams. In his first few months John made as many such excursions as Pius had in the course of one of history's longest pontificates. John visited the sick and the aged. He rubbed elbows with Rome's poorest in parish street processions. The contrasts seemed endless and yet after a few months they dwindled.

"Getting out and around is a good thing," commented one of those most closely associated with Pius's pontificate, "but his tasks eventually keep every pope close to his desk. There are too many matters which he alone must study and act upon. You will see that the trips will become fewer. Even though the new Holy Father does not seem to like staying inside, there is no choice."

Another Vatican aide touched the point differently. He spoke of the Guelphs and Ghibellines, the two factions of the Middle Ages which Italy was torn between: the Guelphs for the Pope; the Ghibellines for the claims of the German Emperor.

"The fact," he said, "is that no pope can be 'Ghibelline' in a certain sense. He must act for the Papacy, for the Church; there isn't a great deal of leeway."

Both aides were right. Gradually as I thought back over the nature of Pius's reign and saw the broader character of John's emerge, the multiplicity of common threads running through all pontificates became more clear.

PART TWO


PIUS XII,
A "BLACK" ROMAN

# 5.  Pius the Unknown

Pius and John, it was clear from the most superficial knowledge of the two, were as one in their devotion to Christ, their reverence for the Papacy as the depository of Biblical heritage, and their loyalty in advanced age to the inspirations of their Catholic boyhoods.

That was the essential, the origin and the conclusion of the story of each. It remained true, however, that no parallel stories could have been written with more contrasting elements.

Just as John soon impressed the papal court with his open fatherliness, Pius was withdrawn. Aides said he was not the person the world thought him to be. Some of his most intimate collaborators admitted that it was bafflingly difficult for even them to penetrate to the depths of his soul.

I had watched Pius XII through many years. One of my first assignments as a reporter on a New York newspaper had been to join the ribald crew of ships' news photographers and writers on a chill morning in 1936, sailing down New York Harbor to interview the arriving Cardinal Secretary of State of the Vatican. I had been covering Catholic news for a year and had been raised in Catholic schools in New York, but the Roman prelate was a stranger to me. The emphasis in Catholic life, despite all the many public ceremonies and the intricately developed hierarchy, is on personal life, on one's own conduct and conscience, one's own ultimate relationship with God. The influence of authorities in Rome was felt only indirectly and invisibly through Cardinal Hayes's chancellery behind Manhattan's St. Patrick's Cathedral. Much Church power was exercised locally and autonomously by the New York cardinal. That part, reserved to Rome and to the predominantly Italian staff of the Vatican, I as a Catholic and even as a journalist rarely observed. I had seen Cardinal Pacelli's name in one-paragraph news items about Catholic devotional congresses in South America and in Europe, but I knew no more of him than that.

There was an air of excitement around the regular morning card game in the cabin of our coast-guard cutter as we bucked and rolled through the restless waters of the Narrows. Ships news was generally good only for an inside-page railing photo of an actress's knees, but this morning we had probable Page One copy. Father Charles Coughlin, of Detroit, a radio preacher, had become an important political figure, ranting against "bankers" and associates of President Franklin D. Roosevelt. A Presidential election was imminent. Father Coughlin's influence on the "Catholic vote" was a factor in whether Alf M. Landon, the Republican, or Roosevelt would win. There was reason to suspect that the Vatican prelate, the main assistant of Pope Pius XI, had come to silence the Michigan priest and to take the Catholic Church out of the American campaign. A church which has lived under most parties and regimes and sees its mission as eternal is never happy to be a campaign issue, and is doubly discontent when the private theories of a priest are confused with what Church leaders consider the essential truths.

We scrambled up the gangplank as the ocean liner slowed to take health inspectors and customs officers aboard at Quarantine. We ducked through narrow hallways and up stairwells. The cardinal awaited us in one of the broader corridors. The principal salons were presumably being used by immigration inspectors. The Vatican dignitary was a tall, thin man of olive complexion. He smiled cordially but a shade coolly, inviting none of the rough camaraderie which the ultrademocratic ships' reporters and cameramen considered their privilege. There was a Continental air of courtesy and dignity which impressed and somewhat repressed all of us.

The interview was over in minutes. The cardinal handed out a prepared statement as a "journalistic tax of entry into the United

States." It told us that he was on vacation and that he was excited
at the thought of seeing such a dynamic and important new part
of the world as the United States had become. There was no
word about the Michigan radio orator. The deans of our press
group tried a few questions about the Detroit priest, but a distant,
inscrutable and determined smile was the only reply. The round-
cheeked young American monsignor at the cardinal's side found
it unnecessary to do any coaching. It was evident that in helping
with the cautiously nonpolitical statement the American priest
had already given ample and shrewd advice. For the sake of one
small detail we asked the priest's name. He would accompany the
Roman cardinal on his 8,000-mile six-week coast-to-coast tour
of the greater part of the American Catholic dioceses, we were
told. The priest's name was Francis Spellman, a Bostonian of
Irish descent. Dealing with us in that unsatisfactory interview had
been two of the dominant figures of American and World
Catholicism of the generation then rising. The help the young
monsignor was giving Cardinal Pacelli was surely one of the
factors the pontiff had in mind three years later, when just after
his own election he appointed the Boston priest Cardinal Hayes's
successor in the internationally important New York Arch-
bishopric.

Cardinal Pacelli had been cautiously uncommunicative. Only
later did I learn that he was no different at home on the Tiber
than he was there on a part of the Hudson.

I was in Rome for Pius's election in 1939, listening and watch-
ing as the highest representatives of World Catholicism discussed
the choice before them. With four years behind me as my paper's
"Catholic expert," I was still unprepared for the old mind of
Rome, but as I stepped ashore in Naples there were many fellow
American Catholics to help me. There is much that is practical
and human in the mind of Rome residents, a young Pittsburgh
priest, Father Walter Carroll, taught me as we met at shipside.
We were part-time correspondents for the same American
Catholic news service and traveled to Rome together. Father
Carroll was still doing advanced theological studies. Later he was

to ride north through Italy in a jeep as the official liaison between
the advancing American Army and the Vatican during World
War II. Still later he was to become the chief American in the
Vatican Secretariate of State—the "prime ministry" of the Catholic Church. A predecessor in that post was the same Monsignor
Spellman whom Cardinal Pacelli had chosen as his American
guide.

I poked among my strange Italian paper money as we came
to the end of an insanely rollicking taxi drive through swarming
Neapolitan streets. I picked out two ten-lire notes, handed them
to the cabdriver, and continued to puzzle over the exchange rate.
Twenty was one dollar, I was figuring out slowly, as the Pitts-
burgher's hand shot out and recaptured a bill from the driver's
still-open palm.

"For a seven-lire ride, ten is enough," the priest told the driver
in Italian, which he later translated, and hurried me into the
station.

"Yes," the driver shouted after us, "but the fact is he gave me
twenty! That other ten is mine!"

The voice held emotion but no conviction. Church and laity
were living together in their own strange Italian equilibrium
compounded of respect and skepticism, affection and cynicism;
at once devout and practical. It was a mixture of faith and real-
ism assembled in proportions strange to an American mind. It was
the background against which the assembling sixty-two cardinals
would scrutinize their own membership and choose Catholicism's
new Pope.

Father Carroll's skirmish with the cabdriver was not his last
tangle before Rome. The sixty-mile-an-hour express, a pride of
Fascism, rocked toward the Eternal City as we took our places in
the restaurant car for dinner. I broke a roll. It was gray, almost
black. Mussolini's efforts to make dependent Italy self-sufficient
in wheat and the other essentials of a nationalistic state had been
a sad failure.

"Take it back and get us white," the Pennsylvania priest told
the steward with the authority of a Rome veteran. The waiter,
with no flicker of expression and without any explanation of

why poor bread had been served, brought something a bit better.

It was the Roman world of hope and few illusions which was to name the new Pope. Again it was a resident American priest who helped me to understand. I felt I was beginning to merge with the people of the Seven Hills a few days later when I visited the ancient Church of Santa Sabina for the services of Ash Wednesday, the first day of the annual Lenten penitential period. For centuries the Roman faithful have visited one of forty old churches each day in turn during Lent. The Mass book used by all Catholics lists the Rome "station churches" along with the special prayers for each Lenten day. A Catholic feels at home in a place of worship he has known for many years through his missal, but there was still a great deal that was strange. The floor was strewn with bay leaves.

"Why is that?" I asked a white-haired priest at my elbow.

"I'll tell you," he whispered solemnly, "when you say what part of Brooklyn you came from!"

I was not so "merged" after all. At the end of the service I told him about the largely Irish Catholic part of Brooklyn, opposite Quarantine on the Narrows, where I had lived for a quarter of a century, and he explained how he knew the gradations of the Brooklyn accent so well. He had taught for years in a Brooklyn Catholic school. He was in Rome as one of the Catholic capital's most eminent educators of student priests from all nations. He had had his joke; he offered to help. He was soon my best source of information. I had only one question. Who would be Pope?

The embarrassment was then his, but quick as he was to tease, he was just as ready to assist. He outlined the cardinals' problem.

"They must decide whether to pick a diplomat—or a parish priest!"

Arguments for a diplomat were many. Mussolini had just violated the 1929 Vatican Peace Agreement by passing a Nazi-type law forbidding marriages between Christians and Jews. The 1929 agreement had given the Catholic Church control of marriage questions. The racist law was thus far the gravest Fascist violation of the Italian-Vatican concordat.

Farther north in Europe there was other bad news. The Nazi hold on Austria was tightening, and the theological faculty at the university in Vienna had been closed. That part of the university was in effect a Catholic seminary. This was a new blow from Hitler against the tens of millions of Catholics behind German borders.

The reasons for choosing a diplomat were quickly appreciated, but another Roman school of thought favored a "parish priest" —a saint. Many remembered humble Pius X who had ruled as Pope during the decade before World War I. By contrast with the socially minded intellectual, Leo XIII, who had preceded him, Pius X had been modest indeed, but his uncomplicated faith and piety had inspired a Catholic religious revival.

Who was "the diplomat"? Who was "the saint"?

Cardinal Pacelli, the Secretary of State, the principal support of Pius XI during years of anguished sparring with Hitler and Mussolini, was without question "the diplomat."

The parish priest? The saint?

My informant's face softened. "Certainly Cardinal dalla Costa in Florence is a saint," he said. "There are even stories that miracles have been worked through his intercession. He has been a parish priest, a pastor, a bishop, an archbishop and a cardinal. He is a true father of his flock. He has not the least diplomatic training. He has never mixed in politics. But what he does have is the moral courage the next pope needs."

I thought I had my story and I filed it. The next pope would be either Cardinal Pacelli or Cardinal Elia dalla Costa, and if I had to sharpen the prediction I would say, cautiously, Cardinal dalla Costa!

I was to meet Cardinal dalla Costa one winter a decade later when I called on him at his episcopal residence opposite the dramatic medieval tiger-striped bell tower and cathedral of Florence. His priest-secretary stopped me as I tried to slip out of my overcoat. There in the dark, high-ceilinged rooms of the prelate's ancient palace it was wiser to keep dressed for outdoors, the priest explained. He led me into the vast hall which was the traditional office of the Florence archbishop. Behind the broad desk huddled the tiny, sunken-cheeked figure of the octogenarian cardinal. He, too, was in an overcoat. He chatted pleasantly for a half hour, but each of us was congealed with cold. Florence is ringed with misery and Communism. In his own way, accepting the architectural glories of a more flamboyant past, the cardinal —without heat in the frigid palace—was sharing the lot of his war-despoiled flock.

Diplomat or parish priest! To one who knew the emphasis every nun in parochial classroom puts on sanctity, it was in-conceivable that the papal electors could choose a foreign-policy expert rather than a saint. To me as an American reporter it seemed equally obvious that diplomacy belonged in worldly foreign offices and that piety was above all the quality appropri-ate to Christianity's main representative.

The cardinals had already decided, and rather differently. I waited at the entrance to the magnificent Renaissance Sistine Chapel for the arrival of the cardinals for the papal election in 1939. I studied the tense, spare figure of Cardinal Pacelli espe-cially. He arrived exactly fifteen minutes before the scheduled time. As Cardinal Chamberlain he was acting *Chef de l'Église* —Chief of the Church, a young Swiss Guard admiringly ex-plained to me. An un-Italian punctuality, the "courtesy of kings," was the odd mark of the Roman-born prelate. It was perhaps a holdover from his twenty-two years as a papal diplomat in Ger-many; a nation the cardinal had admired for its discipline, in-dustry and science.

The cardinal was pale and seemed shaken. I learned afterward that he had tripped and fallen a moment before. The seventy-five-year-old cardinal of Paris, Jean Verdier, had helped him up and had punned prophetically in Latin, *Vicarius Christi in terra!* —"Christ's Vicar on the ground! Vicar of Christ on earth!" Cardinal Pacelli needed no reminder that the main title of the Pope is "Christ's Vicar on Earth," the stand-in—not quite the suc-cessor—of the God-Man at the head of the Christian Church.

Cardinal Verdier, it was commonly said, was one of those who helped rally support for the State Secretary among the twenty-seven non-Italian cardinals.

The faces of the cardinals were inscrutable as they filed past. Most impenetrable was that of Cardinal Pacelli. His head was lowered and his eyes fixed on the cardinal before him. If you could judge by what one Italian illustrated magazine had published you could be sure at least of twenty-seven who would not be chosen. The magazine had run the headline I PAPABILI—"Those eligible for election." Beneath it were thirty-two pictures, those of the Italians! Any Catholic male with the "use of reason," and at least every cardinal, was a potential pope, but the Italian paper had proudly and correctly assumed that, once again, the new Pope would be Italian.

In making their choice the cardinals would have to judge the visible and hidden qualities of many prelates.

"They are ready to take a non-Italian if he is ablest, but there are at least three or four Italians who are considered superior to the foreigners," I was told.

Several names of non-Italians were ticked off. Cardinal Verdier of the prophetic pun and one or two other Frenchmen were mentioned, "But the Germans would not be very happy to have a French Pope! And Germans are not likely candidates, for the same reason in reverse." Another was Cardinal Cerejeira, the impressive young Portuguese primate who had received his red hat at a mere forty-one. The list included even an American, Cardinal Dennis Dougherty of Philadelphia, a bluff, no-nonsense man who, after a violent storm on shipboard, had assured me that any one up and around at such a time was a good sailor.

The deep secrecy that shrouds conclaves may keep us from ever knowing what went on behind the doubly locked doors, but we can assume that Pius XII did not receive two-thirds of the votes on the first ballot. Did he receive almost exactly two-thirds on the second? I have wondered, for one of his first acts as Pope was to change an old rule of papal elections. The provision in 1939 was that the cardinals had to sign their ballots and that in the event of an exact two-thirds vote the elected pontiff had to submit to the humiliating ordeal of having each ballot opened to make sure that he had not voted for himself. The rule derived from an era when leadership of the Church meant sovereignty over central Italy—an age when princely families fought for the throne of Peter as a temporal plum. In a time of greater separation of Church and State the provision had no sense and served only to demean the prelate chosen for the world's most elevated religious mission. Pius's new rule called for an election margin of two-thirds plus one, and suppressed evidence of how each cardinal cast his ballot; not only were the ballots unsigned, but the cardinals were asked to disguise their handwriting so that no one could know how they had voted. The change was the latest of many which new pontiffs made to avoid repetition of what they disapproved of in their own elections. It recalled the act of Pius XI in 1922 in guaranteeing that cardinals of distant countries should be assured a chance to vote. Boston's Cardinal William O'Connell had protested because he missed the 1922 election by hours. It also brought to mind Pius X in 1903. He had been appalled to see one of the most eminent "rival" *papabili*, the reputedly pro-French Cardinal Rampolla, vetoed by Austria. Though the veto assured his own election, Pius X ordered excommunication for any cardinal who brought another "veto" to a conclave.

As a correspondent covering the papal election from the uninformed outside, I had taken the chance that there would be two unsuccessful ballots and a puff of black smoke from the Sistine Chapel chimney at the end of the first morning of voting. Many conclaves have dragged on for a week or more—one in the fourteenth century lasting two years. It seemed clear that neither the saintly Florentine, the diplomatic Vatican State Secretary, or any other could dominate the balloting in a vote or two. The same could be said of the third and fourth ballots in the afternoon, but a qualm beset me. I interrupted the swift sightseeing I was doing in the fear that I would not see Europe again, and hurried to St. Peter's Square. Minutes after getting there I saw the faint gray puff which meant that Pius XII—after one of the shortest papal elections in history—had been chosen on the third ballot. Amid immense excitement the reed-slim Pope appeared on St.

Peter's balcony to bless us. What few knew until after his death nineteen years later was that Pius was found an hour or so after appearing, sobbing as if brokenhearted. Whether the cause of the tears was fear, a sense of inadequacy, mere exhaustion, or all of them is unknown, but the reasons the cardinals so quickly selected the sensitive spirit that was Pius XII is now understood in much detail.

# 6. Pius the Man

During the generation in which Pius was Pope, priests in Rome were impressed by an attitude of many who sought audience with him. They were anxious to get to confession before going into Pius's presence. It was clear that subconsciously they felt that Christ's Vicar, like God, could see through them; could peer with revulsion into the dark corners of their souls.

Pius, according to his nearest assistants, was an unusually sensitive man, alert to the doubts, worries and sufferings of the millions who came to him, but he was not clairvoyant and none of his old cardinal electors thought that he was.

What the pious, practical sages of the Cardinals' College saw in their colleague was hinted at in remarks American electors made to us afterward.

The dilemma "diplomat or saint" was a false one, Roman-trained Cardinal O'Connell of Boston told us.

"We have a Holy Father of vast experience, great ability, great power and," he paused significantly, "great restraint."

The new Pope, with more than four decades' experience in Holy See diplomacy, understood Germany, knew Hitler and Mussolini, comprehended America at least a little after the Monsignor Spellman-guided tour, and was not one to act rashly or delay indefinitely.

"He is above all," the cardinal said, "a man of great piety. He is a saint."

Are there diplomat-saints? Cardinal O'Connell was satisfied that the Papacy had one.

"Everything points to a remarkable reign," the cardinal finished. "We are happy at this elevation. We are confident that the strength of Pius XI's pontificate will be continued."

"Strength" had been the keynote of Pius XI. He had denounced both Communism and Nazism and had grappled boldly with difficult moral problems of capitalism and Socialism in his historic encyclical letter, *Quadragesimo Anno*—"In The Fortieth Year." The encyclical was a sequel to the even greater 1891 labor letter of Leo XIII. The two denounced Marxism in its Communist and Socialist forms as atheistic and materialistic concepts of life, but endorsed many of the aspirations of the unprotected workingman. The two messages closed the door on a feudal past and opened the way to an important Catholic role in labor unions.

In Pius XI's time many had lamented that the ex-mountain climber had been too rough and brusque. Some in the Vatican had felt that he gave too little time to preparation of his chatty talks from the throne, but none denied that he was a man of shrewdness and courage. With a new World War threatening, Catholics of the world had been shocked by Pius XI's loss.

Other aspects of the personality of the new pontiff were underlined by Cardinal Dougherty of Philadelphia.

"From the time he was a young man," the elector said of the new successor of Peter, "he was spoken of as the future hope of the Church. He has a remarkable combination of the highest qualities of body and mind. He is tall, ascetic. His is a Roman face—a face such as one finds on old coins and statues dug up in various parts of the world! He has a most charming manner. His disposition is gentleness personified!"

The Pennsylvania cardinal had never before voted for a pope. For that matter only two Americans had previously cast ballots in a papal election: Cardinals James Gibbons of Baltimore in 1903, and John Farley of New York in 1914. But Cardinal Dougherty had had long experience in choosing curates, parish pastors, monsignors and bishops. He, too, was a product of Roman education and had the Eternal City's mixture of the spiritual and mundane, the supernatural and earthily realistic. He knew, as Rome long has, how well it is that the devout men chosen for bishops should be of a physical appearance handsome

enough to command deference and of a character mild enough
to give a parent's loving leadership.

Nationalist thoughts as an American evidently were not wholly
absent from the mind of the Quaker State cardinal as he weighed
his vote inside the conclave, for he went on with warm approval
to describe "the great satisfaction and wonder" the new Pope
had expressed as he reminisced about the 1936 American trip.

Finally, Cardinal Pacelli's phenomenal command of languages
had captured Cardinal Dougherty's imagination.

"He is a remarkable linguist," he told us. "He is at ease, not
only in Latin but in German, French . . . ! He speaks English
adequately but with the manner of a student rather than of one
who is really at home in it. He only learned English in 1935."

The cardinal, it was plain, would have been happier if the new
Pope had had a completely relaxed command of the English
language, but it was evident that he was awed by the rest of Pius
XII's linguistic accomplishments.

"When he was apostolic nuncio in Germany he frequently
preached and lectured in German," Cardinal Dougherty said.
"He caused great surprise by the fluency and correctness of his
pronunciation and by the elegance of his style in that language!"

Cardinal Dougherty summed up his reaction: Cardinal Pacelli
had obviously enjoyed the broad confidence of a great predecessor who had seen him for a long while at close range. In
frequent travels through Europe and both Americas, Cardinal
Pacelli had made a "deep impression" as "the most outstanding
ecclesiastic."

Master of languages, trusted aid of Pius XI, veteran of the
highest Catholic Church councils, kindly gentleman, diplomat
and man of sanctity; the new Pope was surely all of that. But
we know now from the "White Book" Cardinal Domenico
Tardini published as Vatican Secretary of State in 1960 that a
rumor circulated that some of the cardinals were reluctant to
choose Pacelli because "he is a man of peace and what the
world needs now is a war pope!"

The cardinal's White Book was just that, a brochure with a
white cover. It was presented as a subordinate's intimate impres-

sions of a late eminent superior, but there were some of the over-
tones of the traditional diplomatic White Book as well. The
brochure told much of "the other side" of the late pontiff; the
penetrating personal details which are usually kept away from
public attention during a man's lifetime, but which seem properly
to become part of the public patrimony when one of the world's
great history-makers passes on.

Hitler had already seized several countries. Any new step could
bring another global conflict. Nazi and Communist totalitarianism
were pressing down on the Christian Church. A fighting pope
might have to lead his flock through military and ideological
ruin.

Was the rumor true? Cardinal Tardini insisted that he did not
know. He was not then a member of the Sacred College. It might,
of course, have been one of those concoctions of fertile imagi-
nations which always seem to circulate on such occasions, the
State Secretary of 1960 observed cautiously. But the fact that
he opened his White Book with the account showed that the
cardinal, one of Pius XII's nearest associates, found the story
plausible.

The fact was that the distant, courtly prelate whom I had met
at Quarantine with the ships'-news crew, the linguist whom Pius
XI had called "Our Pentecostal Cardinal"—our cardinal with
the God-given command of the main Western idioms—the
churchman of so many brilliant parts, was a shy, almost timid
man, a person of a meditative and scrupulous character bordering
on the indecisive. Beyond that there was something else obscure
about the character of the Pope of the tormented middle decades
of the twentieth century. He was a man with the strong, clear,
trusting, hopeful faith of a child—that of the altar boy he had
been in the former parish of St. Philip Neri in ancient downtown
Rome. Surely tales of the sixteenth-century Roman saint, a priest
who revived spiritual fervor in a materialistic city, must have
sunk into the future Pope's mind and molded his own devout
ambitions. But Pius was more than a man of piety. He was one
of a practical, even skeptical, turn of mind. Talking to him, a
visitor could find his conclusions about the fate of the twentieth-

century world pessimistic. But his faith saved him from that. God, in his view, could not permit the disaster which cold calculation tended to forecast. A serene confidence thus walked hand in hand with the chilly appraisal of the earth and its problems which was the other side of Pius XII's not easily penetrated character.

The Pius whom the cardinals of the 1939 conclave—like any electors—knew only in part, was the son of one of the "blackest" families of Rome. The "Blacks" were those who remained loyal to the ebony-clad clergy of the Eternal City in 1870 when the red-shirted revolutionary Giuseppe Garibaldi and the blue-bannered dynasty-minded King Victor Emmanuel of the House of Savoy conquered the 1,000-year-old Central Italian Papal State and formed united modern Italy.

The future Pius was born in Rome only six years after the last papal state sovereign was overthrown. The downfall of the king-popes had had deep repercussions inside the Pacelli family. The future pontiff's grandfather had been Acting Minister of the Interior in the Papal State Government for years, and as such, supervisor of much of the law and order in the ancient Church kingdom. He had been offered a post as a counsellor of state in the new united Italy, but outraged by the attack against the Pope, had refused. Grandfather Marcantonio Pacelli had been a petty papal-state nobleman and was co-founder of *L'Osservatore Romano*, the paper which for more than a century has served as the mouthpiece of the Vatican and as a lighthouse of ideas and leadership for Catholics throughout the world.

The father of the future Pope, Filippo Pacelli, had also been eminent in Catholic lay circles in Rome, and as a lawyer at the Papal Consistorial Court few other laymen outranked him in the reduced Vatican world.

Perhaps the greatest influence on the Pacellis' third child and second son was that of his mother's family. She was a minor noblewoman, the Marchioness Virginia Graziosi. Two of her brothers were priests, two of her sisters nuns. The future Pope grew up with clerical relatives all about him. His grandfather's brother,

Don Giuseppe Pacelli, had baptized him, and he had been inspired by tales of his Jesuit uncle, a missionary in Brazil.

It was logical to think of the wistful, silent Eugenio Pacelli as a possible future churchman. It is said, in fact, that an old priest, Don Jacobacci, had picked him up at the time of his baptism and assured the bystanders that "sixty-three years from now all Christians will hail him in St. Peter's!" The day the conclave ended in 1939 proved to be Eugene Pacelli's sixty-third birthday.

Whatever their own views, the Pacelli relatives did nothing to push their child toward the Church. Filippo Pacelli, in fact, enrolled his studious son in the Italian government *lycée*. The excitement of the fall of the theocratic state and the rise of laic liberalism reverberated inside the school walls. The atmosphere was anticlerical. Eugenio, the son of the "Blacks," was forced to take a stand and he did—on the Church's side. It is recalled that he got a bad mark for conduct when he put another student up to answering an assignment by choosing St. Augustine as one of history's greatest figures. It is said that when the teacher objected the young Pacelli argued the case. It was one of the future Pope's few school demerits, for he stayed at the top of his class for years and won a nationwide contest in world history.

Romans who traced back into Eugene Pacelli's childhood report that a favorite pastime of his was to act out religious ceremonies. There must be some added mystic attraction to that in the Italian soul, for one of the very few times I observed children playing at religion was in a hill town west of Rome where four solemn urchins acted out Christ's Passion during the Good Friday season.

Eugenio was a bookworm, but he indulged in some sports— all, however, solitary ones. He rode horseback, swam, rowed and walked. There is no record of any team play or of bodily contact sports such as soccer, ball of any kind, or boxing.

It was in his late teens that he announced that he wanted to be a priest. For a *lycée* student of a broad and modern classical education it was a striking and courageous decision. Priests in the Rome of that day were accustomed to insults on the street. The gulf between "science and religion," all-vanquishing liberalism

PIUS THE MAN    63

and fundamentalist faith, nineteenth-century democracy and authoritarianism, hardly could have been wider.

Eugenio entered the seminary, but for reasons of health lived at home. The camaraderie, the give-and-take which are part of the life of any boarding school, was passed over in his formative years. The seminarian did well; he was so successful, in fact, that he felt able to double up in his studies, following the normal preparation of a priest at the school for clergy and taking courses in literature at the state university. By the time of his ordination the young cleric was one of the few who was trained in the thought both of his Church and of the unfriendly modern world around it.

Even at ordination the future Pope was alone. He was considered too frail for the long joint ceremony at which his contemporaries became priests. Among those at his first Mass, in the 1,500-year-old church of Santa Maria Maggiore—the "major" church of Mary in Rome—was a cardinal friend of the family, Vincenzo Vanutelli. Within months the young "Black," son of two worlds—one ancient and Christian, the other modern and rational—was summoned to the Vatican as the aide of Monsignor Pietro Gasparri, the Church's Director of Diplomatic Affairs, and a future Secretary of State.

It was perhaps from that moment that the character and the future of the Pope of World War II were decided. In the Secretariate of State young Father Pacelli worked with the tireless dedication and talent which had given him perfect scores at the lycée and at the university. He was assigned to the modern rearrangement of the complicated and overlapping old laws of the Church, the "codification of canon law." In connection with that task he had to report progress to the Pope, Pius X, a man he was later to raise to the altars of the Catholic Church as a saint. He studied the Pope with reverence but also with cool appraisal. He knew Pius X's reputation for provincial simplicity, but as he was to tell one of his assistants later when he was Pope, that evaluation did the saint no justice. Pius X showed a quick and canny grasp of the essentials as he reviewed the project's progress, Pius XII said later of his predecessor.

By the time of the coronation of King George V in 1910,

Father Pacelli was so prominent at the papal court that he was chosen as one of Pius X's envoys to the ceremony. Perhaps his respect for Britain and the hope for a better Catholic-British understanding that ran as an important thread through Pius XII's pontificate dated from then. By 1917, at forty-one, the Pope of twenty-two years later seemed the proper choice for one of the main diplomatic assignments of his generation. He was raised to archbishop and sent to Germany as nuncio, or ambassador, of Pope Benedict XV, with a mission to attempt to negotiate the end of World War I. The mission failed. The Vatican's voice under Benedict was far less loud than Pius XII made it during his own reign. He did not succeed then, but in the years following World War I the alumnus of St. Philip Neri's church managed to negotiate two concordats, one of which later limited Hitler in his efforts to use the Catholic clergy as part of the totalitarian Nazi machine.

The archbishop's assignment to Germany was a blow to his mother. At a time of life when most other priests are already a generation removed from their families, Monsignor Pacelli had continued to live at home.

The family influences which were still at work in those final years before the foreign assignment were suggested by the recollections of Brother Clancy, head of the Irish Christian Brothers' School, which the future Pope's young nephews attended. At the time of Pius XII's election in 1939 I asked Brother Clancy what he remembered. "How the Pope's nephews often exulted in school that they would 'stay home next day for Mass!' " he told me.

"Our uncle will celebrate it for us!" the Pacelli boys would boast.

Devotion to the clergy and pride in the priesthood were carrying into another generation of Pacellis, but the isolation which had kept the future pontiff separated from his fellows was also still noticeable.

I visited the Pacelli home in 1939. It was a far cry from the Renaissance glories of flamboyant St. Peter's where preparations for Pius XII's coronation were under way. It was a small, neat house of Pompeian red, the picturesque color which Mussolini was trying to ban as inappropriate for a "warlike nation."

The house was not rich but it had a certain patrician dignity. The walled courtyard was tiny, with a neatly clipped box hedge beside a prim graveled walk; a French garden in microcosm. A gold-woven red tapestry with the new pontiff's coat of arms dominated the small living room. On it two angels in blue held a shield, one part decorated with the dove and olive leaves which have long been the symbols of the Pacellis (*pace* means peace in Italian), the other half adorned with the papal tiara and Peter's heavenly keys.

The wall pictures were religious. One showed Christ in agony. The subjects were traditional and devout. The works were copies without artistic pretensions.

The influences represented by that home seemed evident—a profound dedication to the Catholic Church and to the Papacy, immersion in the middle class, the withdrawn attitude of a family conscious of a worthy past and given to the struggles of a sometimes difficult present.

In Germany, at last away from his family, the Roman priest worked well. He admired much about the Teutons. As Pope there was a great deal about him that was German. In an Italy where five minutes' lateness is considered being on time, Pope Pius was punctual to the second whether he was rising at 6, saying Mass at 7:30, having breakfast at 8:30, or receiving visitors in audience. No German was more scrupulous about checking quotations or correct word usages. Many of Pius's aides were convinced, in fact, that far too many precious hours were lost by the Pope as he himself hunted down references and grammatical constructions.

Even Pius's chief assistants as pontiff could be traced back to the German days. Soon after he reached Germany, Mother Pasqualina, a Bavarian, was sent to him as a housekeeper by her Swiss order. She remained with him four decades until his death. Father Robert Leiber, a German Jesuit historian and professor, joined the nuncio as a secretary and language tutor. A half-dozen other Germans—nuns and priests—made up the bulk of Pius's personal Vatican staff. One was a librarian; one the priest to whom Pius went for confession; two were nuns who served as assistant cooks, laundresses and housekeepers. The language of Pius's small papal household was German. Father Leiber, for one, never acquired complete fluency in Italian.

The German days ended in 1929. The fifty-three-year-old archbishop was recalled to Rome in glory to succeed his old superior, Cardinal Gasparri, as Secretary of State. From there to the Papacy proved a short step. It is said that the ill and aged Pius XI remarked at one time that he would be ready to die if he were sure that his multilingual Secretary of State of the thirties would succeed him. By then the Cardinal's linguistic talents and photographic memory were a legend. It is said that he could read twenty pages three times and then repeat them without a slip. Time and again I followed long texts as he recited them without notes. I never ceased to marvel at the fact that not a syllable was altered. It is said that electricians apologized, at the end of one of Pius's audiences, for moving in front of him to make needed adjustments while he spoke.

"Did you?" he asked. "I didn't see. I was reading."

# 7. Private Life of a Pope

Millions of words have been published about Pius XII, but not one account of his private life in the Papacy is fully accurate.

That at least is the testimony of Father Leiber, Pius's secretary.

Some accounts were ludicrous, the priest adds. The funniest, in his opinion, was by a famous but unidentified journalist who said that the Pope was awakened in his iron bedstead each morning by four bearded brown-robed Franciscan Capuchin monks carrying a cup of coffee.

The truth, according to Father Leiber, was that "everything was as normal as possible."

The Pius who had been a Rome *lycée* pupil and a student of the Italian state university brought a calm practicality to his exalted spiritual office.

The accounts of Pius's private life erred persistently in over-sentimentality. The Pope was devout but he was a realistic diplomat, too. There were occasional stories that he slept on the floor as a penance. The truth is that he was repelled by all extremes, whether of self-mortification, fasting, or even the choice of words in a document. He was forever cutting down the force of expressions in early drafts of Vatican texts. A word with a little less sting might avoid offending someone and good never came of hurting people, the Pope believed.

All was "normal," but if one criticism were to be made—in the view of the Pope's intimate assistants—it was that too little time went to relaxation, too little to general reading. It was too much a life of "all work and no play." It was just the reverse of the criticism which historians level against the Renaissance Popes whose worldly lives helped provoke the Protestant Reformation and the scandal of a divided Western Christianity.

When Archbishop Pacelli became Cardinal Secretary of State his salty predecessor, Cardinal Gasparri, warned him to concentrate on the main problems and to leave details to his subordinates.

"Otherwise," the elderly churchman said, "it will be your skin."

It was advice wasted on the former schoolboy who had always believed that one who could get ten should never be content with nine. Domenico Tardini, Pius's main assistant in the Secretariate of State, said that the Cardinal's associates soon set up what they called "the infirmary." It was a large pocket in the leather folder in which documents were carried each day to the director of Vatican diplomacy. The slightest secretarial flaw would catch the Pope's eye and he would refuse to sign until the paper was redone according to his concept of what was proper. Monsignor Tardini would slide the rejected sheet back into the folder and return with it another day.

Not only did the Cardinal Secretary of State provide a steady flow of small mistakes for the "infirmary," but Pius as Pope used many hours, and in the end many months, checking tiny details—matters of correct form in his half-dozen main languages, errors of punctuation in the galley proofs of papal speeches to be published in the Vatican paper, correct versions of quotations which he wished to use. Pius had the scholar's aversion to garbled references. To make sure that the quotations were accurate he looked them up himself. That, almost alone, gave him rest of a sort. It is said that his only hobby was dictionaries. He had an impressive collection of them.

Pius's day began between 6 and 6:30. Each was the same for years on end. An alarm would waken him in his seven-room middle-class apartment in the Vatican Palace overlooking St. Peter's Square. He would take a cold bath, dress, and then shave with a white electric razor which was said to have been a present from his special friend, Cardinal Spellman. His five German canaries and a goldfinch would fly freely about the room. They, too, were among the few diversions of the sternly self-disciplined son of the Black Pacellis.

Pius said Mass at 7:30. His footman, butler and chauffeur, Giovanni Stefanori, or the latter's alternate, Mario Stoppa—old employees of the Vatican—would serve.

Breakfast would be at 8:30. As "normal as possible," it was the same as most other Romans had at the same hour or a little earlier. There was toast and coffee, sometimes cream of wheat and fruit juice, too. It was not much considering the grind of the audiences which followed immediately. But it was no more or less than most Italians had. Even in the next two meals the Pope did not eat a great deal or very fancily. He was neither a gourmand, a gourmet, or a fanatical devotee of fasting. Eating too much made him ill. He had no interest in the things of the table. He ate what was set before him by Mother Pasqualina and the two other nuns. He would sit silent and alone after the fashion of Popes and probably from his own attraction to solitude. To some extent the unimaginative and limited diet may have been due to a conscious desire to share the sufferings of the world of the underfed, but certainly it is true that one of the few things which struck Pius XII as comical was the elevation of food to the level of an art. One of his favorite stories, according to post-mortem revelations by Cardinal Tardini, was about a gourmet ambassador who, during his time in Berlin, slipped out to the kitchen between courses to be sure that the food was prepared properly.

Soup, meat, fish, eggs, vegetables, fruit, wine, beer, mineral water and coffee were regular items on the papal table. A midafternoon cup of coffee helped restore the aging Pope's strength. Lunch was at 1:30 P.M., the evening meal about 8:30. There was no eating between meals. With so much strain and work, so little diversion and such scant interest in the table, Pius XII weighed only 128 pounds at the end of World War II, next to nothing for so tall a man. He was five feet eleven and one-half, though his frail build made him seem even taller. The Pope listened to doctors who urged that he gain, and in the fifties his weight went up to 169 pounds, but he was never portly.

At breakfast time Pius XII ran through the newspapers. Although he tended more and more to neglect true literature he was as much a reader of newspapers as any journalist. As newsmen study the writings of their colleagues, so did Pius-XII. *Il Tempo*, a conservative Rome newspaper, was one of his favorites but he went through a pile of others. *Unità*—Unity—the Italian Communist newspaper, was understood to be one of those the Pope perused regularly. Vatican correspondents had reason to believe that at least one sports newspaper was also in the stack. Pius saw sports as the road to the hearts of many youths and tried to reach them that way, too. In audiences he showed some knowledge of sports. The Pope was a fan of Gino Bartoli, a rather devout Catholic layman who was a European bicycle champion.

A red pencil lay at the pontiff's elbow as he skimmed the papers. He used it to mark the most significant items for his staff. Monsignor Tardini was often embarrassed when he arrived for the early morning interview he had each day or every other day.

"Did you see that story on Page Three of such-and-such a paper?" the Pope would ask.

The answer was often no. "I get through two or three papers, but I can't see all those things," the abashed monsignor lamented as he discussed the situation.

Pius was interested in anything that concerned himself, the Catholic Church in general, or the main issues touching the United States, Britain, France, Russia and the other principal nations. Italy as the home country of the Papacy and his own native land was the subject of his especially intense study. Popes are not only-heads of the World Catholic Church, but are also primates or leaders of the Church in Italy. For that reason and because of geography, Italy always gets a far more than average attention at the Vatican.

The morning reading of the papers was supplemented through the day by other reports. Sometimes Pius switched on the radio in his dining room to get news broadcasts from Italy or from the British Broadcasting Corporation in London. Monsignor Tardini brought in other items. A staff working at *Osservatore Romano* drew up a digest of a hundred newspapers of the main nations including Russia. The summary had been started at the time of

Pius XI who saw few if any newspapers. Pius XII had acquired the habit of reading it then and ordered that it be continued. In the evening more reports came in. The Vatican Radio monitored the main Catholic and general news items of the world air waves.

Pius needed to be abreast of the news in order to converse usefully with eminent callers from all professions and from all grades of society. All of his visitors agreed that he succeeded.

Pius XII had as Pope the same uncertain health which had caused him to be ordained alone rather than with his contemporaries. Few of those who saw him in audience realized that in later years he regularly went back to his rooms wet with perspiration. He had to change clothes three or four times a day. He suffered from cold and wore a shawl.

The many changes of vestments no doubt put a strain on the papal wardrobe, but the rather limited outlay for the Pope's support was little inflated by the problem of maintaining his clothing. It has been reported that the Pope's daily food costs were as small as $1.50. That may well be too low an estimate, but the three nuns kept down many expenses. At Pius's own wish his vestments were mended time and again. We are indebted to Monsignor Paganuzzi, of the Pope's staff, for the story of what happened when one unnamed member of the pontiff's inner circle —very likely Monsignor Tardini—asked Mother Pasqualina for one of Pius XII's white vestments as a souvenir of his pontificate. Pius had agreed, so Mother Pasqualina ordered a new garment made. In her opinion it was overdue. To keep his promise Pius wore the new one for a day or two and then sent it to the prelate who had requested it. He himself went back to his worn-out vestments. A sparkling white new cassock of Pius XII was on display in 1960 at the orphanage which was Cardinal Tardini's pet charity. It would seem safe to assume that it is the one of Monsignor Paganuzzi's story.

After audiences Pius would slip into a working garment, an ankle-length cassock, of "every-day gray." In place of the gold-woven red velvet pumps of protocol he would ask the nuns for his "round the world" shoes—a well-worn pair long overdue for discard.

Pius, Italian fashion, napped for a half hour after lunch. After that he walked for an hour in the Vatican garden. In his first years as Pope the brother of his brother-in-law, Monsignor Rossignani, strolled with him. After the latter died the Pope walked alone. As with all of the old, death and estrangements added to his loneliness. This, coupled with the aloof dignity of the Papacy, meant that as the years advanced he was more and more by himself.

Eugene Pacelli had an immense respect for the Papacy. As Pius XI's Secretary of State he had filled a sheet a day with notes on the Pope's comments on the world's main problems. There were 1,300 such sheets at the end. Cardinal Pizzardo recalled how Cardinal Pacelli would refer to them to discover some finer shading of the "mind" of the Pope and would then instruct his own subordinates accordingly.

Pius XII permitted even his most intimate associates and members of his family to kneel when they approached him. He was always a Pope. There were no moments when he escaped from a mission that he accepted with full gravity and devotion. His first words after regaining consciousness on the Monday of his first stroke were: "To work—audiences, letters, files."

His life was one of unremitting labor. When he returned from the walks on which he read books or documents, he plunged into a new round of toil. Often he used his telephone, never identifying himself but usually quickly recognized by the few top aides to whom he phoned. Pius XI was the first Pope to have a telephone, but after it was installed remarked that it was nice though something he would "never use." On the contrary he took advantage of it, causing some concern among his devout assistants who were never sure of how to comport themselves while he was telephoning. One solved the problem by kneeling.

The phoning caused other difficulties, as Cardinal Tardini has related. On one occasion a cardinal's butler hung up when the Pope refused to say who was calling. On another evening when Monsignor Tardini was at dinner at the home of the Peruvian Ambassador, a servant—for the sake of a scruple—decided not to put down the receiver. He reported that a man who would not give his name wished to talk to the Pope's main diplomatic aide. Amid general astonishment the monsignor took no offense and answered the phone.

"I knew who it was," he said.

Sometimes the calls were made to order a reversal of some recently decided policy. Worrying over possible repercussions, Pius occasionally changed the policy completely, even vetoing unanimous decisions by a board of cardinals. The sheltered boy who had suffered through the Rome *lycée* endured the same torments as he faced a Pope's decisions.

Often at 6 P.M. Pius turned to a book he had requested through Father Leiber earlier in the afternoon, a volume needed for a speech or document. The Pope may not have realized the scurrying that some of those requests caused, but after his lunch, nap, and walk, the book was usually there so that he could go on with the next lap of his unceasing effort.

Sometimes evening hours brought visits from Count Enrico Galeazzi, the acting governor of the fifth-of-a-square-mile, 1,000-population Vatican State, who would report on affairs in the small kingdom. Occasionally Princes Carlo or Marcantonio Pacelli, sons of Pius's admired older brother, Francesco, would come to call. The princes and their third prince brother, Giulio, were prominent members of Rome's diplomatic and commercial society, in part, certainly, because of the glamor of the revered family name, but Pius must have seen them through other eyes. He must have beheld them as sons of his brother, a layman who lived, as the Pope once said, "as monks ought to." Francesco was the man Pius XI entrusted with the delicate 3-year negotiation ending the 69-year estrangement between the Italian Government and the Catholic Church and creating the Vatican State.

Even with his family Pius relaxed little. Twice a year all the nephews, their princess wives, and the great-nieces and nephews came to call. Once was at Christmas. The other was on June 2nd, the day of St. Eugene, the holy man for whom the future Pope was named at baptism. In Italy it is one's name day rather than one's birthday which is celebrated. This has the advantage that everyone knows his neighbor's feast day and can greet him accordingly. The days of San Giuseppe and San Giovanni are occasions of jubilation, as can well be imagined. Almost every second male in Italy celebrates the occasion.

The families would call for an hour or two but the Pope would promptly return to his heavy routine. I telephoned Marcantonio after one Christmas party. He said the six great-nieces and nephews from five to fifteen years of age had received most of the attention. In previous years they had recited poems for their papal great-uncle but for some reason had decided suddenly that they were too grown up to continue. The Pope had met them in his apartment beside a tiny representation of the Bethlehem Nativity scene. The three German nuns had set it up as they did every year. In another part of the apartment was a Christmas tree, a more typically German emblem of Christmas. The Pope had asked each child in turn how he was doing in school and had distributed "small" presents. Marcantonio would not say what they were.

Through the evenings Pius worked as he did through the day. Sometimes he typed on a white portable, doing first drafts and recopying speeches. More and more in later years he composed in his neat, tiny, orderly, rather timid longhand. His manuscripts showed occasional corrections but usually only in the selection of words.

Once in awhile the aging Pope listened to music. He knew musical theory well and preferred classics—Bach, Beethoven, Wagner, Verdi. Sometimes, but rarely, he read for relaxation. A favorite volume was the Cicero of his school days. Proof that the grave boy was still present in the man was the fact that the school volume stayed with him through his pontificate. St. Augustine, whom he had defended at the *lycée*, Dante, the father of the Italian language, and the great nineteenth-century Catholic writer, Alessandro Manzoni, author of the classic of modern Italian *I Promessi Sposi*—"The Betrothed"—were other favorites. Pius read Latin and Greek fluently. Father Leiber says he remarked once that he had to be careful about picking up Cicero because the noble old Roman cost him too much time. There was an affinity between the two sons of Rome twenty centuries apart, the Pope's secretary felt.

Occasionally Pius would tune in on the B.B.C. British English, rather than the much more widely spoken American version, was his ideal. One American priest of Irish extraction who lived close to the Pope for several years observed the pontiff's taste for the B.B.C. with faint disapproval.

"He likes it," he said a bit sadly, and with wonder. "It must be that British humor."

Pius never smoked. He had an acute dislike for the habit. He drank only wine and beer.

Supper was at 8:30 P.M. The Pope napped briefly again as at midday, recited the rosary at 9:30 P.M. with the three sisters, and then withdrew to his apartment for more study until midnight or later. From eleven to twelve he was often in his private chapel reading the final prayers of his breviary, the book every Catholic priest studies each day. Long before bedtime the papal apartments were darkened. Burdened by the financial worries of a Church which spent billions of dollars a year, Pius XII was like a seminary president or the father of a large family in what aides called his almost fanatical insistence on turning out unneeded lights. When the footmen and the monsignors neglected to turn one out, Pius XII snapped it off for them. It was another detail in a life assiduously attentive to tiny points. Pius's concern for economy was soon a legend. His will was written on the back of an envelope. Italy's great postwar premier, Alcide De Gasperi, who hid out in the Vatican as a librarian during the last years of Fascism, made a collection of odd paper scraps on which Pius used to order the volumes he required. De Gasperi then took charge of tracking down books for the pontiff.

At twelve or one, sometimes as late as three, the Pope's day ended. It was the wearing day of a man, lonely by nature, who had marshaled all the resources of a powerful will in an effort to fully live up to the demands of the world's loftiest spiritual responsibility.

# 8. Apostle of Audiences

It was a paradox that a man as shy as Pius XII was so much the pontiff of the multitudes. The estimates of how many saw "Papa Pacelli" in audiences range from 10,000,000 to 30,000,000. Whichever is true it was far more than had ever visited any other leader of the Catholic Church. The contrast with the mere handfuls who must have gathered for the first Apostles could not have been greater.

"Your audiences are an apostolate," an official of one of the main Catholic religious orders told Pius one day. The Pope's appreciative response made it clear that he agreed.

It was that official who told me that he had "reason" to believe that he knew another principle at the heart of Pius's unparalleled succession of audiences. This was that the Pope could accomplish more "by seeing the American Secretary of State, John Foster Dulles, than by seeing Cardinals Micara or Cicognani"; in the case of the latter "he already knows their views"; in that of the former he could hope to influence a man of power who was not already part of the Catholic community.

The "reason" was surely because of the Pope's own comments on the subject.

"Cardinal Cicognani," incidentally, was Gaetano Cicognani, Supervisor of the Sacred Congregation of Rites, and not his brother Amleto who was not yet a cardinal and was only later to become Holy See Secretary of State, the man who more than any other has the ear of the pontiff.

The Pope the millions saw in audiences was not at all the timid man the few intimates knew. Depending upon the type of audi-

ence and the nature of the visitor, various sides of Pius's character were seen, but few came away without being favorably impressed.

"One hundred times delegates to conventions have told me
that the papal audience was the best part of their congress," I was
told by the dean of the diplomatic corps to the Holy See.

"If only I could stay in Rome and see him once a day—that
would be all," a young navigator on an American Navy ship said
ecstatically. "I've seen the world," he added solemnly, "and Rome
with the Pope is surely the tourist attraction of the future."

The forecast, by the early sixties, even with another pope, was
rather well borne out.

A few other popes had granted audiences but none in the lav-
ish manner of Pius XII. It is said that the nonagenarian Leo XIII
dozed as crowds filed past his throne on the few occasions when
he could be seen. It was not until the time of his successor, Pius X,
in the first decade of the twentieth century that audiences as they
are now known really began. World War I prevented Benedict
XV from having many, and Pius XI had relatively few. It was left
to Pius XII to grant as many as four general audiences in a single
evening at his summer residence at Castel Gandolfo, something
of which Vatican protocol officers would not have dreamed even
in Pius's own first years as Pope. The Castel Gandolfo audiences
reached a peak of fatherly informality and even of familiarity.
No tickets were required. These audiences were so casual from
the very start that *L'Osservatore Romano* suppressed news of
them for almost a year after they began.

The typical audience was a general one in St. Peter's Basilica.
Pius XII would be carried in on the *sedia gestatoria*—the portable
throne. Protestants who may have been troubled at the sight of a
man riding on the shoulders of twelve of his fellows might have
been interested to know that Pius XII, especially in his last years,
was repelled by the idea of the papal litter and mounted it only
with an effort of will. The same distaste for this symbol of more
than regal glory was shared at least by two other Popes of this
century, Saint Pius X and John XXIII.

Americans visiting St. Peter's for the first time never cease to be astonished at the shouts of *Evviva il Papa*—"Long live the Pope"—which roll up from the throngs at the general audiences.

General Mark Clark, Commander of the Allied forces that liberated Rome, had a favorite story for years afterward. He said that he rode into Rome on a jeep and visited Pius XII. The latter had received tens of thousands of Axis soldiers in audience, and now just as cordially welcomed the Allied troops. They were all his children in a fratricidal conflict. Clark arranged for soldiers to go to the Vatican in waves. Some days later Pius XII asked that the Allied commander return.

"They don't like me," the Pope told the general. "They stand silently."

"They think they're in church, Your Holiness," the general replied. "They believe that if they dared make a sound we'd knock their blocks off!"

The Pope usually mounted a throne before the papal altar above the believed tomb of St. Peter and beneath Michelangelo's dome. It was the spot of best visibility. Often he would speak in six languages. Then would come his blessing, his arms stretched out straight so that his frail white figure made a cross, his eyes turned up toward the heavens from which he begged the benediction. He would remount the *sedia gestatoria*, his two hands gesturing toward himself as if to urge all to embrace the religious values he represented.

Pius XII seemed especially distant in the Vatican general audiences. Usually all went as planned, but there were occasional exceptions. Almost all of those who had seats near the Pope's throne were invited guests. Tickets were distributed liberally through the various embassies to the Holy See or through each country's special seminary or national parish church in Rome. For awhile Americans had a choice among all three. Myron C. Taylor presided over a "special Presidential mission" to the person of Pius XII, the rough equivalent of an embassy. The North American College was the United States Seminary, and Santa Susanna's on the edge of the ancient quarter of Rome near the American Embassy was the United States parish church. Any American could have a ticket unless he showed signs of mental unbalance, as a few did. No questions of religion were asked, and letters from Protestant ministers were accepted as valid introductions. Canon Charles Greve of the seventy-five-year-old American Protestant Church, St. Paul's, sent about four such requests for audiences each year to his Catholic opposite number, Father James Cunningham at Santa Susanna's.

The thin screening was not always enough. One American who was certified for a ticket by the North American College shifted from a Jekyll to a Hyde personality after leaving the seminary and getting to the audience. He vaulted the railing separating the crowds from the Pope, and for a change the Swiss Guard protectors of the pontiff had something to do. Another, at the ceremony in which thirty-two prelates were made cardinals in 1946, waited until the Pope mounted the *sedia gestatoria* and then, in full view of the thirty thousand of us at the audience, sprinted up the thirteen red-covered steps to seat himself under the dome on the papal throne. The sacrilege accomplished, he meekly let the Swiss Guards lead him away.

The special and private audiences had another flavor and the person the visitors met on these occasions seemed different.

The man who believed himself Christ's Vicar, God's instrument in the world, "could be very charming," his aides said of him, and I found this myself on several visits to the Pope. The pontiff paid callers several great compliments. He was almost always exactly on time. He checked beforehand on "who was who." He looked his visitors fully in the eyes and gave himself totally to the caller for the seconds or minutes they had together. In photographs Pius had a strange habit of staring away to one side, separating himself from the viewer. I wondered whether it was to limit the value of the photographs as an encouragement to callers of doubtful character who might have slipped through the defenses at the embassies, seminaries, and national parish churches. Many politicians and businessmen wanted pictures for exploitation. Whatever the reason, Pius was not aloof as he talked earnestly and cordially with each of his special visitors in turn.

In such conversations he was frank and showed himself well-informed and practical, a man of the twentieth-century world as well as a believer. Not all of those conversations will be revealed, for they were studded often with the phrase "This is secret, this is secret!" Many will carry small "secrets" to the grave, although what the Pope apparently often meant was merely that "This is not to be attributed to me," a much less grave restriction from a journalist's point of view.

The affable Pius whom the visitors saw was the product of the ceaseless study which made up his life. Callers were perpetually amazed.

"He was aware that the recession is over in the United States," the American Catholic Secretary of Labor James Mitchell said with astonishment in Pius's last months. "Why, we've just learned that ourselves. And he knew all about the International Labor Organization, too!"

The I.L.O., a society of governments, businessmen and labor leaders, was one of the many worthy world groups which rarely made headlines and were known to few outside their own membership.

"Whenever I go in to see him he knows the question," a cardinal said. "He does study the files."

A preference for "Dulleses" over cardinals did not of course mean that Pius XII omitted receiving fellow bishops. Within the limits of the possibilities of each brief day the pontiff saw both "Dulleses" and bishops. The preparation which went into the various audiences was reflected in the experience of a German prelate. He finished reporting to the Pope on the state of moral and political affairs in his diocese and then watched with surprise as Pius drew out a slip on which a half-dozen other topics were noted.

"And about these matters . . . ?" the Pope asked. By the time the catechism was over the pontiff had a good understanding of all the diocese's main problems. It was only one of 1,000 similar sees in the world but the tireless pontiff demanded to know everything in detail.

In those many years of audiences there were surely many strange episodes. No reporter learned more than a few of them. There was the occasion on which Archbishop Spellman pre-

sented sixty of us who were in his party at the time he became
a cardinal: priests, air-line officials, prominent laymen, newspapermen. Each shook hands in turn, the Catholics genuflecting
three times before approaching the sovereign. The Pope reached
over his shoulder to a monsignor behind him who kept him sup-
plied with small silver medals of himself to distribute as souvenirs.

The Pope passed more than an hour with us.

"I'm glad to have seen you all," he told us at the end and then
with a smile, perhaps reading the incredulity in all our faces, "I
mean it!"

There were two schools of thought about a visitor's proper
comportment in a special audience.

"You must be silent unless spoken to," one young Catholic
official advised me. "You must ask no questions. He is a chief of
state. His is the initiative."

"If you stand there saying nothing it will be a mere *baciamano*
[ring-kissing, or literally, hand-kissing audience]," one of those
wiser to Rome's ways warned to the contrary. "Say who you are.
Thank him for receiving you on such a busy day. Speak of his
recent Christmas message. It won't be an interview that you can
publish but it may lead to something interesting."

The latter was the better advice, as my experience with both
methods demonstrated.

Few were permitted to repeat the contents of their talks with
the Pope but many felt free to relate at least what they had said.
Former President Truman was one who was most mum.

"When a gentleman came to call on me," the ex-occupant of
the White House said, "and when he talked afterward about
what we discussed, he didn't get in any more!"

Truman and Herbert Hoover, both of them post-World War II
callers, were the first Presidents or ex-Presidents to visit Rome
for audiences since the time of Woodrow Wilson's call on Benedict XV in 1919.

Hoover, too, was silent on the topic he discussed, but just as
it was a safe guess that Pius and Truman had talked over their ill-
fated joint effort to establish formal Vatican-American diplomatic ties, so was it easy to divine that Hoover asked Pius to help

with his efforts to get Latin America to feed hungry postwar Europe. Hoover interrupted a survey tour of malnutrition areas in Germany to pay a sudden visit to Rome. He "intimated," as his assistants put it, that he would like an audience, and Pius XII sent word that he was always happy to see the former American Chief Executive. In a press conference Hoover appealed to Argentina and other all-Catholic countries of Latin America to cooperate with United States' efforts to feed Europe. The request had no apparent effect but when Pius XII echoed it in a radio address ten days later to his "most dear sons and daughters" of Spanish- and Portuguese-speaking America, shipments of wheat followed promptly.

Some broke faith with the Pope and quoted him. Some merely argued objectionably. A Jew who was a Catholic convert used a special audience just after the war to ask why Pius XII had not spoken out more clearly against concentration camps. The Pope told him that he had condemned cruelty. The visitor was unsatisfied and said so in print. His unauthorized interview mixed up the Pope's words with his own comments and made Vatican indignation all the keener. The man who had arranged for the audience spent an "ugly quarter of an hour" as his Vatican superiors scolded him later for misplacing confidence.

One of those who merely argued was a journalist who is a prominent Catholic layman. He talked over world affairs and then asked permission to repeat the exchange as an interview. The Pope refused. In principle he opposed interviews. Speeches at audiences and encyclical letters to bishops gave him outlet enough for the views he wished to express, and perhaps the concept of "press interview" jarred. The two worlds of Church and press did not, at least at that point, seem to meet.

"Oh but you must let me," the reporter insisted. "I need this for a series I'm doing." He had already interviewed many of the rest of the world's most eminent men.

The reporter reached Pius's limit at that point. As the correspondent told it later, "He took me by the arm and said, 'I must ask you to leave; I've been very good to you.'" The brash journalist was not chagrined. He had one more tale to recount, at least privately. But he left without the interview.

Many who called on Pius were what the world might call nobodies, just people who "come seeking," as one bishop described them—people of all faiths or of none, who wondered what they could learn from the Pope about the spiritual mysteries of existence. Others were more concerned with themselves than with the pontiff. One American woman, a Protestant, obtained a special audience and then wondered desperately what she should say.

"My daughter-in-law," she blurted out finally, "is a Catholic."

A Virginia woman, also Protestant, recounted to her diplomat son-in-law that "After I walked through several rooms I asked a man in white where I'd find the Pope."

"It's I," he said.

A surely apocryphal audience story which became a chestnut joke concerned American Ambassador Clare Booth Luce, an ardent and most articulate Catholic convert. As the tale went, Mrs. Luce had to be interrupted by Pius XII who told her that "I'm Catholic, too."

It was true that after a later audience Mrs. Luce's handsome blue eyes widened as she told her embassy spokesman archly: "You should know that he did most of the talking!"

One visitor who admitted he carried the bulk of the conversation was Manhattan's imaginative young Congressman, Jacob Javits, later a United States Senator. His corner of Manhattan, grouped around Washington Heights, was one-third Catholic and one-third Jewish, so Javits, a freshman member of the House of Representatives, visited Israel and Rome. Javits self-assuredly told the Pope that he had been pleasantly surprised to learn that the labor encyclicals of Leo XIII at the end of the nineteenth century and those of Pius XI in the twenties showed remarkable parallels with the liberal ideas for which he had campaigned successfully in New York.

What went on in Pius's mind during that audience one cannot say, but there were other occasions on which the Pope either could not understand American accents or chose to ignore them. One young American publisher, with the faintest suggestion of condescension, told the Catholic Church's leader that his paper had editorially approved of the pontiff's most recent Christmas speech on problems of peace.

The Pope studied his self-confident and youthful visitor.

"My blessings," he said, "on you and on your family!"

The audience was short-lived.

Former President Roosevelt's son, Franklin D. Jr., a New York Congressman, told the Pope that he had worked out a plan for Catholics and non-Catholics to get along better in his state. It was not a topic that lent itself to a few moments of offhand chatting. Perhaps the Pope did not grasp young Roosevelt's point. His answer in any case changed the subject. "Poland," he said, "is in a sad plight."

Still another type of caller was represented by one of the most successful Vatican correspondents. His technique, he said coolly, was to get a special audience and then to do not most, but all of the talking.

"I just watch the Pope's expression as I tell him what I think to be the case," the bold reporter said. "I can see by how he looks when I am right! The monsignors don't like it and they try to pull him away but that's what I do."

The system was not guaranteed against mistakes but the correspondent at least scored some brilliant near misses.

The recounted episodes of the audiences are in the thousands. There was the sports announcer who destroyed the "poetry" of the moment, as one Vatican staff member said, by the way he answered Pius XII when the latter commented on the immense skill a radio reporter needed in order to describe a complicated contest accurately. It was before television.

"It's not that hard," the flattered and excited reporter answered naively. "Mistakes don't matter. The listeners can't see what really happens!"

A group of nuns from Munich were entranced to think that Pius XII recognized them in the great mass at a general audience. They spoke to a priest on the Pope's small staff and he talked to Mother Pasqualina. She relayed the story to the Pope. "I remember them from Munich," the Pope said in effect, "but I didn't see them there."

A group of pilgrims from Salzburg had a different thought as the Pope passed near them. The pontiff's white cuff was soiled! That too was relayed to one of the staff members.

"I'll tell Mother Pasqualina to be more careful with the laundry," the priest promised.

It was not just laymen who reserved surprises for the hospitable pontiff. Monsignor Angelo Ciuffi, a round, short pastor from Borough Park, Brooklyn, parlayed a series of inspirations into a remarkable audience. During World War II he asked his parishioners to build a new and larger church as a shrine to peace in exchange for the safe return of soldiers. He built the handsome pastel-colored temple and then asked for "a personal gift" to the 8-foot-tall picture of the Madonna and Child which a Rome-born octogenarian, Ilario Panzironi, had painted for him. Rubies, sapphires, amethysts, gem-studded wrist watches and 700 diamonds poured in. Crowns of jewels appraised and insured at $100,000 were made for the two figures and then the monsignor thought of getting the Pope's blessing.

In the anteroom at the Vatican the monsignor had his final inspiration. As quick as it came it was accompanied by another. He would not discuss it with anyone but the Pope.

"I knew that if I asked those monsignors there . . ."

"Your Holiness," the Brooklyn clergyman told the Pope a moment later, "when the picture is installed it would be wonderful if you could preside!"

The Pope refused, but in such a way that it seemed almost as good as an acceptance. The monsignor reported it later in rapt accents.

"He said he had known all about us, that he had read it in the paper. 'Read it in the paper,' he said that textually! He added that 'Nothing would give me greater pleasure.' Those were the words: 'Nothing would give me greater pleasure, but, but . . . I'm a prisoner!' He meant all his obligations."

There was one more small disappointment. The Pope agreed to a group photograph but the cameraman had gone.

"The noon whistle had blown," the Brooklynized Italian-born pastor fumed. "All they think about is their spaghetti!"

Newsmen and statesmen, saints and plotters, housewives and clergy, the Pope who detested the *sedia gestatoria* and longed for solitude, received, blessed and satisfied them all.

# 9. The Mind of Pius XII

A journalist once asked Pius XII what he could do to help him.

Publish his speeches, the Pope answered instantly. All his ideas on all the problems facing a religious man in the midst of the exuberantly scientific twentieth century were there, the Catholic leader indicated.

At least for his final 10 years Pius felt that his mission was his speeches, an adviser reported. In not quite 20 years as Pope he gave 2,300 addresses, one every 3 days. The frequency increased as the pontiff's powers failed. In all his final meetings with the acting Secretary of State, Monsignor Tardini, Pius spoke of his *discorsi*—his discourses. He lamented the burden of them but he drove on harder than ever. In September, his last full month, Pius XII read 13 speeches. In the first 5 days of October, just before his fatal strokes, he gave another 4. Additional talks were ready in the files for the whole of November.

No other Pope fulfilled so thoroughly the first of the three missions of the Papacy: "to teach, to govern and to sanctify." Through his addresses Pius tried to fulfill each of the tasks, for he gave instructions to other Catholic bishops and he labored to bring holiness to all corners of human activity. He talked to beekeepers, lawyers, basketball players, queens, premiers, soldiers and perfume-makers, and to all he pointed a moral tying their callings to the loftiest concepts of piety.

Pius's untiring and variegated message to the world did not go uncriticized.

"It is the habit in Rome to find fault with the Pope," as it was put by one ambassador to the Holy See.

Pius talked too much, some of his assistants judged in effect, however deferentially they phrased it. There was no need to speak at such length about the technical advances in the various fields of his visitors: about isotopes to scientists, offshore platforms to oilmen, or high-speed drills to dentists, critics suggested. The talks were often dry, academic and overly tactful, others objected. On at least one occasion newspapermen reading Pius's speech missed the point entirely. The criticism the pontiff had intended was so cautiously phrased that the fast-working newsmen skipped over it, said one papal diplomat.

Pius's rebukes of Hitlerites, Communists and even Western capitalists were couched in notably mild terms. The same held true in private. Cardinal Tardini, as Pope John's Secretary of State, recalled a papal diplomat who came out of an audience cheerfully convinced that Pius had praised him. The pontiff, on the other hand, felt that he had dressed down the unsatisfactory envoy.

Such were the criticisms, and they were heard so often—especially after Pius's death—that they cannot be ignored; but the argument for the pontiff is far more impressive. He was like a "public fountain," pouring forth good waters at which all the world, great and lowly, could profitably drink, Archbishop Roncalli said often and admiringly during the life of the man he was to succeed.

Pius was a "doctor of the Church," the Venice cardinal added after he became Pope John XXIII. No tribute could be higher. The "Church doctors," for Catholics, are ecclesiastical writers of rare learning and holiness—men such as Saints Thomas Aquinas, Francis of Sales, and Bede the Venerable. In the four most recent centuries only about twenty men had been given the title.

The words of Pius were a *summa*—a masterful summation— of what religion has to say in the face of the issues of the 1900's in the opinion of Federico Alessandrini, assistant editor of the Vatican newspaper.

Pius XII, the serious Rome *lycée* boy who refused to admit that the triumphant science of the nineteenth and twentieth centuries was in necessary conflict with Christian tradition, remained the same in the Papacy. In his thousands of meetings with the eminent and the obscure he preached the point and toiled to prove it. Pius was painstakingly careful as he kept in mind that Catholics, potential Catholics, and good men of all beliefs, lived under every kind of political system, were citizens of countries of all degrees of colonialism and emancipation, and dwelt amid cultures of all the European, American, Asiatic and African varieties. At last, however, he revealed his mind.

What he showed was this: he was convinced that despite the excitement of his own schoolboy years science had never disproved the existence of God, and that it had if anything added new proof of a Creator. It was in a speech of November 22, 1951, to microseismic scientists of the United States and seven other countries in which Pius poured forth some of his deepest convictions on the subject. Whether you study uranium-235 and other radioactive substances, the receding galaxies at the outer edges of space, the composition of meteorites or gravity between "systems of double stars and starry masses," you arrive at the same conclusion. The universe is not infinitely aged; it began at a point in time about five billion years ago; and it will not go on forever but will "grow old" and run down. The Pope insisted that the answer to the mystery of what preceded the events and materials of five billion years ago was the one the Bible gave— God the Creator.

On the subject of Holy Scripture the pontiff made two of the most important statements any of the top Catholic leaders had put forward in generations. One was in the encyclical *Divino Afflante Spiritu* in 1943 and the other in a similar letter, *Humani Generis* in 1950. The first opened the doors to a new interpretation of the Bible in the light of modern science. Behind it was the concession that such passages as the opening chapters of Genesis, with their story of Creation, were next to incomprehensible. It was the Pius of *Divino Afflante Spiritu* who talked later of Creation taking place in the year 5,000,000,000 B.C. *Humani Generis*, somewhat in a reverse direction, warned Catholic theologians against watering down the dogmas of tradition in an effort to make peace between Catholicism and rival philosophies including Communism. For instance, it must be preached that Adam was the first man, and it was not permissible to theorize that there were other men created after Adam who were not his descendants, the Pope said. One could accept the possibility that man evolved from earlier forms of life, but one had to affirm—if one were still to be Catholic—that God intervened at some point in man's development to breathe in the soul that made him human, the Pope proclaimed.

Pius spoke on almost every other problem of modern man. He disappointed many in 1941 and in 1951 by failing to publish a *Quinquagesimo Anno* or a *Sexagesimo Anno* encyclical. Many thought it logical that Pius XI's "In the Fortieth Year" should be followed by an "In the Fiftieth . . ." or "In the Sixtieth Year," partly because the weak labor unions mentioned in 1891 in the first of the eminent social encyclical series had grown strong enough to often indulge in the same abuses of power Leo XIII and Pius XI had condemned in the case of conscienceless capitalist exploiters.

Pius published no encyclical, however. From Father Leiber we know why. The Pope felt that questions of social security, better productivity, stable currencies and full employment which were the catchwords of Western economic thinking during the forties and fifties were surface issues, and that the importance of family, private property and the state as the three essentials of economic society were still as true as they were at the time of the celebrated social encyclicals. Nineteen forty-one in midwar, and 1951 during the tense moments of the Cold War, did not seem the best times for an addition to the Leo XIII and Pius XI series.

It was left to John XXIII in 1961 to finally extend the chain of social letters. It was not an "In the Seventieth Year . . ." but a *Mater et Magister*—"Mother and Teacher" (a reference to the Catholic Church as instructor of the faithful)—that John produced. His emphasis was not quite what was expected. He urged that the benefits for factory hands which Leo and Pius XI had valiantly and successfully demanded should go to farmers, too, and he urged that social thinking reach beyond the limits of a single factory's walls or an individual farm to take in an even more generous international-aid program.

On the issues of labor and capital, Pius XII was neither among the most conservative nor among the most progressive. Some Catholics who wanted a more "social" policy, including even an alliance with Communists, circulated an attack on capitalism which they attributed to Pius XII but the Vatican repudiated the document. Pius did tell some visitors that many of the worst enemies of private property were those who gave it a bad name by wallowing in luxury in a world of need, but the Pope joined predecessors in asserting that at least some individual possession is a necessity of nature.

The character of his office and his vocation for teaching drew Pius into comments on almost every phase of life from the most personal questions of sex to the highest diplomatic issues between East and West.

On sex, as one of the Pontiff's collaborators summed up his preaching, the Pope taught almost exclusively what was "natural," adding from Divine Revelation only that marriage normally is indissoluble, that divorce is forbidden. By "natural" was meant that artificial contraception and abortion were banned, but that man and wife could make use of the woman's monthly sterile period to avoid conceiving children as long as good reasons—such as health conditions and economic need—advised against more babies, and as long as the couple did not avoid having children altogether. Pius XII knew how hard it is for a modern married couple to abide by the ancient marriage prescriptions. He attempted to help. In effect, his talks on the use of the safe period set up a valid Catholic birth control. On childbirth the Pope authorized the use of painkillers and assured mothers who might have troubled consciences that they were not flying in the face of the old words of Genesis: *In dolore paries filios*—"In pain shall you bring forth children." On the terrible dilemma of whether to save mother or child in the fortunately rare cases where the problem arises, the Pope forbade abortion as such but added that it was permissible to save the mother with therapy even though it had the indirect, inevitable effect of killing the fetus.

On World War II and the East-West Cold War Pius was neutral in theory but warmly pro-Western in fact. Count Giuseppe dalla Torre, the aging editor of *L'Osservatore Romano*, urged periodically that the pontiff of the forties and fifties be accepted as an East-West mediator. It was a role Benedict XV had sought when Cardinal Pacelli had been the Holy See's World War I envoy to Germany and when dalla Torre was preparing to take over as director of the Vatican paper. If having the Pope as mediator made a certain sense at the time of the first war between European and American brothers it certainly made none during the Communist Cold War. As *Le Monde* of Paris, one of Europe's most perceptive observers of the Vatican, pointed out at the time of Pius's death, the Papacy was no longer a possible umpire; it was one of the main defenders of a concept of life the Soviets sought to eliminate.

To Americans, including Catholics, it was often baffling that Pius should want to be neutral, but one American priest high in the pontiff's counsels said smilingly: "In World War II he had jurisdiction over both sides—two sides that were killing one another! An unhappy condition!"

In the opinion of others around him the greatest of Pius's achievements was his success in steering the Catholic Church through World War II without catastrophic losses on the one hand, and even with important gains in prestige on the other.

Pius must have struggled with his conscience as he remained silent in World War II during the conflict between the Fascists and the Western and Communist "democrats," for he raised the question in one of the first postwar audiences. It was at a ceremony during which he added 32 members to the College of Cardinals, the largest single addition ever made to that body; in addition to 54 old and new cardinals there were members of the corps of diplomats representing more than 30 countries. He had often remained silent during the war, the Pope told the cardinals and diplomats, because he had feared that worse suffering might befall innocent millions "curbed under the rod of the oppressors."

The fact that Pius was "neutral" in the Cold War was brought out in one of the Christmas messages in which he attempted to point a special moral for the world each year. It was the address of Christmas, 1950. The attitude of the Church, the Pope said, was not that East and West were opposing factions, but rather that each had made great human contributions and would continue to do so. The following Christmas he carried the idea further. He said that "the Church," surely meaning himself in large part, was under pressure, not only from statesmen but also from some of its own high officials, to "abandon neutrality." The Pope appealed to his followers in the old Axis nations, in the democracies, and on both sides of the Iron Curtain to draw on "supernatural faith and hope" in attempting to comprehend the Holy See's position. There is no doubt that many American Catholic churchmen, to cite one group, were finding it hard to understand. The Church, said Pius, would not take sides in the sense of backing one set of material, national and bloc interests against those of another part of the human race (a refusal to make outright common cause with Washington), but on the other hand would not stay neutral in the sense of putting good and evil on the same footing. Pius rejected what the Communists were seeking when they urged the neutrality of the Holy See. The formula meant occasional frustrations for Western diplomats when they asked Pius, during World War II, to condemn the Axis governments to whom tens of millions of German and Italian Catholics looked as civil authorities. But in the long run it meant a virtual wholehearted endorsement of the Allies' World War II Atlantic Charter, the American Marshall Plan for postwar aid to Europe, the United Nations, the Atlantic Alliance, and the American-advocated drive to unite Western Europe economically and politically.

Even that brought criticism of Pius, however. His anti-Communism became ever more clear, so that some French Catholics objected that he was behaving unrealistically in a world where one-third of humanity was under the Marxist flag. The Pope's strong stands in relatively peaceful non-Red Rome meant extra suffering for the seventy million Catholics behind the Iron Curtain, these liberal French murmured.

Pius's view on proper Vatican neutrality was close to his concept on religious toleration. Some Catholic theologians have argued in the past that error has no rights, and that it was the duty of those with the "true Faith" to suppress error when the reins of governmental power gave them the opportunity. It was surely that idea which lay at the root of much of the anti-Catholicism in the United States; the fear that Catholics as a majority, and with a Catholic President, would be far less generous to a Protestant minority than the freedom-revering Protestants were in general toward the Catholic newcomers of the nineteenth and twentieth centuries.

It was not until he had been Pope fourteen years that Pius went to the root of the issue. He spoke to a group of Italian Catholic lawyers and said in effect that he agreed with St. Peter Canisius, the Dutch Jesuit of the time of the Protestant Reformation, who gave moral approval to the Peace of Augsburg of 1555 —the treaty which temporarily quieted Catholic-Protestant turmoil in Germany. Each German prince was told to decide whether Catholicism or Lutheranism was to prevail in his land. The Pope said that Catholics would never "burn incense before the idols" of error, as they had proved gloriously in Rome under the ancient empire, but that they must also recognize that the "greater good" and the "common well-being" often meant that toleration was the proper doctrine. It was especially true, he said, where great masses of differing religions were involved and where Catholic nations were more and more coming out of isolation into federations with non-Catholic states. The hint to doctrinaire Catholics of Spain to soften their attitudes toward Protestants and to move forward into a cordial alliance with the people of other Western nations was clear. It was also evident that as long as Pius's type of thinking remained part of the essential Catholic doctrine no Catholic intolerance of Protestants in the twentieth (or twenty-first or twenty-second) century United States was imaginable. In a steadily shrinking and ever more federated free world of wide religious differences, Pius XII's doctrine of the "greater good" and of tolerance was sure to dominate Catholic thinking in the United States and elsewhere.

He was also concerned with the nature of the Papacy and the qualities of a good Pope. He remembered bitterly that Giuseppe Mazzini, one of the philosophical fathers of modern democratic Italy, had said that not only the Papal States but the Papacy itself was "dead." It was a century after the Mazzini statement that Pius addressed a rally of 200,000 Italian Catholic young women in the square before St. Peter's. This was just before the 1948 Italian elections which stopped the Soviet Communist advance into Europe and helped start a rollback of Moscow influence in Marshal Josip Broz Tito's Yugoslavia.

We know from his aides that Pius was convinced that his diplomatic and professorial manner, his training and his personality kept a gulf between him and the masses he wanted to embrace as a father. It was in this talk on Mazzini at St. Peter's that he tried with special earnestness to reach out to the young women, inviting them to take part in a dialogue.

Mazzini had said that the Papacy was dead, the Pope exclaimed. Did that mean, he asked, that all those scores of thousands of youth beneath his balcony had come to "pay homage, as they say, to something dead 'in blood and in the mud'?"

"No," the thin voices of the women called back.

"Was this a 'dead youth' come to be near a dead thing?"

"No," the women cried.

Both the truth of papal vitality and his own difficulty in building a bridge to the people were reflected on that occasion, for just as the Pope began his speech there was a cloudburst. I was in the crowd that day, as a reporter. Few of us had umbrellas. We huddled under coats and placards. The Pope was slightly protected by a narrow canopy ten feet overhead and by a broad black umbrella held by a monsignor. Even so, side gusts dampened him and direct torrents soaked the rest of us. Unable to improvise, Pius read every word of his protest against Mazzini. The speech took twenty-five minutes, and the rain kept up as long. Several score of the women were treated for exhaustion in first-aid tents. Pius's inability to adapt to a human situation was reflected, but also clear was the hold which he and the Papacy exerted. I asked one peasant girl later how she had taken the downpour.

"What rain?" the ecstatic young woman replied.

The qualities of a good Pope were spelled out at ceremonies in which Pius raised various of his predecessors to the Catholic altars, or dedicated churches to those who were already inscribed as saints. In one such event he named a church for Saint Pope Leo the Great, of the fifth century, on the fifteen hundredth anniversary of Leo's famous meeting with Attila the Hun. The new church was in a largely Communist slum. Pius recalled how the defenseless but daring Leo had met Attila on the outskirts of Rome and had convinced the "scourge of God" to spare the Eternal City. Pius's voice vibrated with admiration for his courageous predecessor, but he said that in a new age he could only pray. The qualities of a good Pope came up for examination again when Pius took part in the beatification of Pope Innocent XI (1676 to 1689). Innocent, said his successor, was a man of dignified, "almost melancholy," appearance, though one who could be "most affable" on the proper occasions. He had been resolute in his decisions though he took them only after "mature reflection and after requests for advice." He bore insults and slanders in silence. He was sensitive to the misfortunes of others, had a clear view of the needs of his age, acted firmly and often alone, and lived in the poverty, simplicity and toil of an apostle. Word for word the description was a portrait of the ideals Pius XII surely held up for himself.

# 10. Pius the Great?

The letters from children which swamped the small Vatican post office at the time of Pius's eightieth birthday in 1956 reflected both the difficulty his contemporaries faced in forming a rounded judgment and the deep-rooted conviction that the first Rome-born Pope in two centuries was one of the great men of his time.

Luciano Casimirri of the press office borrowed packets of the letters from the Secretariate of State to give me the flavor of what the children were saying to the old Pius. The remarks in the flood of mail were often naive and even irrelevant, but all were tender—all reflected devotion and trust.

"I hope you live to 150," Anna Brusi said from medieval Ravenna in Italy. "I have promised (as a sacrifice for you) not to chatter in school, especially with Giulianna, and to give polite answers at home. You are good because you have given all those countries so many things."

"Even if you are a little old," Angela Manzo consoled the Pope from Trieste, Italy, "may you still continue to do good."

"I truthfully hope that you will live to be 100 years of age," Linda Cantlin wrote from Short Hills, New Jersey.

"It must be wonderful to be 80 as I am only ten," Wendy Adamson sent as her message from Sydney, Australia.

Nancy Greene, of Millburn, New Jersey: "We know you are very busy as Pope, but we hope that you will find time to read our letters."

Laura Pallini, Florence, Italy: "I'm glad you were born March 2 like me so that we can celebrate together."

Renzo Uzzan, six, Sardinia: "I would like to drive your car."

Angelo Berillo, Italy: "I am not a very intelligent child. I and my friends go to Mass every Sunday and we pray with faith that the Lord may make me a good young man. I would like to be a priest and if my head can stand the load of the study I would be happy. I would like to go to see you but I can't because I am small and I don't have the money. If something bad happens in the world you will suffer and I will help you with my prayers."

Maria Rosa, Florence: "I pray you become a saint like St. Peter."

Mario Paladino, Sorrento, Italy: "I would like to know what Jesus told you."

The latter was a reference to one of the most mooted aspects of Pius's reign; repeated rumors that he had visions, first of Pius X, then of peculiar sun effects similar to those which occurred in Fatima, Portugal, in 1917 at the time of reported apparitions of the Virgin Mary and finally of Christ himself. There was much skepticism among the Pope's associates, but as one authority said, "By the fact that he himself says that he had a vision [of Christ], the story will be treated with respect."

A typical incident was recounted secondhand. An aide told the Pope that everyone in the Vatican had been amused by news reports of the vision.

"But it's true," the Pope answered.

Cardinal Tardini's account was firsthand. He said that at the time of the Pope's illness in 1956 the pontiff informed him in audience that he had "seen the Lord for an instant, only an instant—but I saw Him well."

The Pope had been running a fever but in the hours of the reported vision he continued to govern the Church and made at least one shrewd decision overruling subordinates. Some of them had wanted to publish a denunciation of Juan Perón in Argentina for devastation of churches and other acts of anticlericalism, but Pius ordered patience for a little longer. Political events took over, and Perón was ousted. At least one Church intrusion in state matters had been avoided; there had been one less quarrel, one less source of bitterness.

The Pope is automatically head of the Congregation of the

Holy Office, the section of the Vatican which concerns itself with matters of faith, but his subordinates were silent on the pontiff's conviction that he had had a vision. It is safe to assume that they quietly assembled evidence, including testimony from the physicians on the state of the pontiff's health, and that they put everything away for judgment far in the future; perhaps as long as fifty years after Pius's time. It is the wisdom of the Vatican that such matters, and in general the holiness of anyone's life, are best weighed well after the person's own generation has gone.

There were many who hoped that Pius XII would be declared a saint. Bishop Peter Van Lierde, Sacristan of the Vatican State, was told by his "superiors," presumably meaning the immediate entourage of the new Pope John, to publish a small picture of Pius with a prayer asking for his canonization as a saint. The prayer called Pius "a fearless defender of the Faith, a courageous struggler for justice and peace . . . a shining model of charity and of every virtue." It asked for miracles as proof from God that Pius was in Heaven.

A million copies of Bishop Van Lierde's prayer were soon in circulation in Europe and the United States, in English, French, German, Spanish, Portuguese, and Maltese. Belgium, the Netherlands, France, Germany, the Iberian Peninsula and Malta reported "favors" received after recitation of the prayer, and many letters from all parts of Europe spoke of the impression of "dignity and holiness" Pius had left even after only brief glimpses at audiences. "Favors" are bits of good fortune perhaps not striking enough to be called miracles. Bishop Van Lierde classified all correspondence according to the importance of what was reported, and Pope John encouraged him by saying in an audience that surely some day Pius XII would be raised to the Catholic altars.

Wendy Adamson, being "only ten," thought that reaching eighty must have been wonderful for the boy of St. Philip Neri's parish, but Pius XII did not feel the same. He weighed the idea of abdicating, as both Father Leiber and Cardinal Tardini have disclosed, and he stayed on in his office only because physicians told him that his repeated spells of bad health would pass and would leave him with unimpaired capacities. Pius had a precedent ready should he decide to lay down his great authority. At least one other Pope had done so, Saint Celestine V in December, 1294. A pious monk, the seventy-nine-year-old Pietro del Murrone had been chosen as a compromise when for two years cardinals had been unable to agree on a successor to Nicholas IV. After only five months in office, convinced that he was a puppet in the hands of less scrupulous men, he resigned. He was named a saint seventeen years later.

The Pope's associates consider it difficult to place the pontiff of the mid-twentieth century in history's perspective. Apart from steering the Church through World War II, Pius had made no very striking reforms and had published no remarkably exceptional encyclicals, some diplomats at the Holy See adjudged. When editorial writers on *L'Osservatore Romano* needed a papal quotation to bolster their political pieces they went back to the encyclicals of frank-spoken Pius XI; to his *Non abbiamo bisogno*—"We have no need . . ." for an excoriation of Fascism (written in the Italian language of the Fascists), to *Mit brennender Sorge*—"With burning heart . . ." for a repudiation of Nazism (in German) and to *Divini redemptoris*—"Of the Divine Redeemer" for a denunciation of Communism (in Latin, a classical world language appropriate to a universal threat).

Was Pius the greatest in the long line of Popes? Certainly it was an eminent company, as some of the pontiff's assistants cautiously pointed out. Pius XI, said one prominent Vatican figure, made the treaty with Mussolini creating the small neutral Vatican State in 1929 at "the last possible moment" in the face of rising Fascist totalitarianism, and thus paved the way for the independence and security of the Holy See during World War II. The courage of Pius XI survived as a Curia legend.

"After forty years we can just manage to put Pius X in perspective," the same prelate added. "We can say now with assurance that he was one of the greats."

It was Pius X who strengthened the flagging spirituality in the Catholic ranks.

Leo XIII, the Pope of the 1891 social encyclical, had been

praised in life and criticized after death, but respect for his role, too, was rising after six decades, the same churchman added.

"We tend to forget it but in writing *Rerum Novarum* Leo had to resist strong pressure in favor of economic paternalism," a Vatican officer said. "We can see now how wise he was to oppose such demands."

Others reached much further back to cite towering figures against whom later pontiffs ought to be measured: Paul III (1534 to 1549), who uncovered a way to turn Renaissance energies into channels useful to his Church; Innocent III (1198 to 1216), who ascended Peter's throne at thirty-seven for an eighteen-year reign during which he won acceptance as head of a medieval European Christian family and set the Franciscan and Dominican orders on a way which they still follow; Saint Gregory VII (Hildebrand), the reformer (1073–1085) who did much to restore celibacy and to suppress financial corruption among the medieval clergy and who made history by humbling Emperor Henry IV at Canossa; Saint Nicholas I, the Great (858 to 867), who was accepted as judge in both civil and religious conflicts; and Saint Gregory I, the Great (590–604), who laid the ground for Papal independence in the Middle Ages by negotiating peace with the Lombards and who fostered monasteries, the conversion of England, and plain song (Gregorian chant).

The brilliant qualities of various of the giants of the Papacy's bewilderingly long history stood in some contrast to various criticisms of Pius: that his was a bright intelligence but not genius; that he was too lenient in appearing at his window during his final year when importunate automobilists blew horns appealing to him to show himself; and that he risked his dignity by patiently exchanging white skullcaps with those in audiences who had bought them as souvenirs or relics from the Sisters of Mary Reparatrix (the seamstresses for the little hats) in Rome's Via Lucchesi. Dozens of the skullcaps are now revered as objects associated with a saint, but the custom of trading them as keepsakes reached a low point when one American woman asked the North American College for six of them "so that I can put lace on them and use them as hats for my daughter's bridesmaids."

The college not only refused, but began making a secret of the Via Lucchesi Convent, naming it only to clergy who could be counted on to revere a souvenir of the Pope. Pope John discontinued the exchanging of skullcaps.

Such were the eminent men of Church history beside whom Pius would be measured, and such were the pontiff's limitations. On balance, many who were in a position to judge decided that Pius did belong among his Church's foremost.

"It will become clearer as time goes on," one of the leading American clergymen in Rome asserted. "His kind comes only once every two centuries."

"I have known most of the top men of our time," said an American statesman, a Catholic. "As a clear thinker I class him with only three others, Churchill, De Valera and Franco."

The list was notably original, but the person who compiled it had a reputation as a judge of men and did have acquaintanceship with most of the chief men of the West.

What his contemporaries thought of Pius was reflected on his eightieth birthday, not only in letters from children but also in a thirty-nine-nation tribute in which the United States took part. John A. McCone of the Atomic Energy Commission, a Catholic businessman of San Francisco, represented President Eisenhower. (McCone was later to become head of the Central Intelligence Agency.) Count Wladimir d'Ormesson of France, dean of the diplomatic corps to the Holy See, a Catholic and admirer of Pius XII, drew up a speech to read in the name of his colleagues and was pleased that none of his fellow diplomats—Protestants from England and Northern Europe, Moslems from the Middle East, liberals from various parts of the world—asked him to change a word. D'Ormesson praised the Pope as one who had defended the rights of the individual and as one whose years of efforts for peace were "of highest importance" to the world.

Holy See prestige, thanks to Pius XII, was at the loftiest peak it had reached, d'Ormesson wrote in *Le Figaro* in Paris when Pius died.

For five successive pontificates the Papacy had climbed from the low point of 1870 when the Pope had had no say in the world of ideas, the English historian, Christopher Dawson, agreed.

Not for centuries had the Vatican enjoyed such a ready hearing, according to Luigi Gedda, the physician who was head of Pius's Italian Catholic Action Organization.

It was Pius who had pushed open the Vatican bronze doors to let in leaders of the world, at least of the non-Communist world, for a two-way exchange of ideas. With Sukarno of Indonesia, Pius agreed that the role of Catholic foreign missionaries would be reduced in favor of the native clergy, while Sukarno pledged that Pius's Christians would enjoy right of citizenship in the new overwhelmingly Moslem nation.

I recall the awed eighteen-year-old Princess Margaret of Britain, dressed head to toe in the black prescribed by protocol, as she came out, chewing her underlip nervously, after a twenty-minute talk alone with the seventy-three-year-old Pius in 1949. She was only the fifth of the British royal family to call on a pope since the cataclysmic split between the Papacy and King Henry VIII which had separated Britain from the Catholic Church in the sixteenth century. Before her had come the Prince of Wales, the future King Edward VII, in the time of Leo XIII; the Prince of Wales, later the Duke of Windsor, in 1918; and Margaret's grandparents, King George V and Queen Mary, in 1923. Margaret's visit soon led to another. Two years later the future Queen, then Princess Elizabeth, and her consort, the Duke of Edinburgh, followed in Margaret's path. That too was memorable. Princess Elizabeth, in black, curtsied deeply, but the Pope seized her right hand in both of his and drew her into his room. "You are very welcome," the pontiff swiftly told the duke as well. Pius plainly longed to end the old English-Italian, Anglican-Catholic division. Twice in his last years in an obvious goodwill gesture he sent messengers to the Oxford-trained English envoy to the Holy See, Sir Marcus Cheke, to tell him appreciatively and enthusiastically that whenever he called he spoke so distinctly that "I understand every word you say." In his long struggles with English in his seventies the Pope had at least mastered the elegant Oxford version of the multiply spoken English language. But I was sure British-Catholic relations, not elocution, were what concerned Pius at that time.

Under Pius the Holy See saw the first visit of a German chief of state—Theodor Heuss, a Lutheran—after a gap of more than half a century. The last before him had been Kaiser Wilhelm II in 1903.

Pius also welcomed the first French chief executive in centuries, the Catholic René Coty, who called in 1957. The Pope ordered the "Marseillaise" played by the papal band. It was believed to be the first time the Vatican ensemble had rendered an anthem associated with revolt against the old French order including the Church. No French chief of state had come to call since Charles VIII in 1495 and that king had made his appearance in a far from auspicious way. He was an invader en route to conquer the kingdom of Naples. Presently, in the face of an alliance of the Pope and of several other kings, Charles was hurriedly on his way out of Italy again. Pius posed smiling with Coty; one of the few times he was photographed that way. Coty was the most eminent Catholic chief of state of his time. Many close to Pius considered him an answer to the accusation that a Catholic in the American White House would be a tool in papal hands. "No one would say that the Pope runs Coty," they said.

Although there was little doubt that Coty was unhindered by Catholic churchmen as he performed his duties in Paris's Elysee Palace it was also evident that the Pope felt close to him. Pius bestowed on him the Vatican's highest honor, the Order of Christ, an elaborate gold necklace supporting an enameled red-and-white cross.

Pius was the man who listened sympathetically to one American statesman as the latter argued for more political unity in Western Europe and then asked for a memorandum on it. The American's ideas were reflected closely in many of Pius's subsequent speeches, although it is also true that the two had seen just about eye to eye on the matter even before they conversed.

Pius was also the Pope who discouraged another Western diplomat who wanted to say something about birth control but did not dare. The two were discussing efforts to foster emigration from such crowded European countries as Italy. The diplomat silently phrased what he would have liked to say:

"Sir, there is something you could do which would help even more than emigration . . ."

The invitation to Pius to reverse the Church condemnation of contraception as something unnatural and immoral went unvoiced. Something in Pius's serene assurance dissuaded the envoy. The two kept to the agreed subject—one on which each could make headway.

Pius, as we know from Father Leiber, was a pope who grieved about the way his predecessors had mistreated the brilliant scientist, Galileo. He was also one who several times weighed the idea of converting Vatican gems into cash for charity, though he eventually heeded those who argued that history and art opposed such a course.

Pius was the Pope who invited basketball players to give a ten-minute exhibition in the great square before St. Peter's as he watched from a throne. He sought a dramatic way to convince young men that there was no gulf between athletics and holiness. Pius also arranged for a statue of St. Joseph the Workman to be carried by helicopter into the Vatican; another public-relations gesture to assure laborers in a semi-Marxist continent that the Vatican was on the side of progress and workers.

One fault of Pius, said one of the foremost diplomats of the West, was that he dissipated energies in receiving visitors and giving specialized talks rather than pondering the principal issues of a Christian civilization now endangered in Asia, Africa, Eastern Europe and in much of the Americas. Unless the Pope found the way, said this Catholic diplomat, no one would.

"If you are waiting for a single great suggestion, I'm not sure it's there," an intimate aide of the Pope retorted. "He has made many recommendations. They have not always been heeded."

It was an attitude a visitor could observe in conversation with the Pope. His duty, as he serenely saw it, was to teach. If the world turned a deaf ear the fault was not his.

To Pius's credit the "world" showed at his death that its attention had not been wholly distracted during his years of sermons.

From Hirohito in Japan to King Gustave in Protestant Sweden, from Eisenhower to Queen Elizabeth, the heads of the non-Communist regions paid tribute. Dr. Geoffry Fisher, chief of the Anglican Church, said that all followers of Christ had honored Pius for "his holiness, his charity, his simplicity and his Christian spirit." The Vatican was gratified to receive messages from many Jews, from officials of the American Baptist and Presbyterian churches, and from the (Protestant and Orthodox) World Council of Churches. Former President Truman, who had been tight-lipped with reporters after his talk with Pius, called him "one of the greatest statesmen" in the Vatican in two centuries. Charles Malik, the President of the United Nations General Assembly, extolled him as "one of the greatest men of our epoch." For my part as a reporter, I had been slow to conclude, but I too was satisfied: Pius, an exceptional man in a line of such men, merited the title of "great" which the Catholic Church only rarely bestows on its pontiffs.

# PART THREE

# JOHN XXIII,
# PEASANT—PRINCE

# 11. The Conclave Secret

The change from the aristocratic, isolated Pius to the amiable, unassuming peasant-born John was "almost too much," as one of those closely associated with the household of the dead Pope commented.

Why, then, did the cardinals choose as they did?

Pope John had told members of the Rome press corps that we had not had "two lines right" as we speculated about what went on during the secret Church election. Cardinal Tisserant, the Dean of the Sacred College, put it a shade less severely two months later when he read the annual Christmas greeting of the cardinals to the new pontiff.

"A great part of what was printed," he said, "was inexact or false."

The American Catholic hierarchy's press section in Washington (at the National Catholic Welfare Conference) watered criticisms down a bit further, and for that matter was even laudatory. All things considered, the staff commented sympathetically, American reporters had done a remarkable job of striking so close to the truth. Few had failed to mention the Venice patriarch as a strong *papabile*.

One reason for the published errors was, of course, the oath every cardinal took as the conclave doors were double-sealed behind him: he and the members of his entourage would "maintain secrecy on everything that in any way concerns the election of the Roman pontiff and on all that is done in the conclave and at the place of election." The one exception would be if the new Pope gave permission for a lifting of the veil.

The reasons for protecting a secret affecting the religious sentiments and convictions of so large a share of the world's Christian
population were evident, but inescapably many details became
known and reflected what the larger picture must have been.

For one thing, the atmosphere inside the conclave, I was assured on excellent authority, was "like a religious retreat." Far
from the fever of a political struggle in which the interests of
world powers are at stake, the air was that of a monastery in
which monks examine the troubled corners of their consciences
and pray for help in living an even more devout life.

"You could feel the Holy Spirit at work," my Vatican confidant said.

We are indebted to Cardinal Tisserant for some details. In a
letter to his diocese on the outskirts of Rome the cardinal said
that he and his colleagues went into the voting with the feeling
that Pius XII had left them without a hint of who he believed
should be his successor. Pius XI had clearly indicated Pius XII
as his own choice, but the latter had not even named a secretary
of state after the death of Archbishop Luigi Maglione in 1943.
A secretary of state is the alter ego of a pope and is often considered as the prelate to follow him. Cardinal Mariano Rampolla,
the Secretary of State of Leo XIII, Merry del Val, the similar aide
of Pius X, and Cardinal Pietro Gasparri, that of Benedict XV,
were all high in the balloting in the first three conclaves of the
twentieth century, although Pius XII was the only occupant of
the top Vatican political office since 1900 actually called to succeed his Pope.

"One fact is certain," Cardinal Tisserant said in the 1958
Christmas speech in talking of John's election, "Almighty God
steered and ratified the choice."

Without any hint of instruction left by the dead Pope Pius,
the cardinals had "found themselves alone with their consciences,
facing the judgment of God," the cardinal added in the letter to
his diocese. Each, he said, felt the weight of the words he uttered
as he dropped his ballot into a chalice. "I call on Our Lord Jesus
Christ who will be my judge to witness that I have chosen the
one who, before God, I believe should be elected." Deepening

the awe was the fact that the chalice stood on an altar before Michelangelo's masterpiece, "The Last Judgment," a magnificent conception of the reward of the good and the damnation of the wicked.

This election was the first under Pius XII's new rules requiring a margin of a two-thirds-plus-one vote and abolishing the old provision that each cardinal sign his ballot inside a flap to be sure he had not voted for himself in the event of an exact two-thirds victory. It was "unimaginable" in the modern era that a cardinal should designate himself, the college's forthright dean commented with an authority and frankness which cannot be questioned.

What did the cardinal mean in saying that Divine inspiration had "steered" and then "ratified" the election? The winning ballot was the first of the two tentatively scheduled for the third afternoon of the election—the eleventh of the conclave. Had votes slowly accumulated for the Venice patriarch through the two ballots of the third morning, ending in overwhelming support on the fateful eleventh round?

As part of the answer we have Pope John's own words to his former neighbors of his native diocese of Bergamo. They visited him just after his election. The new Pope said he was sorry that he would rarely if ever see his Alpine home country again, but "What do you want, after all? God's will was so clearly reflected in the cardinals' vote." A flood of ballots at the end would seem the only interpretation of this.

"From certain signs I could gather what was about to happen," the new Pope added on another occasion. The pontiff did not list these in detail but he smiled over one of them. The quarters he drew in the conclave were those of the office of the Commander of the Pontifical Noble Guard. Over the door was a sign, IL COMANDANTE—the commander.

And on the walls, "perhaps a sign of the immediate future," Pope John later recounted, "were the portraits of all the supreme pontiffs I have known: Leo XIII, St. Pius X, Benedict XV with that deep and penetrating glance of his, on up through the so-venerable Pius XII." The memory of the achievements and virtue of that array of Pontiffs "gave me great peace," the former cardinal of Venice related.

There were other and better reasons for expecting his election. For one, the cardinal, as he talked over the ideal qualifications of the next pontiff, had clear ideas of what was needed. He had a habit of speaking of his own "littleness," but the lofty qualities he saw as desirable in Peter's successor were the same he had been struggling to acquire, with much success, in his own life as a bishop.

"Pray," the cardinal wrote to Bishop Giuseppe Piazza of Bergamo, "for a wise and gentle man who can govern; a saint who will make saints of others. Trust in a new Pentecost . . ."

The new Pope, he said, should "bring new vigor to the victorious struggle for truth, goodness and peace." He should do it through a "revivification of the Church and a reconstruction of the ecclesiastical organization."

Death and old age had created vacancies and slowed down work at the headquarters of the Church. New energy was needed to correct that.

Cardinal Roncalli, it was said from Venice, had left a clean desk; but then, informants added, his workroom was always that way.

He left Venice "with the definite thought of going back quickly," the new Pope told Venetians on his first audience for them after his election. He "certainly did not imagine that the Lord would dispose otherwise." He had chosen his place of burial in Venice near the believed tomb of St. Mark the Evangelist and had expected, perhaps soon, to occupy it.

Cardinal Roncalli was practically unknown as he arrived in Rome, even though the newspapers soon had him at the top of their *papabili* lists. He had passed almost all his life since the middle twenties far from Italy and all of it away from Rome. One of the most famous cardinals asked mutual friends what they knew of the Venetian prelate and admitted that his own knowledge was nearly nil. At least one Venetian insisted later that he had been confident all along that his patriarch would be picked "because he is so good."

Good-natured, modest, manly Cardinal Roncalli quickly became better know as he took part in the discussions of the kind of pope that was needed.

One such talk was with Cardinal Celso Costantini, the head of the Vatican's Congregation for the Propagation of the Faith (missions). The cardinal, a slim earnest man with a white goatee, was known as one of the liberals. He had made strong concessions to local Chinese religious traditions in an effort to introduce the faith of Rome to the Orient, and had laid the foundations for a growth of Catholicism which only the Communists, after World War II, had cut off.

Cardinal Costantini, as it proved, was on his hospital deathbed as the two talked. He died just before the conclave. But in their conversation the pair agreed that the new pontiff had to be a man concerned intimately with the fate of Catholicism's Oriental and African missions. It was easy for Cardinal Roncalli to give his assent. He had worked for several years, before beginning his career as a Vatican diplomat, as director of mission aid work in Italy and in much of the rest of Europe. It was a problem he understood; one that awakened memories of the zeal of younger days. Most of the balance of the cardinal's talks of those days remain secret, but one can be sure that a similar converging of views highlighting the fortuitous combination of qualifications brought by the Venetian patriarch must have occurred often.

A story that flashed through the press corps like a sun ray on a dark afternoon was a remark attributed to a French cardinal. A motion picture cameraman asked him to pose.

"Don't miss Roncalli," the French prelate reportedly said. "He is our Pope."

Cardinal Roncalli had been in France eight years and had won many friendships by his warm understanding of the proud and often difficult French. It was very possibly too far to go from that to the assumption by many correspondents that the six French cardinals, the Belgian Joseph van Roey, and the Lebanese Ignatius Tappouni, could be counted safely in the Roncalli column, but it was equally fair to assume that a substantial number of the eight were looking toward Venice.

There was small surprise in the fact that nine months before the death of Pius XII one of the best-informed Vatican staff members had told me that if the Pope were to die his probable successor would be either the patrician Benedetto Aloisi Masella, who was seventy-nine, or Cardinal Roncalli, two years younger. The prospect would be for a short pontificate in the wake of the rarely precedented two decades of Pius XII. The new Pope's task would be to "speak to the consciences of men," to be a parish priest to the individual souls of the world, and only secondarily to be a statesman negotiating with chiefs of state. Pius had done the latter brilliantly. It would be time for another emphasis.

Silvio Negro, the Italian who impressed me as the finest Vatican reporter of his generation, had told me much the same thing two years earlier. "What is needed," he said, "is a simple good bishop. No diplomat! No Roman!"

What he meant by the latter was that long immersion in the pomp, intrigue, politics and history of Rome is at least a distraction, if not a source of total confusion, to many men and that it may make bureaucrats and skeptics if not cynics out of even devoted persons. A retreat to simpler faith was what the reporter saw as a necessity. Negro's view had been formed in hundreds of talks with Vatican staff members who had confessed their own concerns and convictions.

Cardinal Roncalli was a diplomat but his first speech to his flock in Venice had been to beg them not to think of him as a man of diplomacy but only as a priest.

As the hour for the conclave approached, Cardinal Roncalli knew that many were thinking of him. Every newsstand headline told him that. Father Raimondo Spazzi tells of the few words he and the Venetian patriarch exchanged when they met on the last evening before the election. It was in the entranceway of St. Peter's.

"I'll see you then in Venice on the day for the clergy, on December eighteenth?" the cardinal asked the preacher.

"Yes, Your Eminence," the priest confirmed the appointment, "that is, if things don't change now!"

The patriarch returned his friend's glance.

"Ah yes," he said, "everything in this world can always change. But," he added, "let's hope."

Within four days, inside the Sistine Chapel, the cardinal was telling his brothers of the college that he accepted election out of a sense of duty although fully realizing the burdens which so responsible and controversial an office involved.

In those final moments more and more "signs" indicated the Adriatic cardinal; some grave, some—in the Roman manner—frivolous. The most significant was the speech in St. Peter's by Monsignor Antonio Bacci, the Holy See's Latinist, who had been tapped by the cardinals both in 1939 and in 1958 to give the sermon of exhortation on the eve of the balloting.

"We need a pope gifted with great force of soul and ardent charity . . ." the monsignor said in a long address in Latin which seemed to indicate Cardinal Roncalli in every line. "We need one who will embrace Christians of both East and West, one who will be Pope for all people. We need one whose heart will beat above all for those suffering oppression by an absolutist and persecuting power. We need one, too, who will give his heart to those social classes which are still in great indigence . . . A pope who knows from experience the subtleties of the art and science of politics will not be enough. We need above all a holy pope, one who may get from God what his own natural gifts do not provide."

The fatherly Venetian who had never forgotten the poor men of his home area or the Orientals of his first years of diplomatic service in the Balkans and in the Middle East could scarcely have been better described.

On the less rational side there was the strange divining of the coming great event which has been a characteristic of Rome for as far back as memory can penetrate. How much that may have influenced the atmosphere we can never know, but those signs, too, pointed to Cardinal Roncalli. One was the spurious and oft decried but never forgotten sixteenth-century "Prophecy of St. Malachy," concocted by a clergyman who was at that time attempting to steer a papal election toward the cardinal of his own desires. The "Prophecy," pretending then to be centuries old, accurately "forecast" all elections which were already part of history, neatly designated the enthusiast's own choice for his election, and then went on with glib predictions for the next four centuries. In that list Pius XII would have been a *pastor angelicus*—an "angelic shepherd." However much churchmen in Rome decried the Prophecy, the title finally attached so intimately to Pius that it appeared on his catafalque, officially accepted as apt whether or not the manipulator of the sixteenth century had received holy inspiration in selecting it. The pope of the 1958 conclave was to be *pastor et nauta*—"shepherd and sailor." Some thought that Cardinal Gilroy of Australia, who had been a radio operator on a World War I British troopship, might qualify, but others thought the Cardinal of the Adriatic canals might well be so identified. In Venice he had gone about infrequently by gondola, more often by motorboat. The often irreverent Roman spirit was intrigued by that. "Peter's bark will be a motorboat now," some quipped, to their own delight.

Even John as Pope did not disdain to take note of the curious "Prophecy." He might fly to Venice for a visit one day, and who was to say that a trip by air would not be appropriate for a *nauta?* He laughed.

The most bizarre and original bit of Roman-style tea-leaf reading was done by the weekly magazine *Oggi.* The new Pope, it said, should be a heavy man with a family name including the letter "R." The reason being that for a century there had been a steady alternation between thin men without an R and stout men with. Cardinal Pacelli, Pius XII, had been one of the former, and if you went backward you found Achille Ratti (Pius XI) who was stout; Giacomo della Chiesa (Benedict XV), wispy small; Giuseppe Sarto (Pius X), heavy; Gioacchino Pecci (Leo XIII), reedlike; and Giovanni Mastai-Ferretti (Pius IX), heavy.

Like so many others this "sign" pointed, of course, to the rather rotund Cardinal Roncalli, for as *Oggi* emphasized, Cardinal Aloisi Masella, another eminent possibility, was heavy but had no R, and Valerio Valeri had the R but was a diaphanous figure! A defect of the "sign" was that two other prominent *papabili* qualified: Cardinals Tisserant and Lercaro—both portly.

A few other fallacious signs should be recorded. At the end

of the second day of balloting, someone nervous over the delay noted hopefully, and it seemed at least half seriously, that "tomorrow will be the birthday of Cardinal Lercaro; Pius XII was elected on his birthday!"

Another sign had been found a few days earlier by the children of one European ambassador to the Holy See. Who was the *pastor et nauta?* "Through his mother it applies to Cardinal Costantini!" Presumably she was from a seafaring family.

It was within hours of the discovery of that sign that the earnest and studious Cardinal Costantini died.

Amid all the conflicting indications, the young pastor of Cardinal Roncalli's home town, Don Pietro Bosio, was busy laying in a supply of firecrackers to set off festively in the demonstrative Italian fashion in the event of the village son's designation. The pastor thought there was little doubt, but if not, "We can use them when he comes next time for Confirmation," he told the villagers.

The cardinals filed into the conclave, and their secrets—to a great extent—stayed with them.

Monsignor Loris Capovilla, Cardinal Roncalli's young secretary, speaking at a Catholic Action rally in Venice three months after the election, described the part of the proceedings which he had observed. It was just after the successful ballot had been completed.

"They had told us time and again that the first outsider who would be admitted would be the secretary of the Cardinal who was elected," the young monsignor recalled with an excitement which was still vivid. "I could not bear the anxiety of waiting, so I went to the door and said: 'I am, that is, I have been secretary of the Cardinal Patriarch of Venice!' "

The doors opened without a word and the secretary saw the Sistine Chapel scene in the moments just after the last voting had ended.

All but one canopy over the thrones of the cardinals had been lowered. The one still in place bore the name plate, CARDINAL ANGELO GIUSEPPE RONCALLI. Everyone was smiling and exchanging comments on the brief speech in which the Venetian prelate had protested the humility of his background and qualities and had chosen for his pontificate the internationally popular but, for Popes, all-but-forgotten name of John.

The new Pope was in a side room, already clad in white. He was "calm and smiling."

What had gone on? We know from chance remarks, from notes found among the papers of dead cardinals, or even from open and full reports, what happened at most of the other elections of the past century, and can be sure that much of the same must have occurred. Even in the case of Pius XII's unusually secret election we have Silvio Negro's story of how Cardinal Baudrillart was drawn out by being told that Ambassador Charles Roux's memoirs listed Cardinal Pacelli's victory margin as 52 out of 62.

"Ah? No, not quite that much; it was forty-eight," the cardinal answered spontaneously.

The documents of Cardinal LaFontaine of Venice described Pius XI's election. For the second time the saintly Spaniard, Merry del Val, Secretary of State of Pius X, was prominent in the balloting. He had 17 votes by the end of the first day's voting. Cardinal Pietro Gasparri, Benedict XV's Secretary of State, another leader, had 13. The Archbishop of Milan, Cardinal Ratti, a scholar of strong character but one of whom few had thought during the public speculation before the conclave, had a surprising 5 votes on the first ballot. Cardinal Merry del Val vanished by the end of the second day, replaced by Cardinal LaFontaine whose total rose to 21. Cardinal Gasparri was just ahead with 24.

By the third day Cardinal Gasparri was gone. Cardinal Ratti, whose support had grown steadily, was then up to 27 compared with Cardinal LaFontaine's nearly stationary 22. Next day Cardinal Ratti reached 42 and election.

Benedict XV was another surprise choice. Cardinals Maffi and Ferrari on the one side, and Merry del Val and Loualdi on the other, were seen as favorites but the Bologna prelate got three votes on the first ballot and, like his successor, Pius XI, advanced. His secretary, on news of the cardinals' choice, seemed on the verge of swooning. That prompted a reported remark of Benedict which is now a Rome legend: "Buck up, it's I, after all, that they have made Pope, not you!"

Similarly with Pius X, it was not the two favorites, Cardinal Rampolla, the highly pro-French Secretary of State of Leo XIII, or Cardinal Serafino Vannutelli, who were chosen but the humble country churchman, Archbishop Sarto of Venice. He received 5 ballots on the first round and is said to have murmured that "The Cardinals are having a joke." His support rose successively to 10, 21, 24, 27, 35 and finally a victorious 50.

In the case of the social-minded Leo XIII, the writer of much Catholic and even Western policy with regard to employer-worker relations and Communism, victory was swift. The prelate received 17 votes on the first ballot, 26 on the second, and a victorious 44 on the third.

Cardinals, who had to weigh a score of questions of person and policy, started in each case with a well-divided opinion, and more or less quickly came to a choice, often rejecting leaders who had been strong contenders at the start of the conclave.

In Cardinal Roncalli's election the factor of age, as we newspapermen had speculated, played an important part, for in his pastoral letter Cardinal Tisserant, the college dean, talked of the question at great length.

"Cardinal Roncalli," he said, "was the first Pope since 1730 to be nominated after passing the age of seventy. Clement XII of the famous Corsini family, chosen at that time, was seventy-eight. He ruled ten years.

"Of the fourteen since then, twelve had been between the ages of sixty and seventy and two under sixty. Pius IX was fifty-four and Pius VI, in 1775, fifty-eight.

"If you went back to the seventeenth century, however," the French Cardinal went on, "you found that five of the twelve were over seventy and that Clement X was eighty. Clement ruled for an impressively long six years and three months.

"Now, a year after Cardinal Roncalli's election," he added in a hint of the conclave's considerations, "no one could object to John's age in view of the good health, physical force and capacity for initiative which he has shown."

Cardinal Roncalli, at seventy-six, had seemed old—perhaps too old—but other considerations had overridden that of age.

What those were, the same cardinal indicated in the 1958 Christmas address. If one of them was that a briefer pontificate, after the very long one of Pius XII, could replenish the College of Cardinals and prepare another election, Archbishop Tisserant did not say. His comments on age in the pastoral letter implied that most were agreed that the heir of Pius XII ought not be too much a "pope of transition." As one most closely associated with the election commented, "We cannot do this every three or four years; the world would not understand."

Pius XII's successor had to be a real pope, at least for awhile, and not for a very short while.

"Your Holiness," Cardinal Tisserant told the pontiff in the Christmas speech, "was prepared by Providence with a great variety of occupations: in governing souls as a pastor [in Venice], in work as a teacher [in Italian seminaries around the time of World War I], as a representative of the Holy See abroad."

Shepherd, teacher, diplomat; the makings of a pope were there.

"And everywhere your human and cordial manner won the goodwill of the ordinary people and of the chiefs of state."

The unassuming peasant had become a prince. The unpretentious, scarcely known cardinal was ready to occupy the throne which Pius XII's death had left vacant.

# 12.  *Angelino*–Little Angel

One important factor which Cardinal Tisserant did not mention in listing the qualities which went into the making of the most *papabile* of Catholics in 1958 was the impact a pious, Alpine sharecropper farm family had effected in forming the heart and mind of Angelo Giuseppe Roncalli.

Eugenio Pacelli had been a devout, bright Roman city boy of the late eighteen hundreds, tormented by the seeming conflicts between science and religion; in contrast Angelo Roncalli was a son of the open landscapes and rocky slopes of the Southern Alps, where as on farms everywhere the problems of right and wrong and the mysteries of human origin and destiny seem simpler. From as early as he can remember Angelo wanted to be a priest.

From his first days on Peter's throne Pope John has shown himself a fatherly, rather uncomplicated old man, who enjoys entertaining visitors with reminiscences of his boyhood. Thanks to that we are able to piece together much of his story.

Village records show that his twenty-seven-year-old farmer father reported to the registrar that a son was born and that he wished to call him "Angelo Giuseppe"—our "angel Joseph." As grave, bearded Cardinal Tisserant was to learn with interest three-quarters of a century later, the two names were shrunk soon to "Angelino"—our "little angel."

There is love in *angelino*, but a sturdy boy may have doubts about it. From what Pope John has said we may assume he had mixed feelings. To several thousand Rome street cleaners who were invited to share his name day during his first year as Pope, he talked of both "Angelo" and "Giuseppe." Angelo, he said, was a nice name after all, suggesting as it does "those innocent creatures, so young, so tender, the charm of a family." He must have understood how his parents could have chosen it. But the saint of his name day, March 19th, was the other, Giuseppe. From the time he left home to become a priest and especially after he became a bishop and—Church fashion—began placing more emphasis on his first name, Giuseppe was his preference. Was it because it seemed more robust, more masculine? The Pope did not say but he did tell the sanitation men that he remembered with pleasure that one of the first bits of memorizing he accomplished was a prayer, especially popular in those years in Italy, "I pray to thee, O blessed Joseph."

To himself he was Giuseppe, but his fascination with names did not stop there. To graduates of the Rome college of the Dominican order, the Angelicum, Pope John described how he had used his newly acquired Latin as a schoolboy to compose a prayer to St. John the Evangelist. He recited it every day for long after that and always with "great profit," the old pontiff said.

Biographers who have combed hastily through John XXIII's lifetime papers found a letter he wrote in 1929 to his father, John (Giovanni). The young Roncalli was a papal diplomat in the Balkans by then.

"My dear Father," the bishop wrote, "this feast day of St. John never loses any of its beauty for me as the years pass. Even, as I get older, St. John attracts me more and more. I am devoted to him."

Angelo Giuseppe revered the Giovanni for whom his father was named, but surely a key to his character was the love he had for his father himself. When twelve footmen in maroon knee-breech costumes lifted him aloft for the first time as Pope on the more than regal portable throne, the *sedia gestatoria*, the new pontiff's thoughts went to his father, he told a group of his former Alpine neighbors at an audience given the very afternoon of his coronation. The old peasant had carried him on his shoul-

ders when he was seven years old, taking him to one of the first
large rallies of the young Italian Catholic Action organization,
an association of laymen dedicated to the service of the harassed
clergy of newly united Italy. There on his father's shoulders,
bound for a meeting which meant so much to his little-educated
parent, the boy felt one of the first powerful stirrings of a priestly
vocation.

Now as Pope he felt no incongruity in associating the un-
earthly pomp of the Papacy with his impoverished father.

It was not the first time the new pontiff had turned his
thoughts backward to his family during those first exciting and
demanding days. His immediate thought on being elected was of
his dead "papa and mamma" and of his humble native village of
Sotto il Monte—Under the Mountain—the Pope confided to his
secretary late on the night of his election.

"When I left home at ten," he had written to his parents in another letter from his Balkan post, "I read many books and I
learned many things you were unable to teach me.

"But," he went on, "the few bits I learned from you are still
the most precious and important. They bolster and enliven, they
give warmth to all the many other things I have come to know
since then in so many years of study and teaching."

What were the small fundamental things? Bishop Roncalli
suggested them in another part of the same letter: "The best way
to live is to trust the Lord, to keep peace in one's heart, to accept
all things as being for the best, to be patient and good. Never
to do ill."

Papa Roncalli, according to Pope John's secretary who often
heard descriptions of the old man, was a patriarch of few words.
The best he could provide for his family was a cramped lodging
in a modest farmhouse bulging with 30 tenants. There were about
10 children each in the family of the future Pope and that of his
cousin, and another 10 assorted relatives.

"We were very poor but we were contented," Pope John said
years later. "We never imagined that we lacked anything, and
as a matter of fact we didn't. Ours was a dignified and contented poverty."

"It wasn't truly as poor as some like to say now," the Pope added on another occasion. "It was first and foremost rich in the gifts of heaven, the example of our good parents, Papa and Mamma. We say it with a sense of great emotion and profound thanks to God: we owe a great part of our priestly vocation to our family."

"Fidelity, charity, mutual love and a holy fear of God," those were the marks of his home, Pope John told diplomats from forty nations as he said Mass for them at midnight on Christmas Eve, 1959. Having such a home, he said, had been "a great gift."

As he looked back to those first years, John's fond memory of his father was intermingled with a later episode, the death of one of his sisters at twenty-five. "She was one of God's chosen ones," the pontiff recalled in an audience a half century later. "A girl of truly shining virtue. She hadn't been invited yet to earthly nuptials but she was already ripe for those of heaven."

At the time, in a rare confidence, the grief-stricken father told his priest son that he would have preferred to raise another ten children rather than endure the pain of that one loss. Talking of it on March 1, 1959, to Vatican employees who had three or more children—all of whom had been called together at the Pope's wish—John said that the emotions of that moment had stayed with him through the decades as a mirror of what family can and should be. Deep peace and faith were what he read in the episode.

Angelo Giuseppe was aware of the strain he and his brothers and sisters had meant for his farm-tenant father.

"Ten of us on his back!" he exclaimed years later as he thought of it. It is said that in Venice as patriarch, while emptying his pockets to meet the appeals of beggars, he assured protesting aides that "I'll always have more left than my father had."

Side by side with recollections of that teeming household where no one knew luxury but no one went hungry either, John had other memories: the time when his mother told him to take off the corn meal as soon as it boiled (he ruined it by snatching it from the flames after the first bubble); the way the emigrants

looked as they started off under the kindly ministrations of a
travel agency to seek a better life in the United States or elsewhere (some to succeed and some to fail, as the prelate found
out as he checked up on them on his own annual trips back to
Sotto il Monte); the way he used to fear police even though
he had none but the smallest peculations on his conscience; the
time his cousin got a month in jail for poaching; but, above all,
how the frail old priest of the village looked from the Roncallis'
windows. Angelo Giuseppe could see that the priest's health was
in ruin but he observed also that everyone of every social class
sought out the aged cleric trustingly, and that he welcomed and
consoled all of them. The village pastor was "so affable, serene,
rich in goodness, charitable," John recalled as Pope. It seemed
to the pontiff seven decades later that he had never had any other
thought but to become a priest, that there was "never the least
doubt of it, never any discussion," but it is sure that the sight
of the Sotto il Monte *parroco* helped deepen and confirm the call.

It is for psychologists to say whether the core of the personality which mounted Peter's throne in 1958 was already
formed in childhood. There was little schooling to be had in
Sotto il Monte. Illiteracy was still a plague in villages of that
size all through Italy. At an early age the boy was walking four
hours a day to and from classes in another hamlet. He had a
priest's help with Latin. Formal training was hard to come by,
but what Angelino received he valued.

"All of us," the Pope told an Italian educators' association
at an audience in September, 1959, "carry in our hearts the
memory of our schoolteacher as one of childhood's dearest
recollections. What a high function the teacher has! To mould
souls by word and example, by patience amid so many difficulties
and privations."

The boy's interest in religion was ever clearer. He recited
prayers his fond long-bearded uncle, Barba Zaverio—Xavier, the
whiskered one—had taught him. Prayers revering Jesus's "Sacred
Heart" had moved him first. Others devoted to "the heart of
Mary" followed, the Pope told women of Italian Catholic Ac-

tion on February 24, 1959. His soul, he said, "by God's grace was open to the call of the supernatural; it was already mysteriously on its way toward the Holy Ministry." The typically Catholic devotion to Mary was to take on special significance a half century later as the successor of Peter recognized it for the obstacle it is to a Catholic-Protestant reunion. By then, like Pius XII and other Popes, John had a loyalty he would not renounce.

At the age of eight the future Pope received Holy Communion for the first time, the sacrament of Christ's body and blood, as Catholics believe, "under the appearance of bread and wine." Eight was generally considered too young for the sacrament then. It was not until the days of Saint Pius X in the first decade of the twentieth century that early Communion became the rule. "Happily" his little country parish was in the vanguard of the trend, as John told those at a general audience in September, 1959. It was about the time of that audience that priests in the old Roman slum of Trastevere sent word to the Pope that they had brought together twenty youths from the ages of twelve to twenty-seven who had never received Communion. The youngest was an errand boy in a salami store, the eldest a mechanic. Some were jobless. Would the Pope preside at the ceremony? John agreed. He distributed the Communion himself and then preached a sermon of reminiscences. All he could remember about his own first Communion, he said, was that the church was empty and his family had not come. He could not remember what he had prayed but he could imagine. It could not have been anything but "an act of faith in God."

On this occasion the priest had asked the boys whether they would join the Apostolate of Prayer, a pious organization dedicated to the daily recitation of certain invocations and the occasional addition of others assigned by the movement's leaders. Angelo Giuseppe not only stepped forward but he was given the job of taking down the names of all his comrades of like mind. A voice was whispering, *egredere . . . de doma tua*— "leave thy home." The village church of St. John became the center of the maturing child's affections. When he returned as a priest he wept to find that it had been razed, and he spoke of it to the cardinals in the Sistine Chapel when they elected him. Other religious institutions exerted a fascination for him.

At Baccanello he saw his first monastery, a small Franciscan one where the brothers worked their fields "with that completely naive air of simplicity which has made St. Francis and his sons so endearing." John recounted his Baccanello memories as hundreds of Franciscans joined him in St. John Lateran, his cathedral as Rome's Bishop, on the 750th anniversary of another pope's approval of the Franciscan Code. The Franciscans gave the Pope a handsome container for relics. John sent it to the Baccanello monastery where it became that institution's most unexpected and precious possession.

At fourteen the sharecropper's son donned the austere black cassock of a seminarian, but he never forgot his old home. "One must never lose sight of whence he came and whither he goes," the Pope told one audience. Remembering his simple but God-fearing family gave him a sense of balance in the midst of worldly crises, he stated on another occasion. Each year he vacationed at Sotto il Monte, chatting familiarly in dialect with childhood acquaintances or with their children or grandchildren, taking potluck at the unpretentious Roncalli family table, and getting news of the three nephews and nieces who had entered the clergy and another poor descendant of the family who had married a Communist. Meanwhile in his own villa the signs of ecclesiastical eminence accumulated. Notable was the glass case with two *zucchetti*—skullcaps of churchmen. One was the red of a bishop, that of Monsignor Radini-Tedeschi, who called the young Alpine priest for duty as his secretary soon after his ordination. The other was white, that of St. Pius X, the patriarch from Venice who succeeded Leo XIII as Pope. New heroes were joining earlier ones. The future Pope John, perhaps more than he knew, was by way of emulating them all.

Sotto il Monte went with John to the Vatican. As pontiff he recited each morning the prayers Barba Zaverio had taught him.

Pictures of his father and mother hung in his apartment along with those of the five popes with whom he had had an acquaintance. There was a small oil painting of his village and a picture of him as Paris nuncio with his four farmer brothers. And beside his *prie-dieu* was the portrait of the priest who had baptized him—the kind, ailing veteran he had watched with affectionate awe from his parents' home. The devoted Alpine farm boy knew whence he had come, just as he was confident, as a dedicated Pope, of whither he was going.

# 13. Gay Are the Good

As a newly ordained cleric in Rome in 1904, Father Roncalli was sure of the place he wished to occupy in Church ranks. He told Venetians a half century later in his first talk as patriarch, that he had had his heart set on the lowliest role—that of a country clergyman. Providence, as the patriarch added, decided otherwise.

It could have been no surprise to anyone that young Father Eugenio Pacelli, son of a family dedicated to high Vatican service, should have been taken quickly into the Holy See's Secretariate of State to become the familiar of Church leaders. But only the most extraordinary coincidences explained how Giovanni Roncalli's boy followed a similar path.

The local memory of young Angelo Roncalli is not one of classroom prowess, certainly not in his earliest years. Later his taste for learning and notably his appetite for Church history improved so much that he was singled out at the Bergamo seminary as one to finish his studies in Rome. Bergamo is known as an ever-full reservoir of priestly vocations, and there have long been scholarships for its seminarians in the Eternal City.

In Rome, at eighteen, Roncalli had met Count Giacomo Radini-Tedeschi, a Secretariate of State staff member. It was a meeting which ranks beside Angelo's contemplation of his village pastor as an influence on his character. Father Roncalli was invited to hold the Bible over Father Radini-Tedeschi's shoulders as Pope Saint Pius X consecrated the diplomat a bishop of Bergamo. Shortly afterward the new bishop chose the sharecropper's son as his secretary. Another world opened to the

future Pope. It was a complicated one made up of Church dignitaries and the political and economic controversies of a new era
of Catholic concepts of social justice, but it preserved the spontaneous piety of Sotto il Monte. Father Roncalli was so impressed
with his bishop that he published a 485-page tribute in 1916,
two years after the prelate's death. He kept a book of the bishop's
sayings on his desk for decades. Even in the Vatican, according
to one of the new Pope's closest cardinal collaborators, John
lived with the memory of Bishop Radini-Tedeschi.

Before becoming the bishop's secretary, youthful Father Roncalli had several other experiences in Rome which helped mold
him. He was in an audience held by Leo XIII one day when
several French clergymen cried out a greeting to the "Pope-
King." The Bergamo priest was shocked. Politics did not belong
in church; the French should not have brought the old quarrels
of the fallen eighteenth-century monarchy to the Pope's throne.
Leo himself, a tiny octogenarian, fascinated the youth. "A star
of the greatest magnitude," he described him after succeeding
him as Pope.

Each Sunday during Pius X's reign the young student took
part in audiences in the courtyard of St. Damasus at which the
saint-Pope explained the Gospel to pilgrimages from local
parishes. At the relatively informal audiences at the papal summer residence at Castel Gandolfo, John often thought back to
those receptions and followed the example. Like the devout
parish priest who was the spiritual model for both popes, John
chatted easily about the Gospel of the week or the saint of the
day, obviously convinced that the simplest elements of a faith
are the most important and cannot be repeated too often.

A climactic episode in his youth was an audience with Saint
Pius X just after the celebration of his first Mass, over the tomb
believed to be St. Peter's in the magnificent Vatican Basilica.

"Holy Father," a friend said, as Pope John often afterward
recalled, "here is a young priest from Bergamo who has said his
first Mass today."

"The Pope leaned over me," Cardinal Roncalli related in his
initial speech to his Venetian flock. "I told him words which I

GAY ARE THE GOOD    131

well remember but which are to remain locked away as one of the most precious secrets of my priesthood promises. Pius X put both hands on my head and answered: 'Bravo, my son! I urge you to honor these proposals of yours. I hope that your priesthood will be a success and that it will be a consolation to God's Church.' "

What the young priest whispered we cannot know but we have learned from a talk Pope John gave to seminarians on January 20, 1960, that it was often his custom after that to pray in the four-century-old Church of St. Ignatius beside the tombs of Saints Louis and John Berchmans. He prayed for help in "conserving forever the grace of chastity with no lessening of its delicacy and splendor."

Pius X, a man from the same devout Italian North country, moved on a few steps and then returned to the Bergamo priest.

"When do you say your first Mass in your home village?"

"On the Feast of the Assumption, Holy Father," Father Roncalli responded.

The mid-August holy day commemorating the raising up of the Virgin Mary's body and soul into Heaven is a secular as well as a religious high point in the Italian calendar; the signal for a wholesale closing of shops and for a rushing off for vacations.

"On the Assumption!" The Pope smiled. "Think of what a *festa*—what a celebration! The bells of Bergamo ringing and ringing!"

Pope and priest were from the same area. They were discussing their home. The thrilled young cleric noted nostalgic tones in the elder's voice.

Pius did not let the young clergyman leave without a memento. He gave him an autographed photograph which John displayed as one of his prized possessions in his Vatican apartment when he became Pope. Near it he kept another souvenir of Pius X, an armchair. It shows clearly how one generation influences another. Young seminarian Roncalli was present in St. Peter's for Pius X's coronation as pontiff in 1903 and saw the look of distress on his face when the congregation cheered him. Later Pius X gave in to the applause, recognizing how much it pleased his visitors to express affection. The same shifting attitude toward cheering in church could be observed more than a half century later in John's own first months as Pope.

John's studies in Rome took four years, interrupted briefly by service in 1902 in the Bergamo 73rd Infantry Regiment. It was the custom then, in an Italy of tense relations between the modern laic state and the politically disenfranchised Church, for clerics to do military service along with all other able-bodied youths. It was the first taste of several years of military experience, which according to Cardinal Tisserant made it possible for the developing Angelo Roncalli to understand man's nature and his miseries more intimately and sympathetically. It was the type of human encounter Pius XII had lacked and was therefore all the more desirable in his successor.

At twenty-two the future pontiff lay prostrate on the floor of a Rome chapel as the ancient ceremony of ordination unfolded. He told the story of those moments to a 1959 audience. He thought of "what lay ahead in the service of the Lord." His mind went to the members of his family who had been unable to make the 500-mile trip to the Eternal City. Family funds were even scarcer than in 1958 when there was still one sister who wondered whether she could afford the train ride to see her brother crowned. Angelo Roncalli thought of his "mission."

*"Tu es sacerdos in aeternum"*—"Thou art priest for all eternity!" the presiding officer intoned.

The anointed youth looked up and saw a centuries-old altar picture of Mary. He felt consoled. Later, as Pope, he ordered a reproduction of an ancient image of Christ's mother for his apartment.

One may wonder why Bishop Radini-Tedeschi chose the farm boy to be his secretary. The divergence between their backgrounds was immense. Perhaps it was enough for the prelate that he would have with him in his Bergamo assignment a young man from the area, a good youth whose loyalty could be taken for granted. If that was the bishop's reasoning it was justified. Father Roncalli's affection and admiration for his superior was so great that one who took part in John's election said afterward that the way to know John was to study his 1916 biography of his prelate—a volume of praise so enraptured as to be a paean.

Living with Bishop Radini-Tedeschi was like going to a school of churchmanship and virtue, the secretary found. The bishop was a nobleman dedicated to helping the poor along the lines of Pope Leo XIII's social encyclical, a document which had been received diffidently by many Catholic prelates wedded to a conservative and class-conscious past. A man of broad humanistic culture, Father Radini-Tedeschi had been a staff member of Leo XIII's Secretariate of State for a decade. He was a descendant of an aristocratic family described as the same one which had produced another famous Vatican staff officer, Father Tommaso Radini-Tedeschi, "Master of the Papal Palace" under Clement VII in the early sixteenth century. It was Father Giacomo Radini-Tedeschi who was sent as papal envoy to Paris in 1893 at the time of the French-Holy See concordat to carry the red hat known as the biretta to the newly named Cardinal Donnet. It is old tradition in France for state officials to take part in the biretta-conferral ceremony, and in the momentary peace of Church-State relations in Paris they did so. The future bishop was impressed and described the ceremony in detail later to his secretary in an account which must have stood out in Cardinal Roncalli's mind in 1953 when the ritual was repeated. At that time it was President Vincent Auriol, a Socialist and non-Catholic, who bestowed the biretta of cardinal and Archbishop Roncalli who received it. It was the first time the ceremony had taken place since the occasion Bishop Radini-Tedeschi had described to his young secretary.

A significant member of Father Radini-Tedeschi's entourage was Father Achille Ratti, who became Pope as Pius XI in 1922. There was something rare in the nobleman-priest which brought him future popes as assistants. It was the logic of their relationship that Bishop Radini-Tedeschi should introduce his secretary to the priest who had been his aide on that Paris mission, and it was an important element in the unfolding career of Father Roncalli that he should become the future Pius XI's close friend. One of Pius's first acts was to name Father Roncalli head of the

Catholic Foreign Mission Aid Society, a position of international contacts and influence which proved a quick steppingstone to the episcopacy and to still higher positions.

Bishop Radini-Tedeschi seemed to know and to be beloved by everyone, from everything that his admiring secretary could see. Pius X himself chose to preside at the imposition of hands making Father Radini-Tedeschi a bishop. In a remark which became a legend of John's pontificate, Pius X told Bishop Radini-Tedeschi that he would keep him with him even when the two set off for Paradise. Two days after Pius X expired in 1914, grief-stricken by the start of World War I, Bishop Radini-Tedeschi —still a relatively young man in his fifties—died too. Father Roncalli watched beside his prelate during his dying hours and learned to admire his bishop's serene courage more than ever.

It seemed a step down when Bishop Radini-Tedeschi left the Vatican for Bergamo. He was a man of advanced social ideas. A conservative current was running, with the young Spanish noble, Merry del Val, as successor to the liberal and pro-French Mariano Rampolla in the papal Secretariate of State. Pius X reassured the bishop. For all those things which make a bishop most content Bergamo was best of all, the saintly Pope said of the Alpine diocese. The enthusiasm with which the bishop gave himself to his task offered no suggestion that he felt differently. Radini-Tedeschi, according to Cardinal Tisserant, had reason to fear that his vigorous activities had put him out of step with the Papacy, but the Cardinal testified that all now known demonstrates that the brave and energetic social thinker was always in tune with the true intentions of the progressive Leo XIII and the revered Pius X.

What his contemporaries thought of Bishop Radini-Tedeschi may have been reflected in the pontificate following Pius X's, when Father Roncalli was summoned to Rome. The decision to call him, according to signs at the time, was either made by Benedict XV directly or by his main collaborator, the Cardinal Secretary of State Pietro Gasparri. Benedict XV had ample reason to know Father Roncalli, for he had been "like a brother" to Radini-Tedeschi when they worked together in the Secretariate of State. Both were from the same Po Valley city of Piacenza.

Father Roncalli wrote his biography of his bishop in spare moments on his military assignment during World War I. Churchmen who reread it after John became Pope marveled at the unconscious self-portrait.

"One noticed depths of inexhaustible gaiety in his soul, for his was a spirit alien to the passions which cause sadness," the military clergyman wrote perceptively and lovingly. "His soul was more disposed to point up merits than to exaggerate faults. He treated everything with the greatest reverence and goodness. In highest degree he had from nature that characteristic mentioned by Holy Scripture of being a man made especially to be loved in society. He knew how to enjoy the full charm of a conversation and how to make others share in the pleasure. He had seen and learned much and he spoke in a matchlessly pleasant manner. He was never bored or depressed. He was ever ready to obey his conscience. He possessed the peace of duty done. It was that which shone from his eyes and mouth. His was a perennial and pure joy."

To Father Leone Algisi, a Venetian priest and one of the ablest of John's biographers, no portrait of the pontiff himself could be more apt.

A cardinal of the 1958 conclave put the story of John's episcopal model less lyrically but with no less approval. Bishop Radini-Tedeschi, he said, deserved a place in Church annals as "one of the two or three best Italian bishops of his time."

One of the bishop's first acts as head of the Bergamo diocese was to set out on a visit to parishes. His survey took several years and was followed by another round of visits immediately afterward. For the secretary who went along there was no better way to learn how pastors work out the problems of a variegated ministry. As the climax to the first round of parishes the bishop summoned a synod, a meeting of the prelate with all his clergy. It was the first synod Bergamo had had in 186 years, and we may assume that the priests were surprised and pleased. It was a democratic gesture which Father Roncalli never forgot, for one of his own first measures as pontiff and bishop of Rome was to call the first diocesan synod in the 1,900-year history of the Eternal City See, and the first ecumenical council—something like a synod on the pope and bishop level—in 90 years.

Many years later Cardinal Tisserant suggested that while the bishop and his secretary made their rounds of the Bergamo churches and clergy, Providence shaped the pastor in the soul of Angelo Roncalli, preparing him for that vast part of his papal work. As a spiritual father, Bishop Radini-Tedeschi was peerless, in the opinion of his young assistant.

"I can assure you," Father Roncalli said at memorial ceremonies in Bergamo ten years after Radini-Tedeschi's death, "that even in our most private moments I never saw him fall the least bit short of his high sentiments.

"He was so tall and noble in his person and in his manner. His glance and his smile were sweet but controlled. One said at once that there was a man of command. How he dominated large audiences when he spoke! In another era, under different circumstances, you would have seen him as a commander on his mount leading brave troops into battle!"

He was intransigent, but it was the strength of will "of any self-respecting man," a defense of principles and objectives that held nothing irritating to others. With officials the bishop got on good-naturedly. In short, "Whoever met him, even though he may have been of other ideas and temperaments, believed at once that he was shaking the hand of a gentleman!"

He was the good shepherd, knowing his sheep, leading them to better pastures, and ready if need be to die for them, Pope John recalled in a 1960 audience. It had been a thrill, he added, to go to Venice in 1953, after nearly a forty-year interval, and to imitate in a see of his own the example of his Bergamo superior.

At Bishop Radini-Tedeschi's side "we learned how the fate of the workingman is to be taken to heart," Pope John recounted on his first audience on a May Day—the once revolutionary holiday of Europe's laboring class. The Pope spoke to an organization of Catholic workers, a group Bishop Radini-Tedeschi had helped inspire.

"He gave such a decisive example, he showed such zeal," the

Pope said of the Bergamo clergyman. "In his efforts we had the most eloquent of proofs of how motherly and solicitous the Church is for these working-class children of hers."

Under Radini-Tedeschi, Bergamo had been one of the dioceses to take the lead in shaping a courageous Catholic social program, the Pope added. The Catholic "social renewal" of Italy at mid-century was the fruit of efforts, such as those of the bishop, "which we watched in the springtime of our priesthood." Because of all that, the Pope told the workers, "you are dear to us; know that the Pope is with you!"

What Father Roncalli witnessed was the laying of the foundation for the Catholic Action program which helped the broken Italy of the Fascists to survive the Communist threat in 1945 and create a pro-Western democratic government. He was observing the binding of firmer ties with the working class, the beginning of an answer to the appeal of Marxism, and the start of a revolt against the privilege which had dominated Europe for centuries.

The tireless Bishop Radini-Tedeschi did not limit himself to his own parishes and to local social reform. He organized pilgrimages to the Christian holy places in the Middle East and to the Catholic shrines at Lourdes and other parts of France. His secretary went along. The faith of a village and of seminaries took on additional geographical and historical dimensions.

Nor did Radini-Tedeschi neglect old acquaintances in Church leadership. Father Roncalli was especially impressed one day in an audience with Pius X when the latter told his two callers how a group of solemn and prominent gentlemen had waited on him the day before with a proposal for ending the four-decade-old estrangement between the faith and the nation of the Italian people. The visitors had asked whether Pius X would be willing to settle the dispute by abandoning claims to the 1,000-year old Central-Italian Papal States in exchange for political possession of the city of Rome. Officially Catholics were boycotting modern Italy politically in protest over the 1870 conquest of the pontifical kingdom, but Pius X was already loosening the moral ban, and in talking confidentially to the two Bergamo visitors made it clear that he recognized the loss of political responsibilities as a boon.

"Just imagine, when you think of all the troubles the good people here [inside the autonomous Vatican Palace] already give me; they want me to take Rome, too, to govern!" The old saint shook his head.

He lapsed into dialect, Father Roncalli noted with fascination. "Rome, too, to govern!" *Anca Roma da governar!* (*Anche* [on-kay] and *governare* [go-vair-nah-ray] would have been the proper Italian.)

One canard about Pius X and the Papacy was answered, as far as Bishop Radini-Tedeschi's secretary was concerned. The old pontiff could no longer be called power hungry.

Bishop Radini-Tedeschi, the ever-gay nobleman, amiable associate of the great and friend of the poor, saint in a modern gentleman's form, humanist and traveler, left a bright mark on Father Roncalli's soul. When the latter walked into the Sistine Chapel for the ballot on which he was elected Pope, he was wearing the same purple cassock in which Bishop Radini-Tedeschi had been consecrated in the same room in his presence fifty-three years earlier.

# 14. Home and Saints

When Pope John was carried into St. Peter's on the *sedia gestatoria* for his coronation as Pope, someone shouted: "Hooray for Bergamo!" The Alpine diocese, famous for its vocations for the priesthood, had produced nine cardinals, and at last a pope.

The day was not over before the new Pope chided his Bergamo friends in an audience.

*Evviva* [long live] St. Peter or *Evviva Cristo* were appropriate, but other things, including pride in native area, had to be seen in perspective, the Vicar of Christ gently chided the exultant sons of Bergamo.

In spite of his reprimand, few men were more sensitive to the stirrings of local affection. Still, curiously, his share of provincialism, his *campanilismo*—bell towerism, as Italians call it—was one more part of Monsignor Roncalli's makeup that helped prepare him effectively for the Papacy.

*Campanilismo*, it may be pointed out, is the strangely Italian penchant for knowing nothing and caring nothing about what lies beyond the sound range of one's own village church bell. In a marked way Angelo Roncalli was "campanilistic," but remarkably it led him to the universal.

A capital turning point in his life came during his first months as Bishop Radini-Tedeschi's secretary when the two went to Milan for meetings in preparation for a provincial council. An assembly of that sort brings together a region's bishops and priests and is midway between a diocesan synod and an ecumenical, or universal, council.

Just as Bishop Radini-Tedeschi's Bergamo synod must have

helped nurture ideas which blossomed in John's Rome synod and Roman Catholicism's twenty-first ecumenical council, so did the trips to Milan give the youthful priest valuable free hours while his bishop negotiated with his peers. The young man from a virtually bookless and all but illiterate village had become conscious of the printed page, and used his spare time to browse in the Ambrosian ecclesiastical library. Its director was Father Achille Ratti, the future Pius XI. To Angelo Roncalli's delight a combing of the old stacks turned up a Bergamo gem, thousands of pages and a total of thirty-nine thick volumes of reports telling in his own words what Bishop Charles Borromeo, a canonized saint, had thought of parishes in Roncalli's home area in the course of a three-month inspection in 1575. Here was the very work Father Roncalli and his own bishop were doing! Wouldn't it be interesting to bring out a book telling the story of the diocese seen through the eyes of a late Renaissance saint, in the latter's own words! Father Ratti's reaction was enthusiastic; he was a bibliophile and a vivacious man who had never let his soul dry out amidst the dusty papers of Church archives—as Father Roncalli said of him when Monsignor Ratti became Pope. The older of the two future pontiffs even had a suggestion for a publisher—Leo Olschki of Florence. Bishop Radini-Tedeschi agreed to the project and work began. It proved to be a fifty-year labor. The last of the five volumes was completed two months before the Venetian patriarch was elected Pope. He must have had much just pride of authorship, for even as pontiff John kept a copy of the work in his apartment.

Charles Borromeo had gone from town to town in the Bergamo diocese, studying the fervor and failings of priests and people, patching up some broken marriages and recognizing the impossibility of doing much about others, settling disputes—one of them over the matter of whether military flags should be honored in church. On the latter subject the reigning Pope had said no, but parishioners had been too attached to old banners to obey him. In one such situation the problem had been solved by one of the bishop's assistants who destroyed the offending standards by night. People were indignant but the accomplished fact calmed them, and the Pope had his way.

The core of Bishop Borromeo's mission was to see to it that the reforms demanded by the sixteenth-century ecumenical council of Trent were applied. They were Catholicism's often penitent and assenting response to criticisms made by the newborn Protestantism. Studying those reforms and the uplifting consequences of Catholicism's nineteenth ecumenical council, Father Roncalli was weaned slowly from the parochial Bergamo view of the story to a more universal understanding. Certainly that long contemplation influenced his own decision to call a council in 1959, the act which was considered by far the most important decision of his first years as Pope.

When Father Roncalli was consecrated a bishop in 1925 the ceremony took place beside a relic of the heart of St. Charles Borromeo in the Roman church that had been named for him. When he became Pope his aides were startled at John's insistence that the coronation take place within seven days. There would be scant time for missions from fifty nations to reach Rome, even by jet. John insisted. November 4th was St. Charles Borromeo's day and the pontiff was determined to assume the crown then. Charles, the Pope told the brilliantly arrayed coronation congregation of diplomats and royalty, would be the "protector," the special saint of his pontificate. Using a pope's powers, John inserted a line into the litany of saints recited at the coronation ceremony. He asked the St. Peter's audience to recite the words fervently: *Sancte Carole, tu illum adjuva!*—"O holy Charles, aid thou him!"

Charles Borromeo was an ascetic, severe with himself and very strict with his clergy. The effects of his reforms were still to be seen in Father Roncalli's time.

He was a bishop who deserved to be ranked with "the greatest pastors of souls in the history of the Church in all ages," Pope John said.

His own five books, the new Pope explained on another occasion, showed St. Charles "alive and at work, 300 years afterward," portraying him "the way his contemporaries knew and revered him." He was, said Charles' editor-biographer, "a man with the lofty intelligence of an administrator; one who saw and achieved everything."

"His contemporaries lifted him up for veneration while he was still alive," the pontiff added. "His was an intense religious fervor. He handled everything with exquisite art and with the methods best adapted in each case. He accomplished his goals in an orderly way, with perfect organization, calmly, not without conflicts. But even in the disputes he showed immense dignity and goodness."

What had started as a work of Bergamo scholarship had become a prolonged meditation on a model bishop, an urbane, effective holy man, an example for a kindly but exacting pope. Another of John's preparations was complete.

St. Charles Borromeo was not the only object of Father Roncalli's broadening historical studies. Another churchman of the Venetian area who captured his attention was the Blessed Gregory Barbarigo, who like Father Roncalli was devoted to the memory of Charles Borromeo. One of John's first acts as Pope was to canonize Gregory Barbarigo, waiving the usual requirement of proof of miracles performed since the time of beatification. To add to the drama, John revoked a papal bull of 1741 assigning all canonization ceremonies to St. Peter's Basilica. The Pope held the rite for Gregory Barbarigo at St. John Lateran, his own bishop's cathedral. It was the first such rite to be celebrated there since those in which St. Vincent de Paul, the charity worker, and St. Catherine of Genoa were canonized in 1737.

Pope John gave his views of Gregory Barbarigo before 200 Roman slum women at a party for their children at John's first Christmas in the Papacy.

"Gregory," he said smiling, after he had handed out presents, "twice ran the risk of being Pope, but anyway became one of God's saints."

Gregory lived a century later than Charles. He did his best to imitate him. He, too, like Father Roncalli's superior, Radini-Tedeschi, had been a bishop of Bergamo. Before taking over his diocese he had made a point of praying at St. Charles Borromeo's tomb. His proxy, incidentally, in taking possession of the Bergamo see was a Roncalli—the Archdeacon Rudolfo.

Gregory Barbarigo was born in 1625 to an aristocratic Venetian family. His associations with the Archdeacon Roncalli, Bergamo, Venice, St. Charles Borromeo—everything about the prelate —drew him to Father Roncalli's affectionate attention. A law student, the young Signor Barbarigo was attracted to the life of a monk, but agreed at the urging of papal aides to become a secular priest instead. As such he would be more easily available for important Church service. At thirty-one, Father Barbarigo was a monsignor, at thirty-two bishop of Bergamo, at thirty-five a cardinal and at forty-two, in 1667, he was nearly elected Pope. Repeatedly in the course of five conclaves he was all but elected, while begging that the honor go to another. Of him it could truly be said that he was not Pope only because he did not wish to be, his biographer, Jesuit Father Julius Caesar Cordara stated. The Papacy had had two saints within a few years—Pius V and Innocent XI—and perhaps Providence wanted to leave one for the Cardinals' College, a writer in the Vatican's newspaper L'Osservatore Romano remarked at the time of the canonization. Gregory Barbarigo died at seventy-three in 1697 and was raised to the Catholic altars as a Blessed sixty-four years later. Blesseds are honored locally; saints are revered by the World Church.

Cardinal Barbarigo, called a second Charles Borromeo, visited parishes in the Po Valley area, fining inefficient priests and encouraging religious instruction for children. He developed a printing center famous for its supply of Arabic, Syrian, Armenian and Persian types. Dedicated to higher standards of learning among the clergy, the cardinal was also devoted to the quest for a reunion of Christians of East and West. In canonizing him, Pope John had the satisfaction of raising to universal honor a fellow Venetian dedicated to his own profoundly felt cause of deeper clerical piety and Christian reconciliation.

Remember the words of Gregory Barbarigo, John told the poor women of Rome. One should not fear to have large families, for in Barbarigo's words "God blesses big pots!" Himself a child from a large family, John felt sympathy for those words of three centuries earlier.

However much his home region may have influenced the young priest's first studies, Church history of all sorts quickly absorbed him. In 1908 he published a study on Cardinal Caesar Baronius, an early seventeenth-century Italian historian of ecclesiastical affairs who is famous, according to *The Columbia Encyclopedia*, for never suppressing a fact whether it favored Protestants or Catholics. At the same time he was wholly loyal to the Papacy. From Cardinal Baronius, Pope John borrowed the motto of his cardinalate and pontificate *Oboedientia et pax* —"obedience and peace." "John," said a diplomat admiringly, "knows religious history and has the knack of picking out what is still vital—what still applies: he does not look on it all as if it were a museum of past things."

In addition to his work with Bishop Radini-Tedeschi and his historical studies and writings, young Father Roncalli taught Church history at seminaries. Popes are teachers, so the classroom hours helped him too. The years brought more human contacts, some tears, much laughter. Monsignor Roncalli was once quoted as saying that fellowship came easily to him. There were no tensions, even with the strangest companions. A brother prelate was to notice this when Monsignor Roncalli was nuncio in Paris.

"Every time I had supper with him at the nunciature there was always someone from the far Left also at table," the churchman recalled. John's tastes were catholic with a small c.

Looking back over those years the septuagenarian John found much over which to chuckle: the teacher in the seminary who cried "fire" so earnestly as he described Hell's pains that people next door ran to the street; the seminary financial manager who urged Signor Roncalli and his classmates not to eat much; the way priests from the rival Roman seminary of Capranica had dominated his life so that "all I need now is a Capranica man to show me the gates of Paradise!"

Even when Bishop Radini-Tedeschi died and his secretary was called to duty with the Italian Army as a sergeant in the Medical Corps, the young priest found his situation tolerable at least.

Never did his soldier comrades utter within earshot of him the vulgarities which stud army talk everywhere.

A year or so as a "medics" noncommissioned officer led to his appointment as a chaplain and lieutenant. Father Roncalli was surely thrilled by that assignment, for four decades later, as Pope, he told an audience that he was honored to be the oldest living Italian chaplain and that he felt that a chaplain's being Pope showed the nobility of the military priests' calling.

The war over, Father Roncalli had an emergency assignment to act as spiritual director of the Bergamo seminary, reorienting youths shaken by the war chaos, and also to organize a club for young laymen of the middle class whose religious sentiments had been corroded. On a more sophisticated level, it was work similar to that of the venerated Sotto il Monte parish priest; it is said that Father Roncalli was distressed when he was invited to leave it to go to Rome. The "Red Pope," Cardinal Van Rossum, acting on "personal indications from Pope Benedict XV," wanted Father Roncalli to take over the task of organizing the many little Italian foreign mission aid groups into a single more effective national body. The cardinal was head of the Vatican's Sacred Congregation for the Propagation of the Faith, the Church's mission agency. The red-clad cardinal in charge of that congregation, with his Churchly responsibility for so many teeming millions in un-Christian Asia and Africa, was traditionally known as Rome's "Red Pope."

Father Roncalli, it is said, wrote to the dying Cardinal Ferrari of Milan for counsel. The advice fitted the Baronius motto of "Obedience and Peace."

"Dear Professor Roncalli," the old archbishop is said to have answered, "the will of the Red Pope is the will of the White Pope and therefore the will of God. Leave everything and go. A great blessing of the Lord will go with you."

Father Roncalli went to Rome "out of obedience," as Pope John told an audience in January, 1959. He felt "small" there, as he said in a talk during a brief trip back to Bergamo in 1924. He had been "educated by the church of Bergamo for its sanctuary," but by 1924 he saw that it had been the will of Providence that he should go on to "wider though modest" labors in the Eternal City "where beats the heart of Christianity and of the whole world."

Although he was not important in Rome he was quickly named a monsignor and soon had occasion to see Monsignor Ratti again. The latter was now a cardinal and the two talked just before the 1922 papal election.

Do all you can, the Bergamo priest urged his old friend from the Ambrosian library, to choose a pope who will be "all for peace in the world and for the Church missions."

"Do you imagine we could come out with anyone else?" the cardinal said, smiling.

Whether or not Cardinal Ratti could speak for all other *papabili* he could speak for himself, and within days it was he who was Pope.

The seminarian Roncalli had been close enough at the coronation of Saint Pius X to see his expression of disapproval when crowds cheered the new pontiff; now he was designated to hold a corner of the papal canopy during the procession at the coronation of his friend Pius XI.

Cardinal Ratti has reason to tremble with that immense new responsibility, the newly named monsignor thought to himself.

"But then," he disclosed later before there was any thought of his own accession to the Papacy, "I thought that the whole world was praying for him; the Lord was responsible for the cardinals' choice and would give every help."

Monsignor Roncalli was present as one of the officers of the Congregation for the Propagation of the Faith when Pius XI pronounced his first homily in commemoration of the congregation's 300th anniversary a few days later. The new Pope thrilled his audience with a spontaneous address assuring them that he would see himself on Peter's chair as "Christ's beggar," confidently demanding the co-operation of all.

A few days later Pius XI told Monsignor Roncalli about it during an audience. The monsignor noticed that the new pontiff was already using the papal "we" in a natural manner.

"We were surprised with ourself," Pius XI contentedly recalled the homily. "As we sang the *Credo* we could no longer remember what we had said, but there was joy in our heart from the way we had talked. There was a mystical sweet satisfaction, as if the Lord were saying 'Well done! I am content!' "

The monsignor saw his old friend occasionally after that. Pius XI, he took note, never had an ill word for anyone. His piety shone in one comment he made to his Bergamo confidant. Whenever an especially impressive visitor came, Pius XI prayed to his guardian angel and as the talks proceeded "felt him standing beside us!"

There were more smiles in those years. As Pope John recalled a night he had spent, during his years as a monsignor, at the summer residence of the Mission College in the cool hills outside Rome. The distracted superior gave him a key to a room which had not been used as a dormitory for some time. The young churchman was astounded at what he found. It was used as a storeroom and cluttered from wall to wall. The future Pope pulled out the worst of the debris and managed to find some space for rest. The irony intrigued him next day when Cardinal Camillo Laurenti greeted him in the effusive manner of Italians. "I am sure you are receiving every courtesy," smiled the cardinal, little knowing.

The work of co-ordinating mission-aid activities expanded. Monsignor Roncalli was assigned to transfer the main world center of such activities from France, where it had flourished as a result of local fervor, to Rome where it could be at the Pope's elbow as a more easily manipulated instrument. The new task meant travels across the Continent and frequent communications with missionary bishops throughout the Orient and Black Africa. The horizons of Bishop Radini-Tedeschi's former secretary were still expanding. At the 1925 Holy Year, Monsignor Roncalli was assigned to organize the popular and successful Mission Exhibition, reflecting the many fascinating alien and primitive cultures in which European and American missioners were planting the Gospel seed.

Monsignor Roncalli, under the approving eye of his friend Pius XI, was becoming more prominent, but he did not forget his origins. Bergamo still loomed large with him, as it always continued to. Even as Pope, on May 29, 1959, John found it easy to give a talk on the great men of Bergamo who had often been travelers because of the scarcity of the world's goods in their own homeland, but were also distinguished voyagers such as "Costantino Beltrami, one of the discoverers of the source and course of the Mississippi." On the eve of the conclave, Cardinal Roncalli had written to Bergamo's incumbent bishop that it mattered "little" whether a Bergamo man ascended Peter's throne, but after his election he did tell Romans of Bergamo origin that he had felt it proper to call them together around him and that he did not see it as a conflict with his new universal loyalties. In the album of snapshots of his family and himself which he kept in his apartment as Pope, the last two items were five-cent postcards of Bergamo.

On his coronation day John was deeply moved and wept twice as he talked to a delegation from Bergamo. He caught himself with an effort.

"We don't want to give any more of this spectacle, because we are no longer infants to be seen weeping," he told his fellows from Bergamo, "but our sentiment is what you know and what you can see. Each morning as we prepare to take up our grave task we think of our Bergamo, our homeland, and of our Venice."

In the days just after the opening of the Holy Year Mission Exhibition, another step away from Sotto il Monte and from Bergamo was in preparation. As the Catholic *Tablet* of London related the story on December 13, 1958, brilliant young Father Eugene Tisserant, the future cardinal dean, had come back from the Middle East to confirm a rumor the book-loving Pius XI had heard. It was true, according to the young French linguist, that Kemal Ataturk's drive to make Turkey a modern laic society was forcing Moslem institutions to sell precious ancient religious works. The librarian Pope decided to send a fellow bibliophile as papal envoy to the Eastern Balkans, someone who could be counted on in the course of regular duties to watch for the old volumes valuable to all students of religion. Pius XI recalled the secretary of his former Lombard seminary classmate, the young priest who had been so excited over the Borromeo reports, the monsignor who had done so well on the Mission Exhibition. The Pope promoted Monsignor Roncalli to archbishop and appointed him a Church diplomat for the Balkans. It was one more move in the improbable progress of the sharecropper's boy.

# 15. Reluctant Diplomat

When Pope John received the Rome press corps in one of his first audiences, he told us that no pontiff should be a "political pope," a "scholar pope," a diplomat. He should be a "father." The rest were adornments, but nonessentials.

The same attitude toward diplomacy marked Bishop Roncalli's twenty-eight years as one of the Holy See's gifted international envoys. He was a priest who put the emphasis on what brothers in the human family had in common, while being careful to deny no essential point of his Church's doctrine. In doing that, the unassuming farmer's son succeeded where accomplished linguists and masters of protocol might have failed.

Archbishop Roncalli's first assignment was to Bulgaria. Catholics were only one per cent of the population. The Vatican envoy was not accepted as part of the diplomatic corps. He was treated officially as a civilian with a private religious mission. The same nondiplomatic status was to go with him for the next twenty years of his work as an envoy. Only in Paris was he to receive diplomatic standing, and then in one leap the role of dean of the French capital's markedly sophisticated and worldly diplomatic corps. Paris was one of the capitals which still respected the 1815 Vienna agreement on precedence for papal nuncios. As head of the corps it was Archbishop Roncalli's role to read the diplomats' annual New Year's greeting to the French President.

The glories of such a deanship were far from what Archbishop Roncalli met on arrival at his Sofia post in 1925. He did not know the language. Schooling around Sotto il Monte, such as it was, had included no linguistic pretensions beyond modest local Italian and some Latin, and the years in the Bergamo and Rome seminaries and in Church work had added little. The envoy had no secretary. As he confided after the election of 1958 to Indro Montanelli, the brilliant Italian journalist who managed to get the only exclusive interview, he saw a peach branch in bloom outside his bare room as he offered his first Mass.

"Instead of being cheered by it I wondered whether I would ever see it in blossom another year. It was a moment's pessimism and as if to punish me for it the Lord saw to it that I watched ten springtimes flourish there before I moved on."

Within days the scantily prepared Vatican envoy to overwhelmingly Orthodox Bulgaria comprehended his Church's problem there, as a Vatican Orientalist told me later. Himself a brand-new member of the episcopacy, Archbishop Roncalli quickly looked through the local clergy for one who could take over the native leadership as a bishop, chose Father Cyril Kurteff, and then set off with him for a tour of the back country—an area where little Catholic communities were rare indeed. The trip gave him an opportunity to study both his companion and the nation. It offered a start on learning Bulgarian, too. Perhaps most important, it provided him with the first occasion to ponder on the possibility of a reconciliation of Catholics and Orthodox Christians after a thousand-year estrangement.

That the trip and subsequent years in Sofia went well is attested to by wide evidence. As a reporter covering the festive ceremonies in which Pope John took possession of his Roman Cathedral, St. John Lateran's, I remember an argument with police near the Colosseum as I attempted to trail the Pope back to the Vatican. I wanted to see the public reaction but the police were anxious to keep down the size of the Pope's automobile parade, and anyhow, as they explained, the procession had been blocked for some reason. After a quarter of an hour they relented and I followed the Pope in a procession of a half-dozen cars back through a cheering Rome to St. Peter's.

The reason for the delay, as I learned afterward, was that Pope

John had asked to pay a visit to the ancient church of St. Clement, whose history is identified with Saints Cyril and Methodius, two Roman envoys of the ninth century who did much to Christianize the Balkans and to spread the Cyrillic alphabet—the script form named for St. Cyril and used now by Russians, Serbs and other Balkan peoples. Cyril was Bishop Kurteff's name saint. One can be sure that as papal emissary to the Balkans the future Pope had often thought of this Roman church as a monument to ancient Catholic association with the Balkans and as a symbol of the Catholics' claim to the right of brotherly communion in Orthodox Bulgaria. At St. Clement's John prayed for Bishop Kurteff.

By the time he left Bulgaria, Archbishop Roncalli knew the language well enough to give his farewell speech in it. The tiny Catholic minority gave him a chasuble, a vestment worn during Mass. It was one of those he used regularly in his private chapel when Pope. To remind him of Bulgaria the bishop asked the Vatican to change his honorary diocese from Areopoli, Palestine, to Mesembria, an ancient, no longer Catholic see associated with the Bulgarians.

About then the future Pope rearranged his day's prayers to include the Bulgarians and other Orientals. It was a practice he never suspended even as Pope. He had gone to carry the message of Rome and had ended by acquiring an understanding both of the difficulties of minorities such as the Bulgarian Catholics and also of the virtues of those outside his own Rome communion.

"What fine, hard-working, honest and sincere people those Bulgarians were," John recalled in his first Easter message as Pope. How beautiful was their capital, Sofia, "which carries us back to the ancient Sardica of the first Christian centuries and to noble and glorious epochs of Bulgaria's history!"

The success of the nondiplomat diplomat was repeated on Archbishop Roncalli's next assignment, as Holy See envoy to Turkey and Greece. There too the future Pope had a chance to learn more about the non-Catholic world. The two Balkan and Middle Eastern missions together were to make of John the first

Pope in modern times—and perhaps since the Church's dawn—to live so long amid so small a minority of his fellows.

In Turkey the modernization drive against Mahometanism and all other religions forced Archbishop Roncalli and his fellow Catholic clergy to dress as laymen in public. The Vatican envoy had no official standing and so had to be on his guard against difficulties with the government. Perhaps because of his ten years of experience in Bulgaria, he became the first Vatican agent to get on well with the Orthodox in Turkey. He was given a large share of the credit when the Orthodox patriarch of Istanbul courteously sent a representative to the coronation of Pius XII in 1939.

The good relationship with the Orthodox flowered. Even a strange tragedy seemed to emphasize it. Archbishop Roncalli's successor died three days after the moving experience of exchanging cordial calls with the Orthodox patriarch at the start of his assignment. It seemed in Rome as if the shock of success had overwhelmed the Holy See's envoy.

Orthodox Greece was scarcely an easier assignment than antireligious Turkey, for it was the only country outside the Iron Curtain after World War II to apply a constitutional ban against any religious propaganda other than that for the national Orthodox Church. Archbishop Roncalli made fleeting visits to Athens, and then more extended ones—trips long enough to permit him to do all he wished in the way of bolstering the spirits of the eternally suspect Catholic faithful. Helping him, one can be confident, was his own admiration for Greece. He talked of it to the King and Queen of the Hellenes when the latter called on him as Pope for an unprecedented audience.

From his early school years, the Pope told them, he had treasured "the incomparable masterpieces with which ancient Greece enriched the human cultural patrimony. Plato and Aristotle, immortalized in a famous [Vatican] fresco from the brush of Raphael; Aeschylus, Sophocles, Euripides, Xenophon, Demosthenes! They nourished and fascinated our young years!"

Some of the Greek authors "never have left us since and still have honored places in our library!"

Think of the Greeks who had been martyrs as popes—Evaristus, Telesforus, Iginus, Anterus, Sixtus II, Pope John continued. Recall those who were great teacher-popes—Eusebius, Zosimus, Theoforus, Zaccarius and "two Johns, VI and VII, members of the series whose memory we wished to perpetuate" by choosing the name of John XXIII.

"And we cannot pass over in silence," he went on, "the fact that St. Paul and three of the four evangelists wrote in Greek, and that the early fathers of the Christian church—like St. Gregory Nazianzen, St. Basilius and St. John Chrysostom—used that language for their influential interpretations of traditions handed down from the Apostolic Age." In short, Greece was the land which had thrilled him with "the Acropolis, the Parthenon, the Theatre of Epidaurus," and the route St. Paul had traveled "at Philippi, at Salonika, at Corinth, on the isle of Crete!"

To make the Greek sovereigns more welcome, John gave part of his address in Greek. His intermittent sorties into the Hellenic realm had also given him some competence in that language.

Archbishop Roncalli, the man of broad affections, had found much to love among Balkan and Middle Eastern strangers, and the fondness was repaid. In Istanbul, when envoy Roncalli decided that it was out of place for Catholics to recite public prayers in Western languages—notably French and Italian—Turkish Moslems came to the Catholic Churches to hear the "Our Father" in their own tongue. When Archbishop Roncalli traveled back to the area later on a special papal mission, an Orthodox archbishop paid him the religious tribute of giving him some of the bread the Orthodox use for Communion.

In neutral Turkey during World War II, Archbishop Roncalli got on well with Germans and Allies alike. The Jewish agency of Palestine received his help several times in efforts to save Nazi victims in Bulgaria, Slovakia and Hungary. The Grand Rabbi of Israel, Herzog, called on him. In Greece, in the name of Pius XII, the archbishop managed to open a channel through the Allied blockade to forestall starvation.

What he had done in twenty years as a Church diplomat

had been accomplished on such a muted scale, with so few reports to the Vatican and such humble acceptance of official coolness, the Spanish and French ambassadors are traditionally the most Istanbul envoy when the key Paris nunciature fell vacant. Just as the Spanish and French ambassadors are traditionally the most prominent in the diplomatic corps accredited to the Holy See, so is the nunciature in Paris a star in the crown of Vatican diplomacy. It was Pius XII alone who thought of Archbishop Roncalli.

The Paris nunciature was in a dire situation. Bishop Valerio Valeri, a saintly, frail-figured man who was a prominent 1958 *papabile*, was no longer welcome as nuncio. He had worked closely with Marshal Pétain, the devout Catholic general who had collaborated with German occupiers and attempted to revive religion as one of the few forces left to the vanquished French. In the view of resistance leaders around the Catholics Charles De Gaulle and Georges Bidault, Archbishop Valeri had gone beyond the requirements of his mission and had compromised the nunciature with Vichy. More than that, the resistance demanded that one-third of the ninety French bishops be removed. Good-natured, unobtrusive Archbishop Roncalli was to attempt the miracle of placating De Gaulle, Bidault and the rest, and of welding the Catholics of the resistance with the Pétainists and the men of Vichy as children of the same Church and as brothers willing to forget and to begin a new personal and civic postwar life.

"Are you all crazy?" Archbishop Roncalli asked Monsignor Tardini when he was told of his appointment.

"Be sure, dear friend, that none of us thought of you," replied the next Pope's future Secretary of State, a blunt-spoken man known in Italian as one with "no fur on his tongue [clear talking]."

The story is now a Vatican legend. Archbishop Roncalli never forgot that exchange, but he was able to laugh over it. As Pope he had a moment's fun with it in a characteristically chatty visit to the priests on the Secretariate of State staff. "That was just the way you put it, was it not?" the new Pope asked his Secretary of State. "It was," the latter not very happily replied.

What happened next we have on good authority. Pius XII received the man who would be his successor and told him, apologetically, that he had only ten minutes for the audience but did want to say that it was he who had made the selection. The remaining seven minutes could be dispensed with, the new nuncio answered, for knowing that about the origin of his assignment was all he needed.

In eight years in Paris, it is said, Nuncio Roncalli handed only one note to the Quai d'Orsay. His motto then and always was *Omnia vedere, molto dissimulare, pauca corrigere*—"See all, pass over a great deal, correct just a little." He examined all but two of the ninety French cathedrals.

"Why did you miss them?" a Frenchman asked him.

"Because they didn't invite me," he answered.

French bishops like those in Ireland are known for liking a great deal of local liberty and are not always enthusiastic about inspectors from Rome. French Church history was haunted for generations by "Gallicanism," a heavy emphasis on the first half of the concept of "French Catholic." It was assumed among many Romans that the Gallican current may have run especially strong in the two dioceses which did not urge the future Pope to call.

In other centuries it was the custom for nuncios to stay cautiously inside the walls of their embassies, and one may assume that eyebrows were raised in Rome as Nuncio Roncalli crisscrossed France and all three sections of French North Africa visiting all but two of the bishops. If he ran the risk of irritating Gallicans, he nevertheless reaped a harvest of information and impressions about the country which is known as "the eldest daughter" of the Catholic Church. It was a valuable addition to an education which had begun in Italy and had expanded in an Orient of "separated" Christians. In France the future Pope saw a profoundly troubled Catholic Church at grips with the modern world; an ancient Catholic community beset by the doubts and revolutions of Protestant and Marxist centuries.

The first task of the nuncio was to make himself known. Paris after the liberation was disorganized, and the functionary who received him welcomed him in an unflattering cubbyhole. It was not much of a ceremony but there is a Roncalli legend about what happened then.

"Don't bother," the new nuncio told the troubled official, "I am nuncio only by accident, even by several accidents. And I'll take these carnations with me. I am sure they were meant for me."

He left, so says the often-told tale, carrying the little bouquet which was the only honor France had mustered for the occasion.

His next act, within hours, was to present the greetings of the diplomatic corps to France's President, Charles De Gaulle. The new nuncio made a tactful and amiable speech that resembled many others with which the French were to become familiar. As De Gaulle's successor, Vincent Auriol, was to say later, they were always built around some Gospel reference and appealed constantly for peace. Aware that he spoke for the Soviet Ambassador, too, the nuncio pronounced words of goodwill which only the most irascible could have taken exception to.

The Parisian world into which the Bergamo farm boy went was a land of intellect—dazzlingly brilliant but crippled by discord. It was a city where it was said that the first man to devise the long-sought formula for world government would be a Frenchman and that the first to find why it could not work would be another Frenchman.

Easygoing, slow-moving Nuncio Roncalli, with his imperfect command of French, was a far cry from the widely held image of deft, not to say Machiavellian, Vatican envoys. He soon had some startling successes, however. The first was in the case of the thirty bishops the Gaullists wished to oust. Pursuing a spiritual mission in a land occupied by an enemy must have been an agonizingly difficult responsibility and the new nuncio's sympathies with all bishops, those who had inclined toward Vichy and those who had leaned toward the resistance, was soon apparent. It is said that Nuncio Roncalli protested that a third of the hierarchy was too much to remove and that he would have to resign should the Gaullists persist. Catholics like De Gaulle and Bidault, hard pressed by Communism, would not want so grave a break with the Papacy. Another version of the story is that the nuncio asked documentation on each of the thirty cases reportedly including that of Maurice Feltin in Bordeaux. Months dragged by. New problems in a France haunted by a Marxist Popular Front came to the fore. At the end only two bishops were removed, fewer than 3 per cent of the hierarchy and fewer than a tenth of the first demand. Bishop Feltin went on to become Cardinal of Paris and one of his country's most popular prelates. Years later in the Vatican those who had worked intimately with Pius XII and Nuncio Roncalli chuckled over one tale from France. A Church leader asked one of the Gaullists why there had been such a reversal of attitude toward Monsignor Feltin.

"Oh, times have changed," was the answer.

Emphasizing what united rather than what divided, Nuncio Roncalli was often noticed at the elbow of Ambassador Bogomolov of the Soviet Union. The nuncio was quoted as calling the Soviet envoy "a civilized, courteous and really fine person," but the Russian seemed embarrassed and never opened up in conversation.

Much more success accompanied the nuncio's overtures to the French anticlerical Left. Édouard Herriot, former premier, and head of the Radical Party, a group dedicated to combating Church intrigues in politics, was charmed by the Italian archbishop who always chose the chair in the rear, never seemed to be involved in the controversies that were tearing France, and always had an amiable story or quip. On his deathbed Herriot accepted the Church's blessing.

If all priests were like Nuncio Roncalli there would be no anticlericals, Herriot was once quoted as saying.

On the record Herriot, the grand old man of French anticlerical politics, said of the nuncio that France would "not forget his goodness, his delicate tact, his proof of deep friendship" and that the nuncio was "an apt student of history's pages and of his fellow men."

An aide of the nuncio's in those years tells of one Roncalli-Herriot incident. Talk shifted to the question of the Masonic Order, a group long in conflict with the Catholic Church on many political and other matters.

"Excellency," the nuncio brightened, "you ought to be able to answer on that! You're a good Mason!"

Herriot, according to the story, shook his head.

"Excellency," Herriot is said to have added, "I may end yet Mason. I recall once when we had a cabinet session and someone said that there would be a [Masonic] grand lodge meeting at eight o'clock. One by one the ministers walked out, until at eight there were only three of us left."

"Excellency," Roncalli is said to have added, "I may end yet by serving your Mass!"

Whatever truth there is in such apocryphal stories, the easy cordiality of the nuncio's relations with his presumed enemies is unquestionable.

Another Roncalli story, told this time by French Radicals, was of the nuncio's disarming remark to one of their group.

"What separates us after all?" the archbishop asked the Radical. "Just our ideas! Well, let's admit it. That is not much!"

The story should be taken in the context of a Paris where ideas were often as big and shiny and insubstantial as bubbles in a bath. None but the intellectuals of Paris would appreciate most fully the gentle cynicism of such a remark, or—it is true—would they take it too seriously. One can be sure that after the exchange with his Radical acquaintance the nuncio had made another conquest.

Another man with whom the nuncio got on famously was Vincent Auriol, the Socialist who became President of France. Auriol's background was Marxist and anticlerical, but the nuncio's greeting to him as spokesman for the diplomats was so cordial that the Leftist Chief of State was touched. French diplomats understood that the nuncio and the Socialist President, both warm-hearted, sentimental men of poor families, became faster friends than the nuncio and the two rather severe Catholic intellectuals who dominated other parts of the Paris political

horizon—De Gaulle and the many-times foreign minister, Georges
Bidault.

Auriol said later that although there was a gulf between them
on questions of religion, the President often followed the nuncio's wise, human counsel.

When Nuncio Roncalli knelt before Auriol to receive his red
biretta as cardinal, the Socialist said in affectionate confusion,
"You kneel not to me, an unbeliever, but, through me, to the
Pope. It is we, Eminence, who should kneel to you."

Years later when Auriol, retired, called on Cardinal Roncalli
in Venice, the old Socialist was moved again when Roncalli
swept by a group of the genuflecting faithful in a hotel lobby to
embrace the old agnostic from Paris.

Good relations extended outside politics toward those of other
faiths. The nuncio had cordial contacts with Pastor Boegner, head
of the French Protestant community. When the pastor visited
Rome during John's pontificate it was common to see fifteen or
twenty Catholic bishops at receptions for him at the French
Embassy to the Holy See. The goodwill radiating from Peter's
throne was no doubt one reason for the bishops' friendliness to
the Protestant leader.

The nuncio melted some of the ice in a Paris tormented by
centuries of religious, political and nationalist quarrels but his
work did not go uncriticized. Some in Rome complained that
he waited too long to put a stop to the worker-priest experiment
—the dramatic but ill-starred effort to penetrate the de-Christianized French working class by sending out young priests as
ordinary laborers to factories, for ships' crews and into other
parts of economic life. Many of the priests kept their identities
secret. None of their fellow workers knew that they were ordained, that they said Mass privately in mean working-class flats,
using drinking cups as chalices, and that they had Church authority to preach the Gospel, hear confessions and perform the
rest of a priest's ministry. In an effort to understand the laborers
whom they hoped to convert, many of the young clergy became
converts themselves: to Communism and to sexual relations and
marriage. When the Vatican ban came it struck heavily. For

many of the one hundred worker-priests it meant a heartbreaking choice: disloyalty to "the workers" or to their Church and God. Should the nuncio have acted sooner? Did his willingness to trust the judgment of local bishops go too far? It was a question Church leaders were sure to ponder for long afterward, but the nuncio's success in building a bridge to other leaders was undeniable, and as Cardinal Tisserant indicated, influenced his election.

# 16. Canals of Venice, Road to Rome

"One must never forget the successor of St. Pius X in Venice!" A wise Roman priest was speaking, in October, 1958, of the imminent papal election.

Any list of *papabili* should include the patriarch of the canal city, whoever he was.

Pius XII, whether or not by calculation, named cardinals every seventh year of his pontificate. Elected in 1939, he raised the first group of thirty-two to the Sacred College almost seven years to the day after his election, and in 1953 followed with the next set of appointments. In the remaining five years of his pontificate he named no others.

In 1953 Nuncio Roncalli, at seventy-one, was already rather far along in years for appointment to his Church's supreme council. His rise in the Church had been impressive but slow. Cardinals, as Pius XII saw them, were not men rewarded for achievements, but men selected for greater future service. Nuncio Roncalli was old, but he was chosen. It was then that another of his life's fortunate coincidences intervened.

Cardinals seek three qualities in candidates for the Papacy: knowledge of the unique little world of the Vatican; background in Church diplomacy; and experience in the pastoral ministry. Cardinal-elect Roncalli had the first two but lacked the latter.

The nuncio was sad on the day of his nomination as Cardinal. His fellow cardinal-elect, Archbishop Feltin, whom according to the accounts in Rome he had saved from banishment at Gaullist hands, called to exchange congratulations. The nuncio was reading his breviary.

In his talk with Cardinal Feltin the nuncio made no secret of the reason for his sadness. Nuncios do not stay on in their posts. The appointment would mean leaving Paris.

The back-straining work of constructing bridges of friendship to the Church's many traditional foes had ended as a pleasure, and about that time the noble *Gallorum gens*—the fine French—had taken a place in the nuncio's daily prayers along with the Bulgarians and other Easterners whom he remembered affectionately from his first years abroad.

It was about then that the archbishop-diplomat had written to a nun-missionary niece in Africa that his "little boat" seemed to "sail well on the waters of the Seine." He had added, "I have no wish for aught else in the Church; no change could mean anything but melancholy for me."

The work of pastor was a man's finest ministry, the retiring nuncio told the Paris archbishop.

"It is painful to me to think of ending my life in the paper work of Rome."

The cardinal-elect assumed he would be summoned to the Curia, the group of Church Princes who manage the various congregations.

Going through *Figaro*, the conservative morning newspaper of Paris, the nuncio came on a photograph of the Venetian "gondola of death." Carlo Agostini, Venice's stern patriarch, had died. Many generations earlier Venice had been Bergamo's political ruler, and the prelate from Sotto il Monte thought of it as home. He clipped out the suggestive picture of the slim craft of death and slipped it into his prayer book. Within days he had word of Pius XII's decision. He would not be a Rome ecclesiastical bureaucrat. He would have a man's best mission, that of pastor, and of chief pastor of his own Venetian countryside at that. Whether or not he thought of it, he would have the see of a *papabile*.

Nuncio Roncalli's last act in Paris, it is said, was to ask the band at the station to play the "Marseillaise," the song which once stood for assault on the Crown and on its ally, the Church. Perhaps the reconciliation between the laic ideas associated with the French Revolution and the churchly ones represented by the nuncio was still incomplete, but the envoy wanted no conflict with French or any other nationalism and had made giant strides toward peace with it.

Arriving in Venice was an emotional experience for the new cardinal. He recalled a visit the revered Pius X had made to Bergamo when Angelo Roncalli was a seminarian of seventeen, and told of it later in an audience as Pope.

"He was still a young man, that Venice patriarch. His name, just think of it, was Giuseppe Sarto [a name destined for the Papacy]. He recalled in his sermon that Bergamo had been subject to the government of Venice for 400 years. It was, when all is said and done, a good government. And then Bergamo had been the first to respond to the wave of liberty sweeping through Europe. It cut itself off from Venice."

Bergamo in those moments, as the future saint-Pope talked to its people, might have wondered whether there were still grudges to nurse against the former master-city of Venice, but by the time Cardinal Roncalli received his appointment to the patriarchate the ancient grievances were surely dissolved.

"There was nothing for Bergamo to forgive any more," Pope John recalled, "for Bergamo, with no great effort at all, had succeeded in going back to Venice through its son as patriarch of the lagoon city."

It was at least partly as a triumphant man of Bergamo that the new patriarch of Venice arrived.

With him came his library, a reflection of so many eclectic years: tourist guidebooks to Turkey, Greece and Spain; the works of the superb French preacher, Bossuet; those of the satirical and far from clerical Molière; those of the impressionistic and experimental Rimbaud; and a mass of works on theology and the early "fathers of the Church," the first interpreters of the Christian message. Most were in Latin, Italian or French but the *Imitation of Christ* by St. Thomas à Kempis, a fifteenth-century Latin devotional work, was an English translation. The future Pope was already aware of one of his greatest short-comings as an actor on the world stage—his ignorance of its leading language.

"O Blessed Pius X," the prelate exclaimed in Venice, "here I am in your old place!" Emulating the humble pastor of Sotto il Monte, he had reached the point of filling a post only recently vacated by a saint.

"I was born of poor folk and Providence took me from my native place to travel through the world," the new patriarch told the Venetians. "I journeyed from East to West. My responsibilities placed me in touch with the gravest political and social problems. . . .

"[But] do not look upon your patriarch as a man of politics or as a diplomat! See him only as a pastor of souls, one called to exercise his mission among the lowly, one who is in any case unworthy of the great Shepherd who is Christ and unworthy of him [Pius XII] who represents Him on earth.

"Here is my chance to be wholly a pastor. It is my conviction that the pastor's ministry is the most fascinating and finest a man can be offered in this life."

The new bishop learned that he was St. Mark's 139th successor in Venice and that he was the forty-ninth to follow St. Lawrence Giustinian as patriarch. In the latter he had a new model. He sought out the ascetical works of the austere first patriarch of Venice and learned them well enough to apologize as Pope at the Rome synod for quoting from them. Priests of the Eternal City would understand how "the most recent of Venice's patriarchs" should think of maxims of the lagoon city's first patriarch as he prepared counsels for the clergy of the mid-twentieth century, Pope John remarked. His quotation from St. Lawrence was a warning to curb the tongue—an instrument equipped equally for blessing and for cursing.

In Venice the new patriarch is said to have been known among his priests as the "calm after the storm" and as "no policeman." He visited the many parishes and took in more than he let on, but his reprimands were few. His immediate predecessor, a man very demanding on himself, had also been severe with others. The contrast with the gentle new patriarch was marked and appreciated.

Cardinal Roncalli went to the biennial art show, the first patriarch to do so in half a century. It was an exhibition liberally sprinkled with nudes, but it was also one that reflected the modern artist's anguished but earnest effort to come to grips with all the truths of the century, including those of religion.

The cardinal found himself in conflict with another artistic quarter in Venice. The high altar in St. Mark's Basilica was blocked from view from the nave by magnificent sculptured slabs. They dated back to the days when Mass in the basilica had been for the doge and his small princely court, not for the humble of the city. The new patriarch wanted the slabs removed during services or at least raised on hinges. He wanted the people to see the religious services at which they were now the principal spectators. Venetian artists on the other hand deplored any tampering with an art treasure which ought, in their view, to stay where it was, as it was. The patriarch could have settled the matter in the abrupt way in which the aides of St. Charles Borromeo dealt with the military flags in Bergamo churches, but despite his admiration of almost everything done by St. Charles, the cardinal resolved not to have his way at a price even so small as the killing of a fly. Patience won, and the patriarch, without noticeable community resentment, finally made a slight change, carefully preserving the slabs in position except during services.

A graver question concerned Church relations with Socialism. As nuncio in Paris the prelate had an open-door policy with regard to the world. Anyone, he said, was welcome to see him. It might, he commented, be someone "wishing to confess!"

In Venice the easygoing Paris manner was more difficult to apply. A Communist, Giovanbattista Gianquinto, had dominated local political life for years, much of it as mayor. There was a strong attraction toward Communism inside the left wing of the Catholic party, that of the Christian Democrats. Rome was worried. How much of the patriarch's subsequent behavior was dictated by the slowly formed habits of a markedly liberal lifetime, and how much because of obedience to directives from Pius

XII or from the firmly orthodox Cardinal Alfredo Ottaviani in the Holy Office, we are unlikely ever to know. We can be sure, however, that both liberal instincts and ready obedience to authority prompted the patriarch's steps.

In one of Cardinal Roncalli's first moves, a pastoral letter went to the Left Catholics. It condemned "a very grave doctrinal error"; the idea that one should "virtually share and make common cause with a Marxist ideology which is the negation of Christianity, a doctrine which in practice is irreconcilable with the presuppositions of the Christian gospel."

The patriarch went on:

"It is wrong to say that 'going Left' merely means quicker and bigger economic reforms. The fact is that there will always be the danger that minds will be penetrated by the specious concept that there cannot be social justice, help for all those in misery, and respect for tax laws unless men of goodwill team up with those who deny God and oppose human liberty. The idea can even reach the point of believing that one must submit to the caprices of the deniers of God and oppressors of freedom."

The Cardinal added:

"We no longer bear the name of Catholic if we violate discipline by setting fellow Catholics directly and explicitly against the living, working Church [a possible reference to the French worker-priests who often shunned local parishes in order not to be compromised with 'the bourgeoisie']. We must choose either to be with the Church and to follow its directives and to deserve the name of Catholic, or we may prefer to use our own heads and to cause splits and secessions from the Church. There is no legitimate laic teaching authority in the Church."

This statement made it clear that the patriarch felt not only that he must submit to his superiors in Rome in the event of a conflict between his liberalism and their authority, but also that the same applied to the free currents running among many of the laity in Italy, France and elsewhere. There were thus sharp limits to the archbishop's liberalism. No laymen defying hierarchical conservatism need look to him for support. His hand of friendship held out to those outside his Church did not mean that he would countenance ruptures in the Catholic organization.

In February, 1957, it seemed for a moment that the patriarch's liberal side would dominate. The Left Wing Socialist party of former Foreign Minister Pietro Nenni met in Venice for a national convention. The party had been bound to the Communists by a pact of "unity of action" which meant that the two took the same stand on all issues. The larger and mysteriously well-financed Communist Party, reportedly ever ready to help the Socialists with their bills, almost always had its way. But now in Venice something was changing. At the grass roots there was anti-Communist feeling. The rest of the Socialist parties of Europe had broken with the Communists. Nenni's group, in the face of Communist cruelty in Hungary and oppressiveness everywhere, was feeling the stirrings of independence.

The patriarch published a manifesto. The Nenni Socialists were notorious anticlericals and Marxists but the message he addressed to them was cordial:

"I appreciate the importance of this event [the Nenni convention]. It seems to be one of great importance for the immediate future of our country. As St. Paul said, a bishop should be *hospitalis et benignus*. Every part of Italy will be here. I want to say a word which will be respectful and serene. I, too, am after all a Venetian. I hold hospitality in great honor.

"The [Nenni] meeting is surely inspired, as I very much want to believe, by a desire to work out some system of common understanding with regard to what is worth while in the hunt for better living conditions and for the prosperity of society."

Reaching beyond a past which churchmen could see only as hostile, the patriarch was hoping for a new day in which Catholics and the delegates to the Nenni convention could co-operate cordially.

Cardinal Roncalli was aware how difficult the task was. He said that it was "keenly painful for a pastor of souls" to note, as he had to realistically, how so many "honest and upright intelligences" closed their eyes to "the heavens where shine the truths

CANALS OF VENICE, ROAD TO ROME 169

of religion" and worked at "rebuilding a modern economic, civic and social order on a foundation other than Christ's."

It was a warning to the Socialists that no hospitality or benignity could go so far as to ignore the still yawning gulf between religious and Marxist positions. A few days later in a dry communiqué the cardinal clarified the separation between the two stands. There had been, he said, "no dialog in Venice between Catholics and Marxist forces, nor could there be."

Peace, if there were to be any, would have to be on the basis of a surrender of the more extreme Marxist atheist position. The cardinal and the convention drifted apart. Whether Rome, worried about "blessings to atheism," had intervened will probably remain unknown. About the same time the patriarch, presumably with sadness, adopted another stern measure. He condemned the publication of the extreme Left of the Venice Catholic political movement. Other bishops throughout the area, according to the excellent La Nuova Stampa of Turin, had insisted on the move. Generosity toward others and to their sometimes contradictory ideas had limits which could not be overstepped.

Whether or not Cardinal Ottaviani of the Holy Office was the inspiration for some of the harsher decisions, we can be sure that he was satisfied at last with the Venice patriarch's orthodoxy. At the time of the 1958 papal election when Monsignor Ottaviani's name was often mentioned as that of an erudite young Italian cardinal *papabile*, he worked instead, it is said on good authority, for the election of Cardinal Roncalli.

Difficult moments were compensated for by relaxed ones such as both the gay Bishop Radini-Tedeschi and his secretary-emulator always managed to have. It was in those years that the patriarch is said to have given a speech by mistake in the wrong hamlet and then to have told the right audience tersely but with humor that they should ask their neighboring community what he had said there! It was also at that time that he told the abbot of St. Ambrose's in Milan how he had come by his bishop's pectoral cross. In 1925, newly named an archbishop, he had too few funds to afford a new cross and had shopped for one that was secondhand. A jeweler offered him one for 1,000 lire ($50). It was too much for him then but he went back later and bought it. The heirs of the then abbot of St. Andrews had put it up for sale. Through his years as bishop the future Pope had worn the cross and in Venice had asked another jeweler to add the lion of St. Mark. The patriarch promised the abbot that he would one day restore the object to St. Ambrose's, and within weeks of his election to the Papacy he did so.

As Cardinal-patriarch, Monsignor Roncalli was beginning to attract world attention. A German diplomat visited him to confer the Grand Cross of the Order of Merit of the Bonn Republic in gratitude for what he had done for German prisoners as Paris nuncio. He had worked to prevent the execution of alleged war criminals and had assisted in other ways "materially as well as spiritually."

He did what he did partly as Pius XII's envoy, the cardinal replied. Pius XII, a veteran of many years in Germany, had sympathy for Germans even if he could not, as a Christian, condone Nazi paganism. Much of Nuncio Roncalli's work was still wrapped in secrecy but he did want to say publicly how grateful he had been to French authorities for one mission to German prisoners which they had quietly permitted. It was the task of reassigning all seminarian-prisoners to the same concentration camp near the Cathedral of Chartres. There priests from Germany set up a prison theological school. American Catholic Relief arranged unobtrusively for increased rations. The seminarians had been so hungry they could not study or pray. Getting extra food to them was tricky at a time when the French themselves were not far from starvation and when hatred of all Germans was at a peak.

"I was finally able to perform some ordinations in the prisoner-of-war camp," the cardinal remembered with contentment. "I still have that scene before my mind's eye. It stirs my soul."

The patriarch was happy in his see. He chose the spot where he wanted to be buried. He followed the example of Bishop Radini-Tedeschi by summoning a synod at which all his pastors could comment democratically on the administration of the little spiritual world of the Venice province. He had advice for his aides, a counsel tempered by respect for each assistant's own good conscience. "I don't think we should be too hard on opponents," he told the editor of his paper, "but then, if you are it is because you think you should be." It was advice that might seem confused but it was an example of kindness which called for emulation.

The cardinal thrilled at being Pius X's successor. When ex-President Auriol of France visited him he took the statesman to see the simple room the saint had used as Venice's spiritual leader.

"He, too, was a child of the poor," the patriarch said of his predecessor. "For both of us a little was always enough."

Venice had had one pope in this century and she might well soon have another, Auriol said, as he looked his friend in the eye. Cardinal Roncalli did not answer.

About that time, according to what is understood in Rome, Pius XII invited the Venetian patriarch to join the Curia in Rome. He offered him the management of the Consistorial Congregation which supervises the 2,500 Catholic bishops of the world. Roncalli begged off. He preferred his island see. Pius XII never insisted on appointments. All too many aspired to them. The matter was dropped and the archbishop stayed away from Rome.

Cardinal Roncalli was convinced that he would finish his days in Venice, but as Cardinal Tisserant told his own diocese, Providence had other plans for one with so rich an experience as diplomat, Rome veteran and pastor. Universal applause greeted his election. Even ex-mayor Gianquinto, the Communist, had good words.

"Pope Roncalli," he said, "is a man open to the needs of modern times. I personally am satisfied at his election. In Venice he showed great balance and wisdom, staying away from political factions."

The patriarch's aides gathered up the Venetian souvenirs which were to go to the Vatican to join the rest of the mementoes of a fruitful and happy lifetime. During his pontificate the first thing one saw on entering his suite was the red gonfalon of Venice. Over his bedroom door was a frieze depicting the façade of St. Mark's Basilica.

# 17. John Enthroned

If there were those who were surprised that the peasant from Bergamo, the soft-treading diplomat in the anti-Catholic Balkans and the easy-mannered friend of Paris radicals should be enthroned as Peter's successor, few could have been more astonished than Angelo Roncalli.

"When they say 'Most Holy Father' I turn to see who they mean," the new Pope frankly and appealingly told the staff of the Secretariate of State.

The drama of the choice and the problems John faced were summed up in the coronation service—one of the most brilliant ceremonies Europe had seen in a generation. I watched from a stand off to one side in the apse of St. Peter's Basilica. Across the way, behind a row of red-cassocked cardinals, the air sparkled with the glitter of diamonds in the tiaras of noblewomen. The great of the world were packed into the apse's small area: the American Secretary of Labor James Mitchell, former Ambassador Clare Boothe Luce, and Undersecretary of State Robert Murphy— three of the United States's most eminent Catholics—present on a government mission; Premiers Amintore Fanfani of Italy and Eamon de Valera of Ireland; Chancellor Julius Raab of Austria; former Premier Pierre Pflimlin of France; Foreign Ministers Heinrich von Brentano of West Germany, Fernando Castiello of Spain, and Huang Shao Ku of Nationalist China; former President Enrico Celio of Switzerland; Prince Felix of Luxembourg; the Duke of Norfolk representing Queen Elizabeth of England; General Carlos Cabanillas, chief of Spanish dictator Franco's personal military group; official envoys of another two score countries including Argentina, Australia, Ceylon, South Korea, Japan, Jordan, India, Indonesia, Iran, Israel, Liberia, the United Arab Republic, the Sudan, Vietnam; and representatives of five international organizations including the European Commission for Atomic Energy.

It was a greeting such as no pope had received in generations. It was clear that much of it was a tribute to the dead Pius XII.

Twenty feet from the Pope's rose-and-gold throne, in a better place than that occupied by most royalty, diplomats and cardinals, was a cluster of timid-looking, modest Italians in black—the new Pope's three brothers, a sister, and several nieces and nephews. One of them brushed away a tear as I watched.

The system for assigning seats and standing room broke down. The place before the throne became cluttered with bejeweled late arrivals. A flunky in medieval costume lost patience.

"*Mi dispiace; sgombare!*" he cried in abrupt and not very gentle accents—"I'm sorry; clear it out here!"

Moments later the new Pope arrived and the hours-long ceremony unfolded. A priest sucked wine through a gold tube to be sure that the fluid John used for Communion was not poisoned. Centuries had elapsed since any pope had run such a risk, but the ritual—hallowed by generations of tradition—was performed for the Bergamo prelate just as it had been for so many famous predecessors. John, as custom decreed, waited at his throne for the Communion wafer to be carried to him, but also in the manner decreed by centuries, knelt before his chair to take the Host. John prayed in both Latin and Greek, an outward show of his claim as Pope to be father of all Christians, both those of the Latin West and of the predominantly Orthodox and Greek East. At the Mass's end John accepted, momentarily, the bag of twenty-five gold coins traditionally given to popes by the priests of St. Peter's Basilica for "a well-sung Mass." Outside on the basilica's balcony the new Pope received the three-crowned tiara. It had been brought from the Vatican treasury and was the same one Pius X had used in 1903.

The regal ceremony before so splendid an audience could not have contrasted more with the world of Sotto il Monte which had never left Roncalli's mind. The rude cry *"sgombare,"* on the other hand, underlined the disorganization which had begun to seep into Vatican affairs in the weaker final years of Pius XII. John had to measure up to the glory and to restore order where necessary. He met the first need by staying true to lifelong simplicity, and the latter by a series of fast moves belying a lifetime of obedience and patience. However much the gentle, slow ways of Balkan-formed habits returned to influence later months in his pontificate, John's first hours left a mark on Church history.

The quick promotion of Cardinal di Jorio and the appointment of Secretary of State Tardini, which dominated the news in John's first hours, were not his only prompt assertions of authority. As other members of the conclave streamed out of their quarters after the Pope's election, assuming that they needed no authorization, John good-naturedly but flatly ordered them back. His reason was not explained. Perhaps it was to protect old cardinals against the strain of changing lodgings in the night. More plausibly, many assumed, it was to give the new sovereign the opportunity to hear from the cardinals what they most hoped from his pontificate.

The conversations could not have dragged on interminably that last night of the conclave, however. The story is often told in Rome that when Monsignor Capovilla, the secretary of the new Pope, asked what to do, the reply was, "Let's read the breviary." A priest's required daily prayers had to be recited on all days, even on the one on which a cardinal became Pope.

The way in which he announced Secretary of State Tardini's appointment was typical of the naturalness John brought to Peter's throne. The soul of conversational art is to be uncomplicated, the new Pope told staff members of the State Secretariate. And simplicity, he added, wastes no time on prefixes and suffixes.

He would do away with one prefix immediately, he continued. "Pro-Secretary of State" Tardini would lose the "pro" forthwith. The concentration of diplomatic power in the Pope's hands would end. Just as Pius had told Monsignor Tardini, after the death of Secretary of State Luigi Maglione, that he wanted "executors not collaborators," so John, from his own background, saw cardinals both as "collaborators" and even more than that as "brothers." Each prelate made his own pontificate. For Monsignor Tardini, John's half-joking words about prefixes meant that a life as Pius XII's little-noticed assistant was to be exchanged for a new one in which a large share of the responsibilities of the Holy See were to be delegated to him. A fundamental reorganization was under way.

John had made a fleet start and for months afterward he kept up the rhythm, yet it was long before the old prelate ceased to muse about what it was to be Pope. Seven decades as a subject of Church authority were no full preparation for exercising these immense powers. He was well aware, too, that much talk of "an interim pope," an old man to bridge the gap between the dominant Pius XII and a forceful new Church leader, had preceded his election. For weeks he talked of both subjects: his great age and the problem of being pontiff. Few men in such office have been so candid and disarming. Pope John, whether or not always consciously, was carving for himself a place as a "father" as his role in the scholarly Pius XII's succession.

When he took possession of St. John Lateran's, his cathedral as Rome's bishop, John spoke of his seventy-seven years. "We have no right," he said, "to look forward to a long road ahead. But," he added, "one who trusts God need fear nothing—not even the surprise of death."

Two months later, in January, 1959, the annual commemoration of two saint-Popes, Agatonus and Vitalianus, both of the seventh century, brought up the subject again.

"I who have arrived at the pontificate in such advanced age do not despair of having from the Lord at least the time conceded to St. Agatonus [two years and seven months]. He reigned only briefly, and nearer us there was another who had only twenty-five days, Leo XI, Alessandro de' Medici [1605].

"There are so many things to do," John exclaimed. "But my spiritual disposition is such that if the Lord wishes to call me today, even this very evening, I am ready."

As Rome papers pointed out there had been even shorter pontificates than that of Leo XI, while on the other hand Church history offered greater hopes for an elderly pontiff than so brief a reign as that of St. Agatonus. The shortest pontificate had been that of Stephen II, a Roman, from March 23rd to 25th in 752. He was a layman who died two days after election and before he could be even ordained to the priesthood, let alone consecrated as Rome's bishop. Some Church histories omit him on the grounds that a pontificate cannot begin until a man is at least a priest, but the official list in the *Annuario Pontificio*—Pontifical Yearbook—includes him. Even shorter than Stephen's reign was that of Philip, who is considered an antipope and not part of the legitimate succession. He was elected on July 31, 768, but withdrew the same day and went back to his monastery. The reverse situation, a "transition pope" who remained long, was that of Pope John XXII, the new Pope's immediate predecessor in the legitimate line of Johns. John XXII, elected in 1316 at seventy-three—an especially advanced age in that era—ruled until he was ninety-one.

It was on that occasion that John XXIII disclosed that he had instructed immediate aides who were always genuflecting that they should do so once on greeting him in the morning and once on parting at night and no more.

Another time he said that the spectacle of throngs bowing before him made him feel the need to drop to his own knees "in humble and silent adoration" of God.

Stepping aboard the man-borne papal litter was another psychological problem for the new Pope. He told members of a Catholic Action group that his reaction was similar to that of his revered predecessor, Pius X, who he said seemed stunned, even terrified, when he had to do that for the first time. Aides told Pius that it was not a "human glory" but a device to permit Catholics to "see their father and teacher." The saint-Pope was reassured, and John implied that the same thought satisfied him.

Some months after his election John began to feel that he was no longer the "new" Pope, but—without adjectives—the pontiff. It was clear that he hoped that this feeling was general and that the transfer from Pius XII was over. He talked often of his philosophy of how any man could occupy the awesomely exalted post of "Christ's Vicar."

It was a "position, or better let's say, a service, not without

anxiety, hardships and fatigue, but one that can be met and accomplished with the same serene spirit of bygone times if it is
accepted and performed in a spirit of simplicity." That, the Pope
said, was the "marvelous way in which supernatural grace does
its work."

He was "the humble servant of God's servants," John told the
pastors of Rome's churches.

It was tremendous to think of the grave weight of a pontificate
pressing on the shoulders of "a poor son of an humble worker
of the fields" but with "the old faith, the old principles which
are the foundation of Christian life" it could be done.

Five months after his election John told Venetians, "I am
going my way with the common sense I inherited from home, a
way of looking at things to which I have added Gospel teachings
and the dictates of Christian life. I trust the Lord," he added.
"A loftier teaching than this I cannot give you."

"Simplicity is natural and the divine is in the natural," John
said at another meeting.

To a group of businessmen he put it still another way. Occu-
pying the Papacy, he said, was no enviable position. All had
crosses to bear, but that of the Pope was a great one and "certainly not to be envied." Men to whom he had looked with reverence beheld him now, he said, "with pity and commiseration for
the great burden the Lord has placed upon us. But," John added
characteristically, "that's life's poetry!" Each man bore his "in-
escapable trials with the smile of supernatural understanding and
serenity!"

"May God help me to build nothing on sand and not to agi-
tate myself in vain," the pontiff prayed at another audience.

"The Pope," John said, "is the servant of God's servants. With
that spirit good things are done. It is a work far removed from
politics, from fighting, from wars and from questions of money.
What matters are the things of the spirit, the light of faith."

The two wings of a pontificate, John told us in his first audience to newspapermen, were *veritas et bonitas*—"truth and goodness." On those the modest Pope from Bergamo confidently took
flight.

# 18. Old Tree, New Life

Cardinal Roncalli's prayer, as he wrote to his diocesan seminary just before the 1958 conclave, was that the new Pope would not be a continuance of Pius XII—an impossible ambition—but that he would represent "progress along the line of the eternal youthfulness of the Church": new life in the old tree.

The prayer was answered with John as the agent.

"They are different," one of Pius XII's few intimates told me. "Almost," he added, "too different!"

So much changed so swiftly that John's pontificate seemed even a repudiation of Pius's. There is no doubt that the thought troubled the new Pope. To dispel it he spoke often in his first months of his veneration for Pius as one of the great teachers in the 2,000-year-old Catholic tradition and as a saint. He granted an audience to policemen who had been part of Pius XII's escort on the frequent summer trips back and forth to the suburban residence at Castel Gandolfo, and concluded by taking them down to the crypt under St. Peter's Basilica to pray at Pius's austere white tomb. But even that was revolutionary. The thought of Pius strolling with a group of policemen through St. Peter's to kneel in prayer at another pontiff's bier was inconceivable.

Day after day for weeks the reporters who cover the Vatican had stories of new precedents or breaks with old ones.

"We're working all the time," one of them complained. "We can't go home in the evening. We don't know when something new will happen."

"Here's one pope about whom there's no need to invent legends," one Roman commented wryly. "The truth is enough!"

Pius XII, a son of an upper-middle-class family and a veteran of a generation of diplomacy in Germany, defended the prestige of the papal court jealously, and insisted on the punctilious. It was for that reason that there was consternation in the heart of one papal gendarme when Pope John suddenly appeared before him. The policeman had opened his collar and had taken a seat on the long arm of the Vatican garden's miniature reproduction of the miraculous French grotto of Lourdes. It was 6:30 of a December evening, a little over a month after John's election; a time of night when no one of importance moved in the dark of the Vatican gardens. Pius's walks, as regular as the stars, had always ended at five.

"When they come to fire me I'll ask for a delay because of my eight children," the gendarme is said to have murmured.

"May I go up this way?" the Pope asked, pointing to the Vatican radio station at the top of the gardens.

The flabbergasted policeman gave the little state's sovereign permission to stroll forward inside his realm and the incident ended there. One may assume that the gendarme kept his collar buttoned after six in the future.

The story is told, too, of what happened just after John was elected. He wanted to telephone north, perhaps to his patriarchate at Venice, perhaps to friends at the Bishopric of Bergamo. All lines had been cut off in obedience to tradition in order to isolate the meditating cardinals from the rest of the world. The repairman from the Vatican switchboard was summoned. "How are things going?" the new Pope is said to have asked.

"*Male, male, Eminenza!*" the man reportedly replied—"Bad, bad, your Eminence!"

The prelate, long known as the cardinal from Venice, was certainly not the late Pius XII, and the Vatican laborer had no other instinctive manner of address than *eminence*—cardinal.

The new Pope probed gently. The man had been on the work crew for a generation and was still not officially enrolled; still had no claim to the various benefits provided for the regular staff. His pay was meager. Twenty dollars a week was a common pay check for the ordinary laborer on the Vatican staff. There were a few extras such as small additional sums for the wife and children, but it was a sunken-cheeked existence at best.

"Just between us two," the new Pope is said to have told the man as the phone job was finished, "I'm not *Eminenza* now; I'm the Pope!"

However true the story may be, one of the new sovereign's first acts was to raise wages, nearly doubling some of the lower, and curiously, slightly reducing those of a few unmarried laymen who were at the summit of the papal wage scale. John, we can be sure, was advised that income from Vatican investments would not cover the increases, but he persisted. If voluntary contributions from Catholics throughout the world, especially from those in the United States, did not cover the expanded payroll, the Vatican would cut back on its $1,600,000-a-year direct charities. In response to common sense, charity was starting at home.

The cardinals in Curia, all of whom receive a papal stipend, were given an advance of 15 per cent. That meant that they received about $640 a month plus a housing allowance of $96. With it they were expected to maintain rather princely homes, usually suites in middle-class apartment houses—some in the Vatican, some in other parts of Rome. In each there were handsome red wall decorations prescribed by custom and a chair ready for the Pope should he ever, though it was most unlikely, pay a call. In view of the standards a prince of the Church was expected to meet it was not a very large allowance, and in terms of American pay it was small. Even many of the American newspapermen who interviewed cardinals had larger incomes.

The poorest laborers were raised to $112 a month plus $16 for a wife and $20 for each child. In addition the old custom of giving 3 raises at 5-year intervals was changed to 10 increases over a 20-year period. The highest paid received biennial step-ups of $9.60 and the poorest $4.80.

The raises did not go without some criticism.

"The difference between me and those I supervise is very narrow now," one lay functionary complained. "How am I to maintain dignity?"

Monsignors with many years of training may have wondered

why simple laborers with large families should have incomes equivalent to about $50 a week.

Pope John's comment on such situations was straightforward, Cardinal Tardini told a group of us in a rare press conference. "He said that one man's learning calls for reward but another's problem can be even more urgent, a half-dozen mouths to feed! There were a good fourteen under his own roof," the cardinal said of the Pope. "He knows all about the beauties of family life!"

The ironic inflections in the word "beauties" as the cardinal pronounced it took in all the worries of a father with large needs and small income.

The new pay scale still seemed modest by American standards, but the right to use the tax-free Vatican grocery and pharmacy, and access (at least for some of the Vatican hands) to low-rent apartments owned by the Holy See raised the bottom rates so high that Cardinal Tardini had to give food baskets to eighty outside laborers who were at work on modernizing the apartments of the Pope and his chief assistants. The gulf between the pay of the temporary workers and those of the regular staff was too large not to call for the goodwill gift as a supplement.

Pope John's new way made the biggest headlines at his first Christmas on his visit to two hospitals and to the Rome jail. Nothing similar had been seen in a century. Three of the five previous popes had not even set foot outside the Vatican after their elections. They were voluntary prisoners protesting what they considered the sacrilegious absorption of the 1,000-year-old papal states by modern Italy. Pius XI, after the 1929 settlement which obtained Italian recognition of the 105-acre Vatican as an independent country, had made frequent trips to and from Castel Gandolfo but had made only 5 or 6 other appearances outside the Vatican and always inside the city of Rome. Pius XII made 18 excursions to points away from the Vatican and Castel Gandolfo residences, but they, too, were all in Rome. None had been to places so dramatic and even controversial as those chosen by John. Within a few weeks John was to make more sorties away from his two residences than all the Popes who had preceded him for 100 years. In 22 months he made 64 such journeys, the last to Sabina, a 120-mile round trip from Castel Gandolfo. It was the first time a Pope had been out of the province of Rome since Pius IX's four-months' tour of his rebellious Romagna provinces 103 years before.

The visit to the jail was a prototype of the many extraordinary excursions which followed. Accompanied by Italy's minister of justice, the pontiff walked into the dismal penitentiary a quarter of a mile from the Vatican. Named for a religious institution which used to occupy the same Tiber bank site it is called with mordant inappropriateness Regina Coeli—the Queen of Heaven.

Prison authorities, nervous about what might happen, had combed out a few Communist troublemakers, but the 1,000 inmates in pajamalike striped uniforms who were there to greet the Pope were all but delirious with enthusiasm. A crèche had been set up in the central part from which the prison arms radiated. The prisoners sang *Adeste Fidelis* and the emotion was overpowering. Perhaps some remembered an amnesty which had followed a similar visit by Pius IX when the popes were the kings of the papal states. Possibly that fostered some hopes. Certainly the manly words of the pontiff must have touched the men, too. "Dear sons and dear brothers," he called them. He appealed to them to take their punishment as an amendment for faults, and he told them he well knew how many a father of starving children could be tempted to steal a bit of bread. He talked to them of their children, at once the reason for their keenest pain and the source of their greatest joy.

"In your first letter home, say that the Pope came to see you," the pontiff urged. "Say he was here among you. And in my Holy Mass and in my daily breviary I will have a special thought and intense affection for each of you and for all your dear ones."

A red carpet had been put down to show John the part of the jail it was thought advisable for him to visit, but he left it to go down the long corridors shaking hands and letting the kneeling prisoners kiss his ring. Next day the first women in memory visited the jail. The Pope sent 1,000 chicken dinners and nuns to serve it.

Both the prisoners of Regina Coeli and those of Melun Penitentiary in France sent the Pope missals—books for saying Mass. They were the only two the pontiff used in his Vatican chapel after that. To Melun the Pope sent word that he could not visit there, but that he did want the inmates to believe that "through our humble person" they received "a pledge of Divine mercy" and that "your unseen sorrows, offered up for the greater good of your fatherland, will be a benediction for each of your families in its trial."

After that visit John set out on dozens of others. The wife of the assistant editor of *L'Osservatore Romano*, Mrs. Cesidio Lolli, was a chronic invalid. He called on her. His chauffeur, Mario Stoppa, took ill. He visited him, too. Stoppa could not have been much surprised. He had by then grown used to having the august sovereign of the Vatican State remark to him after a wait: "Sorry to have kept you so long!" John visited Via di Trasone, which I knew as the humble, half-paved road on the edge of Rome where I had lived during my first half decade in Italy. The British Minister to the Holy See, Sir Marcus Cheke, was mortally ill in a small hospital there. The Queen of England took note of that call, sending word to the Pope how much she had appreciated this unique gesture to a member of the Holy See's diplomatic corps.

In one of his first audiences after election a churchman told Pope John that one of his old friends from diplomatic life was a resident of a Rome hotel and was sorry that he had not seen the new pontiff.

"Well, tell him to come over," John replied with the faintest hint of exasperation. "I can't go to the hotel to see him!"

Having uttered the words John may have set to wondering whether they were true. Certainly it was not Roman custom to see a pope strolling through a hotel lobby, but presently for the first time in a century Rome got used to seeing a pope pay many of the calls which generations of visitors had made to the Vatican.

One of the first was just a month after John's election. He left the Vatican at 7 A.M., the earliest papal sortie in Roman memory, and went to the Urban College of the Propagation of the Faith, a seminary for youth of fifty-one nations. The Pope said Mass for the young men. His gesture, he told them, was deliberate, to show at the outset of his pontificate how much he appreciated young clerics who had come from every race and corner of the world to absorb the Roman faith and to be its missionaries.

There was no mistaking the fact that this seemingly casual visit to the seminarians was an important part of the new Pope's policy when an even more unlikely episode occurred two months later. Monsignor Mario Nasalli Rocca, supervisor of the papal court, asked an old friend, Father Joseph Bergeron of Canada, why he had not asked for an audience. Father Bergeron managed a home for old and ill priests. An audience would be a delight, but priests in such a modest capacity could not presume to ask for part of the busy Pope's time, the Canadian answered. A few days later reporters covering the Vatican were alarmed to hear that the Pope had started out on what appeared to be his afternoon drive into the Vatican garden but had curved around St. Peter's and out into Rome instead. He had no motorcycle escort. He was up against the same snarled traffic and halts for red lights as any other motorist. For a Rome accustomed to popes sweeping by with police help in the manner appropriate to a "visiting chief of state" the situation was unimaginable.

John was on his way to Father Bergeron's. For an hour he stayed there, first visiting the infirmary, then chatting from an armchair with those of the twenty-two priest inmates who were well enough to join him. One of the old priests was a seventy-seven-year-old contemporary, Monsignor Virgilio Valcelli, whom John had known in his youth. The two had a warm reunion. Another was Monsignor Alberto Piermattei, one of the "secret chaplains" of Pius XII, a coveted honor that permitted the priest to assist the pontiff at ceremonies. Secret chaplains hold their offices only for the lifetime of the reigning pope. With a gesture which surely touched the old priest, John told him that he was reinstated. It was not an empty comment for the *Pontificio Annuario* thereafter listed the monsignor once again as part of the papal court.

There seemed to be no limit to John's imagination as he chose places to visit. He drove to distant Bellegra in the hills made famous by the Roman poet Horace. He called there at the Benedictine monastery where St. Francis of Assisi, the apostle of poverty and "the most Italian of saints," had been a distinguished visitor. The same day he dropped by at the convent of the Sisters of Bergamo at San Vito. He asked each nun her home town and reminisced about clergymen and the long-past Church events associated with each area.

John's scheme of visits evolved according to a logic of its own. In each missal, Catholics of all seven continents are reminded during Lent that there is a church in Rome which is normally visited on Lenten Sundays. At the "station" church there are special prayers and sometimes a procession through the neighboring streets. No pope in generations had walked in such parades, but John did so. News photographers got unusual shots of the pontiff strolling solemnly in front of coffee bars and unpainted houses—a far cry from the pomp of St. Peter's. One thought suggested another. It came to him as an inspiration one day, the Pope said later, that the better place for him on Lenten Sundays was not in the middle-class and rather devout central parishes hallowed by the centuries and listed in the missal but rather in the new, largely Communist slums around the edges of rapidly expanding modern Rome. The worst Roman misery was there in an area of poor water supply, inadequate schooling, little paving, few sewers and rare churches. There lay the greatest need for a Christian reminder.

I followed John on several of the slum visits. The government had no taste for taking chances and turned out substantial police details. Even so, lines broke and his limousine only squeezed through with difficulty. At Centocelle the markedly Communist but also still largely devout population had hung rugs from windows in an Arab-style salute, and gas stations and house walls were covered with signs: LONG LIVE THE POPE, LONG LIVE OUR BISHOP.

"I really had to go some to get here," John told an overflow congregation at a newly built church, "but this is a triumph!" The almost slangy phrase delighted the crowd. Beware of the "enemy." The Pope sobered. "You know who I mean," he added. "You know him by his last name and his first name! Beware! He works his way in among us!"

For that congregation the appeal for religion and against Communism could not have been better phrased.

Another extraordinary slum visit was to Tiburtina the Third, a community so poor it lacked even a name or a secondhand name. Its designation was thirdhand! As the poor of the Italian hills streamed down toward the bright lights and uncertain hopes of the Eternal City they squatted in fields, put up shanties or even walled up arches of the 2,000-year-old aqueducts, making homes as best they could in structures little better than packing cases. Tiburtina was one such slum and when another grew up a little farther out it called itself Tiburtina the Second. The place the Pope visited was one step farther along the road away from the long-settled and comfortable heart of Rome. I parked on a mudbank which served as a sidewalk and hurried through the rain to the new church, the proudest structure in the community. Like Centocelle, Tiburtina the Third was one of the few such neighborhoods with a place of worship. The sky was gray but the air was bright with bedspreads dangling festively from windows. One shack, an eyesore, hid its sufferings from the Pope's eyes; its occupants had added to the cheer by stringing a clothesline across the front of the narrow property and hanging a colorful bedcovering on that.

The Pope took a seat in the small sanctuary. The church shook with applause as he rose to speak. John frowned and then crossed his lips with a chubby forefinger.

"I must compliment you," he said a moment later. "You did stop quickly, but just keep in mind: in church you must have two things, prayer and silence!" The crowd had the collective expression of a child chided by an indulgent parent.

All went well at Tiburtina the Third, too, as the Father visited with his spiritual children. What an uncommonly rough papal congregation it was I did not realize until all of us in the church tried to burst out simultaneously to see the Pope off. A desperate young woman beside me shoved vigorously at the helplessly pinned-in lady in front of her and then turned to another at her side.

"You," she cried, her voice quivering with indignation at the discovery, "aren't pushing!"

With a heave here, a quick step there, and the passage of enough minutes, we all got out in time to receive the pontiff's final blessing.

These visits took their place beside many other innovations, or really revivals, of half-forgotten papal customs from other centuries. For the first time in a hundred years John resumed the practice of washing the feet of thirteen young priests and seminarians on the day before Good Friday; an imitation of the example of Christ reported in the Gospel of St. John. It was an ancient Christian gesture of humility yet there was a certain twentieth-century humor in it, too, as the much-honored pontiff, nearly eighty, went to his knees before the elegantly dressed diplomatic corps to bathe and kiss the foot of a young African Negro. I managed to get a place in the choir three feet from the Pope at one such ceremony and saw his momentary broad grin after the ceremonial caress of the foot of the fourth young Negro in line. The smile remained only an instant. John's lively sense of the incongruous had been touched, but his piety and earnestness —his stronger emotions—dominated again at once.

He revived the custom of walking unshod at Holy Week ceremonies commemorating the death of Christ. Cardinals followed his example. He revived the practice of kissing the toe of the 1,000-year-old bronze statue of St. Peter in the Vatican Basilica, a tradition few but peasants had respected in recent generations. The statue's toe is worn down by centuries of veneration. John wanted a place in that millenary procession of devotion.

On Ash Wednesday John knelt to have the remains of burned palm rubbed on his forehead by his secretary, Monsignor Capovilla, a reminder that he was "dust" and "unto dust" would return. That, too, was an observance which was general among the faithful but long disassociated from the Pope.

One day a visitor congratulated John on all he had done that was new. To this man's astonishment John denied that he had done anything novel. He added that if he had he deplored it. His only wish, he said, was to emphasize simple, pious customs, to encourage his fellows to practice the ancient Christian "Works of Mercy." "Ransoming captives" is one of them. Visiting Regina Coeli jail and writing to Melun prison must have seemed to John the next best thing to pleading hopelessly and perhaps illogically for a freeing of prisoners. Visiting the sick was another. The many hospital calls were a direct answer to that. The other twelve were: to feed the hungry; give drink to the thirsty; clothe the naked; harbor the stranger; bury the dead; instruct the ignorant; counsel the doubtful; admonish sinners; bear wrongs patiently; forgive offenses; comfort the afflicted; and pray for the living and dead. The mystery of John, if there was one, was largely explained in studying the "Mercy Work" table.

A diplomat accredited to the Holy See put it a bit differently. John, he said, was a student of Church history who had read the pages of the past, not like a wanderer in a museum but as one in search of what was still vital. Parts of the old tree which had lain dormant under the rough bark had sprouted anew.

# 19. Host to the World

Pius XII had had his apostolate of austere audiences, and Nuncio Roncalli his own experience as a genial member of various diplomatic corps, a relaxed guest, a cheery host. Reconciling the two traditions—that of a generation of Vatican life and his own—was not easy, but John managed it with an instinctive, ingenious combination which astonished many and charmed most.

For one thing John rearranged the "private library" where kings, presidents, premiers and others of the world's great were received. Few others ever saw the room but several dozen of us who were members of the press were permitted to examine it at the time of the historic visit of the Anglican Archbishop of Canterbury just before Christmas in 1960. It was the first time since the Protestant Reformation that the primate of the 35,000,-000 Anglicans had called on a pope, and in deference to the democratic English and their vigorous free press the Vatican lifted the veil covering the heart of the Pope's official apartments. The English primate had come in the hope that quarreling Christendom might make peace. The Vatican recognized that the right of the public to know and judge almost everything was at the center of the Protestant ideas with which Catholics would have to come to terms if there were to be any agreement.

I had been in the room once before, fourteen years earlier, when Archbishop Spellman had become a cardinal and had presented all sixty in his entourage—press and all—to his friend, Pius XII. The new cardinal had introduced each of us in turn. Pius sat behind his desk.

In the one and a half intervening decades, and especially in John's two years, great changes had been made.

The most significant was a half circle of thirteen armchairs at the formerly empty far end of the room. Twelve were of a light wine-red. The center one, for the Pope, was dark maroon. The modification spoke volumes. No longer did all visitors have to take a seat beside the Pope's table as the latter sat formally behind it. Now the pontiff could invite callers to the other end of the room to chat, as casually as in any nuncio's or government member's sitting room.

The tall bookcases filled with Pius XII's dictionaries of many languages and encyclopedias of Catholic doctrine still lined the shaded wall between the windows, but the rest of the space glowed with new color and warmth. A brilliant, thick rose-colored carpet bearing the coat of arms of Saint Pius X covered the floor. From the ceiling hung a gay eight-foot chandelier of Venetian glass—a sparkling marvel of clear, transparent material decorated with touches of red and blue. It was the Advent season, the prelude to Christmas, so beneath the chandelier was the Pope's crèche, a masterpiece of Italian glassblowing art. The Infant of clear glass—three inches long—was in His manger. There was an ass of green glass, an ox of gold, and Mary, Joseph and the three Wise Men in stiff flaring, translucent capes.

The walls were recovered with maroon damask woven with the Pope's coat of arms marked prominently with the Venetian lion and the Roncalli tower. The same damask half concealed a door at the far end opening into the Pope's private elevator. This connected with the bedroom and private suite on the floor just above.

Competing for my attention were the sense of hospitality the changes had created and the opportunity to study the Pope through the objects on his desk.

"He passes at least an hour of every day here," said Monsignor William Carew, a Canadian, one of the State Secretariate's few representatives from the English-speaking world, emphasizing the importance of the place as a papal work chamber.

In the center of the desk was a large crucifix, a constant reminder of the Savior's sacrifice. Beyond it, across almost the whole of the wall at the far end of the room, was a tapestry showing Christ giving Peter the keys of Church authority. That, too, was a persistent suggestion of the burden and privilege which, in Catholic eyes, are the Pope's.

There were two French telephones, one black, one a papal white. At the left was a clock, its pendulum swinging nervously. On the right was a well-handled white-bound copy of the *Annuario Pontificio,* the pontifical yearbook—a "Who's Who" of the Vatican and of the World Catholic hierarchy.

In the center was a shallow tray with a half-dozen well-sharpened pencils. Two were double-ended combination red-and-blue markers, presumably for Yeses and Noes on the thousands of papers requiring decisions. One was a plain pencil with a well-worn eraser. Two other rubbers showed signs of hard usage. Amid all the polished marble, blown glass and damask glories, one further addition seemed strangely out of place—a half-empty flimsy cardboard box of paper clips, just as they would come from the simplest stationery store.

One other notable new item in the room, off to the left of the desk, was a three-foot internally lighted plexiglass globe showing the boundaries of the 2,000 Catholic bishoprics.

The room gave a far warmer impression than I had remembered, but Monsignor Carew advised us that the chamber I knew in 1946 had been even less inviting under Pius XI (1922–1939). At that time the Pope's desk was behind a screen. Visitors did not see him until they rounded the barrier. Then they talked with the light of St. Peter's Plaza shining in their eyes. Visitors to Pius XII, and especially to John, were at no such disadvantage.

Much of what happens in the private audiences of any pontiff remains a secret, but enough was divulged to assure us that they had elements of informality inconceivable in many other pontificates. Priests told of John's remark to one archbishop. In effect the invitation went:

"I'm going to have some coffee. I'm old and I need the energy. Will you join me?"

Relaxing with a cup of coffee and being granted an audience

were two ideas that did not seem to go together, but the presumably startled prelate accepted.

"I've just done a broadcast and they're ready with the playback," John went on. "Would you like to listen?"

The answer, of course, was yes. The recording ended with the papal blessing. John and the archbishop rose to their feet and crossed themselves. A recorded papal benediction was still a pontifical blessing, and even though he had himself made the disk some time earlier; John's reverent instincts impelled him to make the same devout response of all fellow Catholics.

When Daniel-Rops, the French Catholic writer, asked to call, John reportedly replied that such a devout layman should have no less cordial a reception than "the King of Jordan," a Moslem potentate who had been given highest honors shortly before. The Pope, by the same report, recalled with a smile the Italian noodle dinners the two had shared in the Paris nunciature, but he plucked at his flapping cassock to show the seven pounds he had willingly lost in the first tense weeks of his pontificate when he had been troubled by indigestion.

Whatever went on it was noted that many visitors entered John's apartment gravely and left in smiles. A prize photograph of the first months of the pontificate was that of the Pope smiling crookedly and the American President Eisenhower guffawing. News editors queried their correspondents about what had provoked the Presidential hilarity. My own best efforts to find out through those who were present or those who were in their immediate parties indicated that John had flapped the text of his formal address in English and then assured the President that he was about to hear *di bello*—"A real beaut!" John had no illusions about his uncertain English accent.

Just as the great came to Pius they followed in procession to John: Presidents De Gaulle of France, Sukarno of Moslem Indonesia, Giovanni Gronchi of Italy, the royal family of Greece on the first such visit since 1439, President Celal Bayer, the first Turkish ruler ever to call on a Roman pontiff, the Queen Mother of England, the Premier of Japan, the Shah of Persia.

Not all of those who tried to see John succeeded. Sometimes

there were religious or political reasons which are valid for all pontiffs. Occasionally John's easy way of giving each visitor the time he needed and making time for "Work-of-Mercy" excursions forced a more severe tightening of the calendar of callers than Pius XII had permitted. Sometimes, too, visitors were disappointed as precious minutes slipped by pleasantly without their getting to points they wished to discuss.

The call of the Anglican primate was an example of one that involved problems which would have existed for any pope. Under the terms of Leo XIII's still-valid 1896 bull (edict) the Catholic Church refused to recognize the legitimacy of the priesthood of the Church of England. The Anglican communion was seen in Rome as schismatic and heretical: schismatic in the sense that it was no longer united to the Roman Church; heretical because of teachings contrary to that of Rome on dozens of issues ranging from the meaning of the Mass to the rightness or wrongness of birth control.

Cardinal Roncalli's motto that he would "receive anyone since he might want to come to confession" held for John in the Papacy: the doors were open to all, and in a special way to the other leaders of divided Christendom. They, too, might "want to confess" and it was soon reported in the highest Church circles in Rome that John had assured one Catholic Action audience that in a sense a two-way confession was in order—a joint admission that wrongs on all sides had led to the scandal of splintered, feuding Christianity.

Dr. Geoffry Fisher, the Anglican primate, was welcome but how could he be received without doing violence to the spirit of Leo's bull? How could scandal be avoided among English Catholics who were taught that there was but one true Church, one other than the established communion of their Queen and of the majority of their countrymen? The problem was solved in part by excluding the press. No witnesses, and especially no photographers, were allowed. We shivered a little in St. Peter's open square for one and a half hours in the cool of a December noon while the Anglican leader was in the Vatican. The primate went in his robes of archbishop, a purple cassock brightened by the same sort of pectoral cross worn by a Catholic prelate. He came and went giving his three-fingered blessing. In its carefully worded report on the "cordial" fifty-minute exchange between the two men, the Vatican called the visitor by his Anglican title of "His Grace," referring to him first as the "Anglican" Archbishop of Canterbury and thereafter without the adjective as "The Archbishop." In his turn the primate talked warmly of "His Holiness." It represented a careful patching together of conflicting loyalties but it also emphasized the open-armed, extroverted welcome characteristic of John's pontificate.

However willing John was to receive almost everyone, the limits were seen soon after his pontificate began. One United States Senator, a Protestant with a heavily Catholic constituency, waited ninety minutes to see the pontiff and then was amazed to have the audience finish in thirty seconds. He concealed his emotions, but his wife was indignant.

"My husband," she said of the distinguished legislator, "has never been treated that way before."

A governor of one of the states along the North-South line of the United States, an area of tense Catholic-Protestant relations, was surprised when American intermediaries in Rome told him that it was not definite that he could see John in a "special" audience—a small group which was a bridge between the private and public ceremonies.

"But I was told by Italian diplomats that I could have a special audience," the eminent figure protested. "It was one of my reasons for coming!"

He did not get it.

One of the greatest American newspapers tried to get a private audience for its managing editor, a man with much influence on public opinion. The prominence he gave to news stories often determined what other policy-formers thought about them. It is true that the newspaper official would never consciously have allowed his judgment of news values to be affected, but a happy encounter with the pontiff would presumably have disposed him a shade more favorably toward Vatican City dispatches. The editor, too, was denied a private talk.

Just as Pius in his late years put the emphasis on receiving men of importance outside his own Church hierarchy, so did John reserve much of his time during his first months for the cardinals and bishops who were his immediate subordinates. Pius felt, after two decades on the papal throne, that his time could best be used to bridge the gap between the Catholic idea and the rest of an evolving world. John, new to the supreme Vatican authority, saw his task as one of familiarizing himself with global problems inside his church and with the men who looked to him for their leadership.

John was the first to concede his own insufficiencies, and even with his audiences for churchmen there were surprises that were not always happy. Whereas Pius XII did research beforehand on the problems of prominent ecclesiastical callers, ticking off the difficult subjects toward the end of the interview if his visitor had not already touched on them, John surprised one eminent Church caller by giving him no directives. The visitor, spiritual administrator in an area of an especially difficult political situation, had come docilely prepared to carry out whatever order John gave him, but the Pope handed him none. Whether or not the aged John felt the complexities of the situation beyond him, the young bishop left with John's implied confidence in him to tackle according to his own conscience a situation which he knew, of course, in much more intimate detail.

In another audience with a bishop, John astonished the latter by saying little or nothing about the prelate's region. He asked instead what the visitor thought about a request which had come from a twice-divorced Oriental potentate who wished to marry a Catholic princess. Instead of instructing his caller John was soliciting the reaction of a fellow bishop with regard to a problem of his own. The marriage to the Oriental would help the country of the Catholic princess politically. How the exchange between the Pope and the bishop went from there on was unreported, but a few weeks later the Vatican spoke out against the marriage, and the Moslem monarch married a young woman of his own religion. John's visitor had been a bit dismayed that he had received no guidance but he may have helped his leader more than he knew in making a delicate decision of broad implications.

Many diplomats accredited to the Holy See had hoped, at the end of Pius's long pontificate, that the new reign of relatively easygoing Pope John would mean more frequent, productive contacts with the pontiff.

"I think he may do more in the private audiences," the ambassador of one of the largest Western powers speculated.

Pius, in his few confidential exchanges with the same diplomat, had frustrated him repeatedly. The Pope would glance upward as the envoy put demands, and would not commit himself. One may presume he wanted time to consult aides and documents, but the envoy, unable to send news scoops in his dispatches to his government, felt discontentedly that Pius wanted to hoard announcements for the speeches which were such a key part of his pontificate.

The same diplomat soon found that he accomplished little, if anything more, in his talks with John. On one of his first encounters the new Pope put him off with a smile and with a typical comment.

"I'm not broken in yet," he said. "Ask me later."

Later talks, the envoy implied, were not much better.

"He is charming, with a fund of anecdotes," the diplomat said, "but they are little stories which do not commit the future!"

John had pleased him, but the substance of the two popes' careful approach to tricky State-Church issues had been little different.

For all his almost casual manner, the diplomats found John no more frequently approachable than Pius and perhaps even less so. Some were chagrined.

"But what they forget," it was pointed out by a leader of the corps of diplomats to the Holy See, "is that they would be unlikely to see the sovereign of any other court or the chief of any other state more than twice during the whole of their stay— once to present credentials and again on leaving. They would be happy to see a foreign ministry's second secretary."

The envoy of one of the most important nations accredited to the pontiff arranges to see the Cardinal Secretary of State only once every two months, and admitted that "I would not dream of asking to see the Pope except on instructions from my government." He never called on Cardinal Tardini for a mere exchange of pleasantries. He had a dossier of problems each time. He saw the Pope about twice a year.

To content his many would-be callers was no easy task for the man who had become Pope at nearly eighty, nor did he attempt it. Some were turned aside firmly. As had been customary in all pontificates, the Pope's aides were warned by churchmen of various nationalities against certain potential callers—persons whose reception would provoke scandal in their home areas. An example was one generously proportioned, provocative young actress who was considered by some churchmen of her own country as little better than a prostitute. She toured Italy. On the mere chance that she might ask for an audience, a churchman who knew of her saw to it that her name went on the list of ineligibles. In his view the news of her audience, should she get one, would be a mockery.

Sometimes the No came from the Vatican. One priest agreed to relay an audience request from a politician of a Catholic area. The man was a nominal Catholic but had outraged local Church officials by a series of liberal measures, including one regarding the diffusion of contraceptive information—something new in his part of the world. A papal audience was politically important to the man. He was due to face his Catholic electorate and their bishops soon again at the polls. Within less than a half hour a Vatican monsignor had the answer. The audience was denied for a series of reasons, each of them listed. A crowded dossier must have been on file in the Secretariate of State. The politician was stunned. John's good nature did not mean indifference on matters his Church considered moral essentials.

The ability to say No showed up in other ways. John did not like the idea of exchanging skullcaps as souvenirs or relics, something Pius XII had well-intentionedly permitted despite the disapproval of some of those close to him. When Cardinal Spellman called on the new Pope just after his election, the secretary of the New York prelate, Monsignor Edwin Broderick, a burly cheerful priest, stepped forward with one of the first requests for one of John's *zucchetti*. Monsignor Broderick had obtained the new pontiff's hat measurements and was ready with a white skullcap to swap.

*Misura propria e justa!*—"The exact right measurement!"—the New York monsignor told the Pope in carefully prepared Italian.

John made the exchange but what the monsignor could not know at the time was that he was getting a rarer keepsake than he realized. Shortly after that the new Pope made it clear that he disapproved the practice. It did not seem to him appropriate. Occasionally he would touch a proffered *zucchetto* but he would not don it or make an exchange.

Often "very grave matters" were treated in private audiences, but there was a "special charm" about the huge, weekly "general" meetings to which anyone could come, John confided at one such gathering in November, 1960. Watching the Pope at many such meetings, I had the impression that one could go even further—that it could be said that it was his encounters with the largest groups of the world's poorest which pleased him most.

"The Pope is with you," John told Italian Catholic laborers at his first May Day audience inside St. Peter's. The next May Day meeting, in 1960, was even more memorable. It was in St. Peter's Square. John said Mass at an altar on the basilica steps. The partly de-Christianized, partly Communized workers were grouped in the square by the thousands. Some smoked cigarettes. Some handsomely proportioned peasant girls in costume posed for their photographs as the Pope reached the sacred moment of the Consecration. Workers who thought themselves Catholic held aloft placards which would have been appropriate at a Communist rally: DOWN WITH PRIVILEGE, DOWN WITH THE DUKEDOM OF CIOCIARA WHICH IS ROOTED IN VIOLENCE, WE WANT BETTER ECONOMIC AND SOCIAL CONDITIONS, THE ITALIAN WORKERS' FEDERATION (Catholic-led) OF TERAMO DECLARES WAR ON PROFITEERING.

Above the Pope's head was a huge blood-red banner bearing his lion-and-tower insignia. It was the cardinals' color, the symbol of sacrifice, but it was also one with which the troubled workers of Italy had become familiar on many a Marxist May Day. In a way the red of the workers was being baptized. Without quarrels over details, the discontented poor were being invited back toward the half-lost faith of their fathers. For all its incongruities it seemed to me the audience which must have pleased the Pope the most. Despite all there was in it to trouble the orthodox, it summed up the effort the sixth of the twentieth-century popes was making to meet the problem of faith and of the impoverished in what might prove to be the century of the poor.

# 20. As John Saw It

"The anecdotes and flashes of jollity which were part of this Pope were recounted time and again and distorted in the process. Taken at face value they tended to lessen his stature as a man, as a distinguished churchman, and as a shepherd of souls. But over all loomed the true pontiff, his piety and severity tempered by immense understanding. His capacity for comprehension shone through in his smile and warm words."

The words are Pope John's, part of a message he sent to priests in Venice in April, 1959. They were intended to describe Saint Pius X but could also have served as a self-portrait. The two men resembled one another both in physique and character.

John was a new Pius X in the way he went back to the simplest Biblical virtues. Where Pius XII manned the frontier between traditional Catholic, Christian and Biblical concepts and those of a Sputnik-minded modern world, John spent many a night reading both Testaments of the Bible, hunting for the old, ever-fresh, concepts of the Judaeo-Christian inheritance to pass on to mid-twentieth-century contemporaries.

How he felt about the *Magisterium*—the Pope's role as the "teacher" of Catholics—John revealed in a speech to Roman Lenten preachers in February, 1960.

"There are three types of people, as San Bernardino says," the Pope told the orators of the penitential period. "There are the *simplices*, the *mediocres* and the *perfectiores*."

To be sure of reaching the *simplices* it was essential to devote part of one's sermon to the fundamental things, "the matters that are absolutely necessary for salvation, for receiving the Church sacraments, for being holy," the pontiff said.

All such subjects, John interjected, had to be set forth with the simplest figures of speech "as if you were talking to children."

As for the rest, those of average mental capacity and those of superior intellect, "a pious bishop and excellent orator once told us that as the years had gone by he had learned that extremely simple speech is the best way to reach them, too; though erudite in things of the world they often know less about lofty and sacred things than the humblest teacher of catechism."

A priest's or a pope's talks should concentrate on fundamentals plainly expressed, but that does not mean that even the least of them should be unprepared, John told younger clergymen on one occasion. His own speeches seemed a cross between the last day's and evening's meditative reading, and improvisations of expression worked out as he smiled down on his audience. Pius XII had leaned heavily on studies of a thousand topics prepared at his precise instruction by Jesuits, but John seemed unhappy with texts sent up from below. One reporter watched with astonishment as John glanced through a prepared speech at the start of an audience and then handed it back to an aide with a gesture that spoke volumes.

"It isn't worth it!" the pontiff seemed to say.

"I don't want to be a *papa-gallo*," John was quoted another time. *Papagallo* is Italian for parrot.

There was never any fear that John was a parrot Pope. He drew on all his years of experience among small Catholic minorities, as a strong man from the Alpine farmland, and as a prelate who had lived among the sophisticates of Paris. From it all he preached a liberalism wedded to Catholic conservatism. It was, to be sure, a combination sometimes puzzling to churchmen accustomed to sharp distinctions and a cautious detachment from "error." Some murmured disapprovingly that the Vatican could not recall similar confusion. Others thought that they detected trends only to soon behold a quick reversal of the tendencies. Others opined that certain fine points were violated, such as ascribing the title of saint to his predecessors—Popes Pius IX and

XII—without awaiting the usual long enquiries. Through it, however, shone the faith of one who had always been Catholic and
devoutly so, while at the same time wholly loving all his fellow
men. Perhaps John groped with a sometimes imperfect vision, but
no one doubted that his heart was good.

Typical of John's thinking and the most important decision of
his first months of pontificate was the summoning of Catholicism's
twenty-first ecumenical council. Churchmen called it daring.
Instead of using the nearly limitless authority conferred by the
1870 council of papal infallibility, the democratic John chose to
summon the 2,500 Catholic bishops of the world to Rome where
all could speak their minds, and where all—taken as a council—
would have an infallibility of their own. The council could resist John's own view of the world. It could march down paths
Rome's cautious theologians and ecclesiastical bureaucrats might
fear to venture. It might take steps with unforeseeable consequences for future generations of Catholics. In his mountainman's
faith and in his respect for the minds and goodwill of others,
John had no fear.

The council would have its own life but it was also plain that
it would make its proclamations on Church discipline and morals
under the influence of the strong personality of the Pope.

What that personality was the Pope's secretary, Monsignor
Capovilla, suggested in his 1959 talk in Venice.

"His is a great heart," the secretary said. "It is without calculation, without ties to one current of political thought or another.
His mind is open with regard to method and he has no taste
for anything that sets itself up as infallible, irreplaceable or
monopolistic."

Was there a contradiction in an infallible pope shy of the concept of infallibility, of the chief of the "one, true Church" opposed in principle to the "irreplaceable and monopolistic?" Love
and charity, in John's view, were the core of the Christian and
Catholic doctrine. Without repudiating what he and his intimate
associates considered the essentials of the Catholic tradition, John
as Pope was determined to break through incrustations which
had led to a divided Christianity. John was sure there was no

contradiction. Pragmatically, case by case, he made his pontifical way.

Every word Pius XII had spoken in public audiences was published afterward. The Pope himself would type the final draft of a speech which might have started with his own idea, and then been worked over by theologians. During the speech Pius might change a word or two. He would then insist that the release of the text be held up until he could go over it one more time. A classic illustration was the time a few months before his death when Pius spoke to aviation writers at ceremonies inaugurating a new air service between America, Europe and Australia. To the dismay of the air-line press agent, Pius slipped the text into the wide sleeve of his white cassock as the talk ended. The publicity man reached for it and the Pope pulled back. The reporters needed it for their stories, the worried press agent explained.

"No," Pius said, "revision, revision!"

By contrast, the Vatican has seldom published any but indirect quotations from John's speeches. It was rumored that the Pope himself had objected to textual reports. Most of the gay turns of phrase, much of the jollity, was lost in the process. At audiences few but Italians understand the pontiff's familiar chatter. Monsignors translating into French, German, and as a rule into English, too, combed out almost everything that was lighthearted. Some on the Vatican staff deplored that much of John's originality was lost in the process. However someone, perhaps John himself, had decided that spontaneous good cheer should not be permitted to shrink the figure of John as it had that of St. Pius X.

Despite the screen between the pontiff's words and the world, John shone through and what could be seen was edifying.

For one thing, he was an optimist. He felt that religion meant joy, not gloom. A favorite story of his was of the time when he and Bishop Radini-Tedeschi took 25,000 lire to Pius X. That was only $40 in the days after World War II, but in the days of the saint-Pope it meant many thousands of dollars. Pius was so busy during the audience, lamenting antireligious trends of the contemporary cultured world, that he almost forgot to acknowledge the gift. Young Father Roncalli walked out, objecting that

the Pope might have had a happy word or two for his visitors.
The bishop scolded his secretary for his liberty in criticizing a
pope and the young priest repented, but John made sure as pontiff that he, in his turn, did not depress his callers.

"Some imagine Christianity as lugubrious," John told visitors
in December, 1958. "No, it is joy! It is the jubilation of order,
of peace, of the right relationship to God, to oneself and to one's
neighbor."

Another time he said, "Christianity is peace, joy, love and a
life that is ever renewed."

"There is no melancholy," the Pope put it yet again. "One
walks in the path of the Lord missing no chance to do good. But
of course there is no reason for exaggerated optimism or for joy
out of proportion."

John was one of the elderly who did not feel that "the world
always grows worse as it gets older." So he confided to visitors
at the start of 1959.

Surely one of the reasons why he felt that was because of his
own thorough dedication to the ancient virtues, especially charity.
In the years before he became Pope, Monsignor Capovilla often
heard the future pontiff express himself:

"I don't care what they think or say about me. I don't care
whether I get there late or not at all. What matters is to be true
to my own good intentions, whatever the cost. I want to be good
all the time and with everyone."

In an audience in Latin to priests, John urged: "Cultivate charity! It sums up all the virtues, all good things."

To Catholic newspapermen in a 1959 audience he said: "There
is a duty, as Alessandro Manzoni remarked, to speak up for the
truth, but always in a charitable way. We must be fearless in
defense of truth, but never unfair or without generosity to opponents."

The Catholic Church's "great merit," John advised Roman
priests in February, 1959, is "the triumph of charity."

"When you are charitable," John told Venetian visitors in
March, 1959, "you are sure of never being mistaken. Learn how
to understand, to forgive, to be gracious. That's Christianity.

By contrast it is the way of the world to push, to parade, to use
violence. That's all wrong. The force we possess is the truth
and the charity of Jesus Christ."

John's charity did not stop short of the Protestants, the traditional foes of Catholicism since the Reformation. In a talk to
Roman priests behind closed doors in January, 1960, in a monastery overlooking the Colosseum, John reportedly told the
clergymen that Catholic-Protestant bickering about historic
rights and wrongs was no longer tolerable and "all sides" might
well accept a share in the responsibility for the disintegration of
the Christian fold.

While Pius had wanted the widest possible diffusion of each of
his delicately weighed words, John was opposed to "notary pub-
lics in the audience," as he once said to a Venetian group, men
taking down each word and holding the Pope to unintended implications. Without texts, Rome's word-weighers could not determine how much of the Catholic historical and scholastic tradition John was minimizing or rejecting, but his friendly goodwill
and the charity of his instincts were evident.

He was humble as well as charitable. The Orfei Circus troupe
saw that in one of his first audiences.

"Come back and see me," the Pope said in the easy manner of
a Bergamo farmer. "I'm always here. You mention me in your
prayers and I'll pray for you."

Success always goes to those "humble in heart," John assured
student priests at the large mission college of the *Propaganda
Fide*—the Propagation of the Faith.

"On the contrary," he added, "those who give in to the temptations of presumptuous grandeur are doomed to live bitter days."
Vatican attachés observed quickly that John rarely if ever said
*voglio*—"I want." His phrase instead was *mi sembra*—"the way
it seems to me." That this was modesty not weakness was reflected in what happened after that. However much traditionalists
resisted the ideas that "seemed" right to John, such as the reform
of the priests' prayer book, the changes somehow found their
way into effect.

In addition to charity and modesty, he emphasized other merits.

On his visit to ill priests in one of his first unannounced excursions outside the Vatican, he told of a baptistery he had seen on his travels. It had eight columns adorned with statues depicting each of the three virtues Catholics call "theological" (faith, hope and charity), and each of the four virtues known as "cardinal" (prudence, justice, fortitude, temperance).

The eighth?

The designer of the baptismal font, unguided by tradition, had picked "patience." Earnestly the thoughtful pontiff pressed that thought on these clergymen who were enduring waning days.

*Veritas, justititia, sanctitas*—"Truth, justice, holiness"—John told newly consecrated bishops in May, 1960, are the Catholic apostolate's force. Notably absent, he said, was "any mirage of glory or of material interests."

Plain "goodness" was the finest of all human attributes, the Pope remarked in one of his 1960 Lenten slum sermons. "The human intellect," he said, "can list other eminent qualities but none compares with mere goodness."

"Always respect everyone's dignity, from the highest to the lowliest," John urged on another occasion. "Especially respect every man's liberty. God Himself honors that."

In that evidently lay the roots of John's liberalism. It was a quality deserving the closest study, for no attribute was more exceptional in one sworn to preserve the essence of the Christian heritage. Obviously alert to it as a key problem, John treated the question in his first encyclical in July, 1959. "Many points of doctrine," he said, were open to debate by theologians. So long as the arguments did not corrode the foundations of the unity of faith they could shed light on the proper interpretation of dogmas. The remark opened the door to peace talks with Protestant theologians, but the insistence on a preservation of "faith unity" underscored the orthodoxy which was as much a part of John as his liberalism.

In December, 1958, John called his predecessor, Leo XIII, into evidence to demonstrate that it is Catholic doctrine that "in merely political matters" contrasting views were permitted to Church followers. At about that time John made up his mind to remove the powerful Catholic Action organization of Italy from politics. Despite a 1929 agreement with Italy barring Church interference in politics, the Catholic Action machine, under the dour Dr. Luigi Gedda, had become perhaps the strongest single political force in the country. Many Catholic laymen had objected that it was no proper role for a Church organization, and John agreed.

His liberalism permeated his approach to art, too. He spoke on that in January, 1959:

"Artists find the Church door not only open but wide open. The Pope encourages and blesses. He is pleased to contemplate calmly even some rather extreme experiments, for some things surprise one at first, only to become generally accepted later on. There are on the other hand, it is true, certain things to which one never grows accustomed, for they are distortions which conflict with nature. They are to be rejected."

In his talk at a rather modernistic church in the Primavalle slum John said: "There are those who say that only the ancients knew how to build beautiful churches. It isn't true. Moderns do also. They are a bit after their own fashion, reflecting feelings of the moment, but they, too, are handsome."

For pastors throughout the world debating whether to put up another poor copy of the Gothic, the remark was encouraging.

Hand and hand with his liberalism, however, walked John's veneration of obedience as a capital virtue. Even before becoming Pope he chose that word for his coat of arms. He gave obedience freely in his decades subject to Church superiors and he demanded it from subordinates from the start of his own long climb up the ladder of Church authority. The unity, strength and durability of the Catholic Church from Roman times to the present are inconceivable without obedience. John never doubted that the quality was needed.

In an audience for the Vatican's Swiss Guard, he told the men in their early twenties:

"One must know how to take orders, and one must see the value of submitting to the decisions of superiors."

To the proverbially obedient Jesuits of *Civilta Cattolica*, a publication written by talented priests of the Society of Jesus but with a policy dictated by the Pope and Cardinal Secretary of State, John added:

"I too am of the 'party' [of those who obey, and stand for obedience]. Obedience is a source above all of peace and tranquility."

The Pope told the priests to look up the twenty-third chapter of the third book of St. Thomas à Kempis's *Imitation of Christ*. They did so at once after getting back to the villa they occupy in the heart of Rome overlooking the gardens where Lucullus had his epicurean feasts. In the quotation the influential Church writers thought they saw the reflection of much of John's mind:

"Seek, my son, the will of others rather than your own. Seek always to have less rather than more. Seek always the lowest place, to be below others. Desire and pray always that the Divine Will may be fully accomplished in you. The man who lives that way enters the kingdom of heaven and tranquility."

Side by side with his insistence on obedience, John placed his concept of the role of the laity in the Church. However displeasing it might be in a democratic age where men were accustomed to vote on all things—whether they be jurors at a trial or members of the electorate at the polls—John insisted that Pius XII was exactly right in 1954 in saying that "there never has been nor can there ever be a legitimate *magisterium* of the laity inside the Church." The interpretation of the Christian inheritance belonged to the bishops and priests, to the dedicated men who had given up a great share of the world's pleasures to accept consecration and ordination as the Heirs of Christ's Apostles. Laymen would have to content themselves with a lesser role. Like the rest of John's ideas, the principle found a quick, far-reaching application. European laymen who defied the Vatican's Holy Office to ally with Communists in the name of social justice found themselves outside the Church pale. Opinionated laymen like Dr. Gedda who had the right of standing on the lower steps of the Pope's throne, higher than priests and monsignors, found themselves back down with the rest of the laity, while the power

of such organizations as Dr. Gedda's Italian Catholic Action
went back to control by a committee of bishops.

John's hope, as he said in the summer of 1959, was for the reunion of all those who "agree on the most memorable fact of
human history," Christ as the Light of civilization. What he
wished, he had said a half year earlier, was "the return of the
spirit of friendliness and of amiable brotherliness among those
who—thanks be to God, hundreds of millions—are outstanding
for their love of the cross."

Having the wish for reunion and achieving it were two separate things, as John well knew. Ideas of a secondary place for the
laity, of obedience as a capital principle, and so many other controversial doctrines such as the high place given Mary by Catholics and the key role accorded the Pope, stood as obstacles despite the generosity of John's feelings toward Protestants, toward
Jews, and toward men of all other religions.

The ecumenical council might help, John thought, but not even
that, he conceded, could "do away in one sweep with all the
divisions among Christians." The road was long, but John was
sure that "God's grace is at work in souls and all of us must
multiply our faith in Him and in the abundant grace He is sure
to concede."

Pius's utterances had been from the mind; John's were from
the heart. Who was to say which spoke more clearly to modern
man?

# 21. The Last Shall Be First

Cardinal Angelo Roncalli was far from last among the church-men of Catholicism when he was chosen in 1958 as Christendom's foremost spiritual leader, but his abilities in his late seventies were limited. No one was more conscious of his shortcomings than he.

His knowledge of "littleness" was enough to explain how con-fused he felt, the patriarch told fellow cardinals just after his election.

At seventy-seven it was hard, indeed, for John to take up the complicated and heavy papal work load. Pius XII had had the relative vigor of sixty-three when he assumed the Church com-mand and had fourteen years of experience behind him by the time he entered his own seventy-eighth year. John's assistants no-ticed that the pontiff could work only irregularly. By contrast with meticulous Pius XII who even checked 25,000-lire ($40) expenditures, John had little strength for detail.

The lack of persistence in his work efforts was reflected in his sleep habits.

"He got up to work at two o'clock this morning," the then Vatican Secretary of State Tardini told us in the course of an unprecedented visit to the Rome foreign press club.

"He has a guardian angel who wakes him when it's time to work." The cardinal smiled. "He is disorderly in his work habits. He may go to bed at ten, get up at two to work until four, and then go back to bed for three hours. I, fortunately, have a guard-ian angel who lets me sleep through the night," the State Secretary added.

John's difficulties with his task were reflected in other ways.

In audiences the pontiff sometimes showed either inadequate preparation or weariness, sometimes making small mistakes, sometimes disappointing visitors by repeating homilies heard before. To a priest born in 1886 and thus five years his junior, John said, "I see you are eighty-six" which would have made the visitor a decade older than the pontiff. To a group of Irish pilgrims the Pope spoke fondly of "St. Bridget of Scotland" meaning "St. Bridget of Sweden." The Pope's American aide, well knowing the tension between southern Irish and Scottish, grimaced but could not interrupt.

Giulio Barteloni, a news tipster at the Vatican, obtained a special audience for himself and his family on his twenty-fifth wedding anniversary, hoping, too, for usable exclusive comments from the pontiff. John merely repeated what he had said on such occasions before—that he did not object to newswork but that truth was holy and that reporters should not betray it.

John's limitations were real, but he was relentless in seeking them out, confessing them, perhaps even exaggerating them. His humbleness was a match for anything he lacked. Again it was in writing about another that he clearly portrayed himself. This time the text was from 1924 when he read a eulogy on the tenth anniversary of the death of Bishop Radini-Tedeschi. All he had to say then about his beloved bishop's outward appearance of strength and his inner struggles against imperfections could well describe his own life in the decades before and after the 1924 commemoration:

"I can assure you," the Pope said of his former bishop, "that this prelate who seemed like a dominant personality was profoundly modest. He thought so poorly of himself, he had so low an opinion of his own physical and moral qualities, that it was a source of astonishment—especially for those close to him. From all this he drew an iron discipline which he imposed on himself before asking it of others. His was a day-by-day struggle to be strong and courageous, to be of value in God's service. At the same time there was an increase in his gentle esteem and sympathy for others."

An example of John's own drive to improve was his heroic

effort to master English during the final months of his seventies. To a French diplomat, John explained that despite his smoothly literary command of his native Italian, his almost equal fluency in Latin, his competent French reflecting wide reading in that language, his fair Bulgarian and Turkish, his smattering of Greek, and his slight understanding of Russian, he suffered from the poverty of his English. The pontiff "felt cut off from a very important part of the world and from so many of his visitors," the French diplomat understood. Characteristically, too, John did not neglect the matter for long. With the help of his Irish secretary, Monsignor Thomas Ryan, he resumed lessons which the Tipperary priest had given him sporadically two decades earlier when the two were together in the papal nunciature in Turkey. Cardinal Amleto Cicognani, the former Washington envoy of the Vatican, was astonished one day to hear from Pope John that the pontiff was using one of the cardinal's own brief writings in English as an exercise for translation into Italian. The passage was a preface the Apostolic Delegate had written for prize essays by United States seminarians. The episode, incidentally, was one of the first signs of the interest the pontiff was taking in the prelate he was to make his Secretary of State following the death of Cardinal Tardini in 1961.

"My horse is grazing so the grass will grow," the rural-minded pontiff told English-speaking visitors at that time. Farmers, at least, understood that English lessons were under way and that John hoped for progress. To those of us who were in Cardinal Spellman's party just after John's election, the pontiff promised that he would speak "American" on our next visit or "anyway, in Paradise!" Wishing and trying were easier at his age than doing, and John had to admit later to a group of American bishops that even the first lesson in English had baffled him. With a native language in which each syllable is pronounced and every vowel has only one sound, it was hard to understand how "a" could be pronounced one way in "park" and another in "flat," let alone all the rest of the bewildering variations which followed.

The aged John struggled with Spanish and German, too. At the end of one earnest but imperfect attempt he prompted general laughter by his remark: "If there are any here expert in these languages, please realize that we all start somewhere. With God's grace I'll do better."

Probably few who shared in the amusement had a linguistic roster that equaled his.

Popes, even such self-demeaning ones as John, mount at last an eminence on which few even of their associates can reach them, so one young monsignor who translated at audiences never was able to tell the old Pope what he longed to say: "Holy Father, just tell the people in English: 'God bless you.' That's all they ask."

As he worked in his late seventies to overcome deficiencies he may have first observed in his teens, Pope John never relented in his stern and disarming appraisals of his own shortcomings.

In referring to himself he one day observed, "God made a lot out of a little."

One might think, he said, that Providence had guided the cardinals to pick "a brother of theirs who was already old and of modest proportions" in order to "show how It could intervene with more than enough grace to cover up the deficiencies."

Certainly if the years of study, travel and diplomatic experience away from Sotto il Monte had not polished over every imperfection, John succeeded in the Vatican far better than an insomniac tired with the weight of many years could have been expected to. For all his sporadic ways, a routine of sorts was established as the foundation on which the Pope could perform his high service. As a rule he rose at 4 A.M. and retired at ten. He dressed himself, calling for no help from his valet, Guido Gusso. He read his priest's prayer book, recited a few psalms and hymns aloud, repeated a few prayers from his childhood, and then said Mass at about 6:30 A.M. Breakfast at eight was light: coffee and milk, bread and fruit. Audiences started at nine with a briefing from the Secretary of State on the main events of the day. Supplementing the report was a stack of newspapers and clippings underlined in blue and red, depending on the importance of the various items. After that came audiences, dragging on sometimes until two. A medically prescribed, nonfattening lunch followed:

meat or cheese, fruit, mineral water, coffee—but no cakes, pies, ice cream or after-meal cordials. Often there was a guest. John is said to have decided that there is nothing in Sacred Scripture compelling popes to eat alone "like punished seminarians." Whether or not he did reason in that typically popular way, one custom of many generations that sets the Holy Fathers of Catholicism apart from their fellow humans fell into disuse. The Pope's own peasant brothers and sister, many of the cardinals and numerous bishops were among those who were invited to dine. A gregarious nature may have been bolstered in that decision by a memory from ambassadorial years that often the easiest way to achieve a meeting of minds, whatever the problem, is at meals. Certainly the table Nuncio Roncalli set during his Paris days was sophisticated, known both for hearty portions of his own Italian spaghetti and also for the host's good knowledge of wines. Where there were no guests at the Vatican there was occasional background classical music: Brahms, Mozart, Handel. After lunch Pope John napped in an armchair for a half hour.

Visitors to the Paris legation recalled Nuncio Roncalli as one who smoked cigars, and more frequently cigarettes, but in the Vatican Pope John was a nonsmoker. Some insisted that he had never smoked, that he had merely sometimes held a lighted cigarette to put others at ease. It is hard to credit that, but cards and chess, at least, were two pastimes in which the peasant-born Pope never indulged. He had never learned either.

As his Vatican day ended, John liked an occasional hour with Church history, a mine of experiences and suggestions which never failed to inspire him and perhaps strengthened his conviction that no problem would prove great enough to destroy the Church and religion of which he was momentarily leader.

Sometime during the day John said the first two couplets of the Rosary, a series of prayers recalling the main events of the life of Christ and of His mother, the Virgin Mary. The last of these selections was recited with the three nuns from Bergamo who were his cooks and housemaids. They had succeeded two unmarried sisters of the pontiff who had done the same service for him and had given him a link with his farm home when he was a papal diplomat. The last couplet of the Rosary was told at 7:45 P.M. followed by a supper of soup, vegetables, bread and fruit.

Of all the moments of his Vatican day those passed reciting the Hail Mary's and the other Rosary couplet prayers were certainly among those John found the most consoling. Of all the Catholic devotions the Rosary is one of the most modest. Few but priests can read the Latin of the breviary, and only the moderately well educated can follow the changing devotions of the missal, but children old enough for Communion can share in the Rosary. The old prelate was united spiritually with the least of his flock as the beads slipped through his fingers. He made a point of offering one decade of the Rosary decades for each of the continents. "America," as he told the daughter of a New York newspaperman, "is fifth."

Saying the prayers to the Virgin over and over and meditating on Christ's life and the hopes and fears of the five continents was a persistent source, the Pope remarked in a 1960 audience, of "patience, sweetness, and resignation, and at the same time of enthusiasm for the wars without cannons and horror which the Church wages to affirm the truth."

John's election had inspired a flood of jokes, provoked evidently by the contrast between the stocky child of peasants and the slender partrician who had preceded him. "There are signs in downtown Rome now," some said after John began his frequent excursions, "reading LOOK OUT FOR THE POPE." "The Spanish call him 'Juan two-three,'" said others bemused at the highest numeral in papal history. "Vat 69," is his phone number said still others. "Johnny Walker," agreed others. "S. C. V.! *Se Cristo Venisse!*"—"If Christ were to return"—others repeated an old Roman jibe about the license plate letters on the limousines John used for his various trips (s. c. v., *Stato della Citta del Vaticano* —the State of Vatican City). Further jests concerned the many other cardinals who had been considered *papabili*, and quoted one as saying to John in the words of an advertisement for a detergent, "I thought my cassock was white until I saw yours!"

If the jokes reflected the strain of a mundane world adapting to the concept of another in the chain of "Vicars of Christ," the fact that they soon vanished was a tribute to the impression the unpretentious John presently created.

Sometimes it was his amiable but meticulous honesty that struck callers such as Ernest A. Kehr, Cardinal Spellman's stamp adviser, who thanked the Pope for "the first" sheet of a new Vatican series.

"It's not first, it's second," John answered unexpectedly. "I kept the first for myself."

At other times it was his casual, fatherly way. When Augustus Velletri, the American Embassy's unofficial liaison with the Holy See, called for a farewell audience, John saw a hole in the mouth of one of the Velletri children.

"What did you do with the tooth?" he demanded.

"Threw it away," the boy answered, in an exchange which no doubt will long be remembered in the diplomat's family.

On other occasions it was the way the aged pontiff comported himself as some of the most pitifully ill persons came to him in audience, perhaps hoping secretly for one of the miracles described in Christ's story. One such was Katherine Hudson, an Oklahoma girl of ten, dying slowly of leukemia. She fell into a coma on the plane flying to Rome, but revived, and with her all but moneyless mother called on John for one of the latter's rare afternoon audiences. The child was in her white dress for First Communion. A Vatican priest said that the half-hour talk through an interpreter between the old Italian of nearly eighty and the little American girl went heavily but the child seemed comforted.

"He let me kiss his pectoral cross," she said. "He talked to me about the Madonna. He asked about school. He wanted to know whether I liked St. Peter's. He said he would pray for me and he asked me to pray for him." The child assured her mother that she would be well, but within a few weeks she was dead.

To call someone "Holiness" is easy but to live up to it is hard, John said after his first months in the pontificate. Each man peering into his own conscience sees a sinner, he added.

He charmed a vaguely anticlerical peasant of the Roman hills by his neighborly conversation from the throne during a Castel Gandolfo audience. "He talks just like us," the farmer marveled.

To merit the awesome title of "Holiness" is probably more than a modern mind can comprehend, but month by month in his familiar ways John moved nearer to it.

In his first Christmas as Pope, John said Mass for only a handful of communicants. Romans were not accustomed to a papal Christmas and some Vatican staff members wondered privately whether the pontiff had not imprudently brought humiliation on himself and the Papacy.

"But then as the Mass went on those who were there began reciting the responses from their missals," one of the doubters related. "There were no cardinals present; no court. It was just a bishop with his flock—a pastor with his parish. It was one of the most edifying spectacles I remember."

Sometimes John vanished from his quarters on the top of the Papal Palace to pray for as long as two hours at the Vatican garden's miniature reproduction of the shrine to Mary at Lourdes. Prayer, he was sure, was a stronger weapon than political cunning or a dozen other tactics.

More insights into his character came as the Pope of 1958 talked of occupations he considered best. The priesthood, he insisted, was first, but schoolteaching followed closely in his estimation. Teachers, he thought, shared a little of the priesthood. Whether one remembered instructors from childhood or contemplated them in the present, one was sure that "the gates of heaven swung ajar when good teachers arrived."

Doctors were the third of a triumvirate dedicated to man's body and soul. John linked them reverently with priests and teachers.

Newspapermen, too, received the Roncalli prelate's accolade. The same eternal quest for information which is the role of the reporter was his task as a churchman trying to relate Biblical verities to modern conditions, the Pope felt.

Factfinder, preacher, moral healer, John shared the American national trait of friendship for underdogs. In his case the inclination was to open his heart to the new, poor "third-force" nations. For those of us who could follow the byplay in Italian and English, one of the pontiff's first audiences with Cardinal

Spellman was revealing. John urged the Americans to value things of the spirit and appealed to them to share their wealth. The patriotic New York cardinal translated for the benefit of his entourage, as John requested him to do, but interjected that Americans certainly did share their good fortune. "Cardinals advise and the Pope decides," John coolly rejoined.

John's feeling for the poor, his sympathy for Socialists, his friendly way with anticlerical Leftists of the French stripe, spread some fears among diplomats at the time of his election that he might lend at least a bit of an ear to Moscow for the first time in the Holy See's history. One journalist whose work it is to defend the Vatican confided that he was preparing to defend John against the charge of softness toward Communism but that he could not do so until the uneasy fear broke into print in a concrete and answerable form. The defense was never written, for as one ambassador told me, "I checked with one of those closest to the new Pope and he assures me that there is nothing to it." The ambassador was embarrassed to even put into words what, on the face of it, seemed preposterous.

The truth, as all learned, was that John's goodwill knew no frontiers. Just as he offered a decade of his Rosary three times each day for "America," so did he pray for Russians, Chinese of the mainland, African Negroes, and all others as he told his beads. He was "for" the Communists of Russia precisely because he was against Communist hatred and for Christian brotherly affection. When Russians and men of five satellite nations visited him as part of an international technical delegation, John offered his blessing "to all who wish to accept it," but at the same time the Pope joined his predecessors in decrying Communism as an enemy of inalienable human liberties and as "unmodern" as well as immoral.

He was not the intellectual Pius XII had been. In his late seventies John was not the same untiring worker. But few years of his pontificate had passed before he had proved to the satisfaction of skeptical Rome that even so depleted a College of Cardinals as the one left by the lonely Pius XII could work the marvel of producing with evident ease another great Christian shepherd.

# PART FOUR

# ETERNAL CITY

# 22.  Christian-Pagan Rome

There is a Roman equivalent of the Anglo-Saxon, "The king is dead, long live the king." It is *"Morto il papa, si fa un altro"*— "When the Pope dies, you make [elect] another." The immediate meaning is that life must go on despite all disillusions. But perhaps there is a subtler further thought—that the important things in which a man trusts cannot fail.

Of all the things I learned as a reporter covering such different pontificates as those of Pius XII and of John XXIII, the most appealing and remarkable was the mood of Rome: human, confident, eternal. Pacellis and Roncallis, Piuses and Johns, come and go, but Rome with its saints and its scoundrels, its cynicism and its faith, seems fated to go on forever.

In a way this observation can be expanded to take in all of Italy—the perplexing, paradoxical country which has traditionally given Catholicism a third of its cardinals, and for four centuries all of its popes.

The rascalry of Rome and of Italy is easy to observe, as I saw in my first hours in the peninsula when Monsignor Carroll battled the Neapolitan driver for my ten-lire note and fought the train waiter for white bread instead of black. Even the Vatican police like tips from news photographers in exchange for good shooting positions, and sometimes pious pilgrims are tempted to believe that the Romans await them like vultures: the porters and cabdrivers at the main railroad station who shout as they try to get double the official rate; the dignified guides who demand prices that would make an Italian quail; the companies with limousines who charge old ladies five times as much for a ride to a papal audience at Castel Gandolfo as any local resident would dream of spending. I watched a souvenir peddler working on two Italian newlyweds at the Colosseum at the time of Pope John's election. They were from North Italy so they were fair game for the Roman.

"Take a nice medal of the Pope," the hustler urged the embarrassed couple. "Take one of Pope John. Take one of Pope Pius, too. You have two mothers-in-law. Take one for each!"

The two shuffled off, already a bit inured to the Roman attack. The peddler took the repulse with the Eternal City's rich philosophy. He was trying to get rid of his store of Pius XII medals, he confessed, but admitted that it was not going well. In his voice were both the resignation and the ever-fresh hope and determination of Rome. He would keep trying to sell the medals of the old pontificate for a while and then he would take the rest of the loss with a shrug.

It is said that "Paris is where a good American goes when he dies," and by the same token Rome is the city every Catholic longs to visit. Few pilgrims admit it back home and many perhaps not even to themselves, but the human side of Rome and Italy almost always comes to the devout as a shock. Dirt, poverty, anticlericalism, inefficiency, thievery—Rome and Italy have all of these in good measure. The faithful traveler seeking a heaven on earth such as he has never found at home does not encounter it in Italy's capital city either. Many turn back sadly.

That is the first impression, yet I feel that many of us in Rome's permanent American colony of 10,000 have learned something more.

Pope John touched on it in a talk with a visitor. He remarked that Piazza del Popolo—the People's Square—where the ancient Flaminian Way goes through the 1,700-year-old city walls has statues of Peter and Paul. Peter's hand points downward as if to say, "Here is where the laws are made for the whole Christian world." Paul's gestures far down the departing Via Flaminia. "That," he seems to say, gesticulating toward the world away from Rome, "is where the laws are obeyed."

The joke was an old one in Rome and had a shade too much

truth in it, John indicated to his caller. For that reason, he went on, he had summoned Rome's first diocesan synod, its first partially democratic assembly of parish priests around the Pope as their bishop. The intention was to spur a new moral and religious upsurge. The thought was similar to that of Pius XII who had doubled the number of parishes in Rome during his pontificate.

If thievery is a measure of depravity, sacred Rome—stained with the blood of many of Christianity's first martyrs—has an all too disturbing share of it. One group of Irish pilgrims at St. Peter's were thunderstruck to discover that several dozen of them had lost their wallets to light-fingered neighbors in the closely packed congregation. Attachés at the Irish Embassy told me later how hard it was to explain that not everyone who crossed St. Peter's threshold did so with pure intentions, and that St. Peter's was notorious among Roman police as a mecca for Italy's petty thieves.

Rome's dignified *Il Messaggero* was moved at one point in the late fifties to an editorial of protest:

"They're not just taking the traditional things like purses, handbags and the contents of cash registers," the newspaper lamented. "The news of the past week indicates that they steal everything now: phonograph records, slugs for juke boxes, even canaries. The way it is going we'll soon have 500,000 thieves in Rome!"

It reminded me of a visit I made just after World War II to Borbona, a mountain village threatened with starvation. I asked the pastor, Don Giuseppe, what would happen. "No one will leave anything around to be stolen," he answered.

Behind the remark I thought I observed two things: the conviction that the people stoically somehow would pull through; and also that the right of a starving family to survival would impress villagers as greater than the property privilege of careless owners who left things "to be stolen."

The source of the thievery, *Messaggero* felt, were the shantytowns and cave dwellings around the ancient city. Eternal Rome had had a population of 2,000,000 at the height of the empire, had sunk to being a community of 17,000 in rags and ruin during the Middle Ages, had returned to 250,000 at the time of the fall of the Papal States in 1870, and then—from just before World War II to the end of the fifties—had blown up from 1,000,000 to the old peak of 2,000,000 once again. As the sixties started, Rome was on the way to 3,000,000 for the first time in its "perpetual" history.

The slum dwellers came from the eroded, backward and miserable hills of the poor Italian south. They hoped for bright lights, jobs and security in the capital, and found squalor, disease and the lure of prostitution and theft instead. The scandal of wealth beside poverty, of social injustice and great temptation, were brought forcibly to Rome's attention: Communists claimed 100,000 recruits inside the Eternal City and even succeeded in thrusting a pro-Communist administration on the province of Rome.

Yet even in the misery of the Red belt, some inheritance from the ancient Christians remained. I walked along the ruins of the ancient aqueduct, seeing the one-room homes made by walling up 2,000-year-old arches. Boys in their teens melted lead in a bonfire. The stealing of lead pipe for the metal was a postwar plague in Rome. A pretty girl of four caught my eye. Her mother had draped three miniature bulls' horns around her neck, a pagan protection against the evil eye Romans have dreaded since the time of Caesar. She wore a replica of a horseshoe, too. But beside them all was a cross. The mother was appealing to all the gods—to Jupiter and to Jesus—to spare her little girl. It was not orthodox piety but it came from a desperate and prayerful heart.

I went to a Communist cell meeting one night a hundred yards from the Vatican. St. Peter's was the source of all troubles, and one day "we'll go up there and burn it down," the shabby young orator assured his excited audience. The forty present in the cramped, narrow room nodded approval, but even they were far less Communist and more Christian than they knew. They welcomed me, a fact-collecting American reporter, with all the gentility that Rome has learned through her many human and

Christian centuries, and we all parted in a glow of good fellowship. St. Peter's received no calls from arsonists, and no doubt all those who crowded the cell meeting have been up to the Vatican Basilica for frequent papal blessings since.

Just what one is to make of the Roman and the Italian is a subject to which Pope John put his mind on at least one occasion when he was welcoming Giovanni Gronchi, the Italian President, on an official call.

"It is still earth here after all, Mr. President," the Pope said of Italy. "In that it is the same as everywhere else. But the reasons for hope are more valid than those for fearing."

Italy, John added, has a good people "still inspired by the religion of their fathers."

By and large there is little cruelty among the Italians, a converted rabbi and priest told me as we foreign residents discussed our fellow Romans.

After the extraordinary event of the Christian victory of nearly 2,000 years ago, Rome—deep down—was Christian in its attitudes even if Italian Catholicism was all but incomprehensible to Americans, the ex-rabbi said.

One close friend, a Communist, always crossed himself before meals, the priest recalled. "He told me he didn't know why; it just seemed the right thing to do."

Only about a third of the Italians went to Sunday Mass, although only a fraction of one per cent considered themselves non-Catholic. Many were "wheel" or even "horizontal" Catholics. They had nothing to do with church except to go there on the wheels of a baby carriage for baptism, on those of a hired car for marriage, and on those of a hearse for the final rites. The "horizontal" Christians skipped the church weddings and contented themselves with baptismal and funeral contacts with spiritual ministration.

To an American Catholic accustomed to the idea that Sunday Mass is a grave obligation, the Italian catalogue of kinds of Catholics was astonishing. Less than half were *pratticanti*—practicing Catholics—who obeyed the main church rules about annual confession and regular mass attendance, and only about 5 per cent were *fanatici*—literally, fanatical Catholics—who took Church injunctions earnestly, worked in the "Catholic Action" organization as helpers of the penniless clergy, and in general tried to be what Americans call "good Catholics."

One could say that the center of gravity in Italy after the ancient marvel of the conversion of the Emperor Constantine had shifted back a bit toward paganism, even if not far enough to actually offer incense to the old gods overthrown by heroic Christian martyrs.

There was, for instance, a flavor of paganism or at least of devotion bordering on hysteria in the semiannual pilgrimages to Mount Autore in the Abruzzi east of Rome. My wife Mary and I made the pilgrimage one night. Our goal was a cave about 1,000 feet up the wall of a cliff. For as long as any peasants of the area could remember, it had been the custom to climb to the cave on two annual feast days—those of the Holy Trinity and of Saint Anna, the Madonna's mother. Paul Geier, an American Embassy attaché, and his aristocratic Austrian wife Gabriella came with us. We started in from Vallepietra, an 800-year-old village of fieldstone and cobbled walks which has never risen above its farm origins. A parish church was crowded with an excited congregation. One man in an ecstasy of anguished devotion kissed the dusty floor, begging the divine powers to help him with his insuperable problems. Women held sick, tired, weeping babies aloft in prayers for miraculous healings.

To one of a cooler Anglo-Saxon background the scene was disturbing, unattractive. We left the church quickly, had thick, black coffees for the long night road ahead of us, and asked the man behind the shiny coffee machine whether we would find our way.

"Find your way?" He was astounded.

"The trail," he said, "will be as crowded as this." He held up two fingers side by side.

He was right. In the whole of the ascent, from midnight to 3 A.M., we were unable to take more than three long strides without having to hold back again to keep from stepping on the feet ahead of us. Thousands were on their way through the moonless night heading for the same mountainside grotto. The men who exploit piety were there, too. Beside bonfires at the trail's edge were a legion of horrors, men with all sorts of mutilations and cripplings, begging for our pennies. The peasants gave them a cent or two at a time, in the same way that the Arab conquerors of the area had done 1,000 years earlier and still do on the Mediterranean's south shore. Italy has known everything and forgets nothing. Perhaps that part of our night was Saracen.

Many carried four-foot candles. Most chanted over and over again the hymn of the Trinity, a strange melody not unlike the songs of the Arab casbahs:

> *Viva, viva, sempre viva,*
> *Quelle tre Persone Divine!*
> May they live, may they live,
> May they live on forever,
> Those three Divine Persons!

A leader would sing a verse, and then the whole of a hamlet would chant the refrain again. The song beat into the brain until it was inaudible, but for a day later it echoed in the mind.

Each hamlet was led by a standard bearer with the community's name and the picture of the Trinity—three Christs side by side. That concept of God the Father, God the Son, and God the Holy Spirit still prevails at Mount Autore, although it has been banned elsewhere in the Catholic Church since the Renaissance.

Periodically a husky man at the head of his village group would bawl instructions:

"San Felice! [The people of the village of San Felice] *Reposo*"—Rest.

There was something Arabic in that, too. The cry of authority of a strong man. Cardboard suitcases would come down off women's bandannaed heads and there would be five minutes of repose.

All ages and both sexes were in the line. On one steep stretch a heavy old woman assured me she would make it.

"Saint Anna," she said, "will get me there."

Some on the road told me they were Communists. They were willing, they implied, to try anything.

We reached the frozen ledge just before dawn. Scores sprawled next to great bonfires, fighting off the chill. We had made the climb the right way—neither in the heat of a sunny midsummer day, or lounging in the icy cliff-edge night air. Mass was at dawn and we were all soon on our way home again. Before going we saw the triple Christ of 1450 on the cave wall—the object of the devotion. Nearby were Roman ruins which have made some scholars think that the strange cave has been a place of prayer since pagan times, perhaps originally to the gods of Greece. For all that is known, the pilgrimage may be another of the relics of pagan antiquity baptized as Christian and converted to Jesus's cult.

It is thus a strange land of paradoxes in which Peter's successor has his see, a land pagan and Christian, often illiterate but frequently wise, prey to many of the failings of the flesh but deeply human; a land with a rich share of wrongdoers but with saints in every post-Constantine generation. Even as a reporter in a mere dozen years in Rome I met some of the saints: Alcide de Gasperi, the writer on foreign affairs in *L'Osservatore Romano* who saved Italy from Communism as Premier after World War II, and passed a half hour each morning meditating some passage of St. Paul recommended to him by his nun daughter; Giorgio La Pira, the eccentric mayor of Florence, who wore the dazzling white socks of a Dominican, lived in Savonarola's old monastery, and successfully fought Communism by well-motivated but quixotic and illegal appropriations of empty private houses for the homeless; Giuseppe Dossetti, a Catholic party deputy, whose friends read their prayer books during dull moments in the parliament, and who decided at forty-six to be a priest. In a land so often and so well attuned to what is kind, gentle and serene, it was easy as a foreigner to begin thinking, as I did after a few years, that I was at "home in Rome."

# 23. Vatican State, Minute and Mighty

The improbable is always possible in the strange little world of the Pope's 108-acre Vatican kingdom, so I should not have been surprised one day to find myself and a shirt-sleeved priest bombing beside St. Peter's Basilica for the lost stadium of Nero. Past and future, science and faith, the greatest concepts and many humble people, meet and mix among astonishing contrasts in the tiny area where the spiritual sovereigns of Catholicism are also earthly kings.

The priest was erudite J. Joseph Lynch, a New York Jesuit who had been my college professor of physics, and who had long directed the earthquake-detecting station at Fordham University, one of America's and the world's main observatories of the type. Father Lynch knew, of course, that diggers who removed 3,000 truckloads of earth from beneath St. Peter's during the forties and fifties had not found the Circus of Nero beside which St. Peter is said to have been crucified and buried. An old Roman Christian tradition had it that St. Peter's itself rested on the walls of the old circus. The excavators, encouraged by the science-minded Pius XII, had probed 20 feet down to the virgin clay of Vatican Hill and had found no masonry earlier than the fourth century A.D. It had been a disappointment to many who had hoped for a dramatic proof of the Catholic tradition that the first of Christ's Apostles had ruled in Rome as the first Christian bishop and that he had died there. It was Father Lynch's idea that by setting off miniature earthquakes—small dynamite charges—

he could "read" the underground contours, perhaps detecting the buried stadium that way. We bombed all one afternoon but the circus remained hidden.

Bombing for the relics of Nero struck lounging nearby Swiss Guards and pontifical gendarmes as no more unlikely than a thousand other occurrences in a little state midway between earth and heaven where so many apparent irreconcilables, so many opposed aspects of life, meet and somehow mold. If all Rome and Italy have their paradoxes, the tiny Vatican State sees them multiplied.

Pius IX had explained to diplomats in the final disillusioned hours of the 1,000-year-old Papal States that as a churchman he felt that he needed political and territorial independence in order to exercise an impartial spiritual mission. He had been arrested as a young priest on a trip to Spain and had learned the harshness of the captive's lot as he smuggled out messages inside loaves of bread.

If political independence was desirable, it was well to have the Pope relieved of the tax-collecting, judging, punishing and general administration of a large state, as Pius X indicated to the future Pope John XXIII. What was the happy medium? One of Pius XII's most intimate associates felt that although the 108 Vatican acres were "perhaps too small," it was high good fortune that Mussolini had not restored the whole city of Rome in 1929. For years that possibility had been discussed.

"During World War II," he said, "Italy would have had tremendous leverage against the Pope if all the supplies for more than one million Romans had to come through the Italian lines. As it is, the Vatican is so small that supplies reach it almost unnoticed."

For years I wondered how independent the 108-acre state really was. Fifty nations from Protestant England to Catholic France, Moslem Egypt and Shintoist Japan sent diplomatic envoys in implicit recognition of Vatican Hill independence, but the United States limited itself during the war and immediate postwar period to sending a "personal Presidential representative" to the Pope. The reality of Vatican independence remained in a cloud as far as American official policy was concerned.

I was convinced finally that the Vatican did have its independence. It was swallowed up inside the western side of the city of Rome, and its military defenses and relationship with diplomats were beset by a thousand peculiarities, but the moral guaranty of world opinion was a protection which surely daunted Italy and even gave Germany pause during World War II.

Aides of Pius XII told of one incident when Nazis took prisoners at the Russicum, the seminary for priests who may one day be sent to convert an ex-Communist Russia. This seminary, like many other Catholic institutions in Rome, had given asylum to men fleeing wartime Europe's Axis masters. Pius XII gave the German commander of Rome a twelve-hour ultimatum and the captives were returned. The Germans dared not arouse the tens of millions of Catholics behind their lines.

When in the late fifties Italian troops surrounded tiny San Marino, a village-sized ancient republic in the Central Italian Apennines, forcing the downfall of a Communist Government, Western diplomats murmured that the measures were highhanded.

"Imagine if Italy dared do that to the Vatican," they said.

It was inconceivable that the Italians should.

Inside their little state the popes had all the attributes of independence, lawyers pointed out. They had territory, citizens to govern, an armed force, coinage, postage stamps. Most spectacularly there were the accredited ambassadors and ministers plenipotentiary. There was the world's fourth most powerful shortwave radio installation (after America's, Russia's and Britain's). And there was also the groundwork for the Vatican's own merchant navy and civil air force. In 1951 the Vatican signed the 1921 Barcelona Agreement on shipping for landlocked nations, and in the fifties Vatican officials insisted that the wording of the 1929 pact with Italy allowed an air force "of, say, one plane for the Pope and one for the Secretary of State." This has remained theoretical.

The Vatican diplomatic corps well illustrated the anomalies of the small state.

Although Britain, France and other nations sent some of their shrewdest career officers, all envoys had to live in a "foreign country" while serving near the pontifical court. There was no room in the Vatican, so all the diplomats dwelt in "foreign" Rome. "All" is not quite the right word, since some lived farther away. Because the Vatican refused to let the same man double as envoy to Italy and to the Holy See, a duplication which might belittle Vatican independence, the not very richly financed diplomatic corps of Pakistan—as one example—had to tell its ambassador to Rome to ignore the Vatican officially, while the Pakistan envoy to Madrid was instructed to function as the formal tie with the Holy See. There was no objection to diplomats away from Italy doubling as legates to the papal court. El Salvador, too, told its Madrid envoy to represent it at the Vatican. India's envoy doubled in Switzerland, and Liberia's in France.

Italy and the Holy See exchanged ambassadors, and it was no secret that many pious laymen in the Italian Diplomatic Corps longed for the Holy See post. Not only did it mean contact with the placid spiritual world around St. Peter's, but it meant living at home in the rich Roman sunshine. To one ambassador in an important but depressing Communist capital, postwar Premier De Gasperi gave a tart refusal when the envoy begged for the Rome assignment.

"You're selfish," the Catholic Premier said. "Whenever I want anything from the Vatican I can always use the telephone."

The papal nuncio to Italy was one of the very few envoys of the world who could report home with a local telephone call. Perhaps the only other one was the French Ambassador to the North Atlantic Treaty Organization, the Western military alliance, in Paris.

The nuncio's situation was matched by that of the Italian Ambassador in the late fifties, Bartolomeo Migone. His own foreign office was nearer to his residence than the Secretariate of State, and as a matter of fact he had to drive past his ministry to get to the Holy See.

The military defenses of the little Vatican State contained their own great share of oddities. The Vatican was at once the most militarized and most peaceful, the best-defended and the least-defended of states. A third of its 1,000 citizens were under arms. The 100 Swiss Guards enjoyed a double citizenship while on duty—the Vatican's and their own native Swiss. The three Vatican entrances were watched closely, but as the head of the 150-man Vatican gendarmerie admitted, it was nearly impossible to screen the thousands of daily visitors, taking care to treat bishops and other dignitaries properly and managing at the same time to comb out those with unwholesome intentions.

"I wish the regulations were stricter," Major Balthazar Dieter, Assistant Commander of the Swiss Guard, confided.

Although the gendarmes and Swiss, backed by the fifty-man Noble Guard and the several score members of the Palatine Guard, volunteer Roman laymen, provided fairly tight defenses inside the Vatican walls, a further peculiarity was that a substantial part of the "national" territory was patrolled by another state. The huge St. Peter's Square was in the Pope's kingdom, but by agreement was generally controlled by Italian police. The Vatican could reclaim the area for ceremonies at will. A white line on the pavement at the edge of the Square marked the frontier. Anyone could wander across, making it one of the world's least watched borders, but those who wanted to go farther inside the walls had to wait while police telephoned Vatican officials to be sure the visitor was welcome.

How serious were the ceremonial swords and helmets of the Pope's Noble Guard attendants? How much martial determination lay behind the antique steel breastplates of the yellow-gold-red-suited Swiss? More, perhaps, than camera-minded tourists would think. The new recruits from the German and French cantons of the Catholic part of Switzerland were sworn in each year on June 6th, the anniversary of the battle of St. Peter's Square in 1527 when the Swiss Guard was almost wiped out. The Swiss mercenaries, with a tradition of scarcely one generation behind them at the time, fought successfully to cover the flight of Giulio de' Medici, Pope Clement VII. The gendarmes, too, looked back to battles against brigands and others in the middle of the nineteenth century when the popes still ruled central Italy. The Swiss generally carried their medieval spears—halberds—which were not much of a twentieth-century weapon, but they also had automatic pistols and periodically held unpublicized target practice.

Philosophers and college professors, as well as veterans of the Swiss Army top command, find their way into the leadership of the Swiss Guards. It was one of the former who assured me that "although we are the most peaceful soldiers in the world, we are sworn to defend the Pope and his successors to the death and there is no doubt we would do it."

A painting of the 1527 massacre looked down on the young Swiss as they ate in their private beer hall just west of St. Peter's. Their discipline was harsh, with 48 hours on call alternating with 24 hours of often interrupted rest. Language classes and organized sports often interfered with their time off. Pay, even with Pope John's raises, was only $125 a month. Few men re-enlisted after the minimum two-years service, but most of them were proud and often sent younger brothers or sons to succeed them.

"We would fight only if attacked, and even then we would be very careful," the Swiss officer said. "For we know we are the soldiers of the Pope. We know that he does not defend himself with arms. His defenses are prayers—those of the spirit."

Even so the Vatican maintained a jail though it was reportedly used mostly as a storeroom. One of the few postwar inmates was a young man of otherwise good record and background who was caught pilfering in the Vatican Museum. Church authorities were moved to compassion, and to spare the youth worse at the hands of Italian justice, locked him up in the Vatican for thirty fairly tranquil and relatively contented days.

Most of the other attributes of a state were crowded into the small territory. There was a pharmacy run by the Fatebene Fratelli—the do-good brotherhood—nurses to popes, and merchants of such implausible home-produced articles as a stomach pacifier ("fifteen drops in water") sold under the national coat of arms, the papal crown and keys. That was not all, for there was also the pharmacy's own rum in bottles decorated with pictures of a swaggering pirate.

The pharmacy reflected the tax-free condition of the little state. There and at the grocery across the street prices were 15 per cent under Rome's. Only Vatican employees and accredited diplomats were allowed to shop, but business never slackened. The finances of the Vatican, eternally touch and go and especially so in the wake of Pope John's $1,000,000-a-year in raises, drew no supplement from the low-paid, untaxed Vatican citizens, but depended largely, as it had since the fall of the Papal States, on the annual offering—Peter's Pence—from Catholics of the world. There were some earnings from the $85,000,000 Italy gave the Vatican in 1929 in exchange for a waiver of claims on the lost Papal States, but the whole invested Vatican capital was under $100,000,000, according to Cardinal Domenico Tardini. For the headquarters of a Church of 500,000,000 it was small, and the frayed cuffs and chipped paint to be seen everywhere in the state reflected it. That was so despite the eternal and universal suspicion that a Church with so many chapels, schools, hospitals, asylums and monasteries must be rich in capital.

Since the sixteenth century the Augustinian Order of priests had had the privilege of guarding the Vatican treasures. It was one young American of that society who took us to see them. There was the gold tube for tasting the Pope's wine as an ancient safeguard against poisoning at solemn masses. There was a set of lace and embroidered vestments on which thirty subjects of the Austrian Emperor had reportedly toiled for sixteen years. There was a tiara studded with bits of colored paper to represent gems stolen by Napoleon. Perhaps most impressive was a chalice covered with diamonds and rubies which had been pried from a saddle and bridle a Turkish sultan had given to a pope. All in all it was not such an overwhelming collection, certainly not when compared with others I had seen at Versailles or even at the Kremlin. Perhaps my twelve-year-old son Bill was justified in letting his mind wander.

"What became of the saddle?" he wanted to know.

In the early fifties the Vatican population over whom the Pope maintained total executive, legislative and judicial power consisted of 1,031 persons. Three-quarters were men, and there were 57 children. Cardinals, Vatican department heads including laymen, the Swiss Guards, and wives and children of the laymen made up

the bulk of the citizenry. There was no military draft, even for
young men in the families of the laymen, but most of the Vatican's younger subjects lost citizenship and became Italians at
twenty-five. In one way it was a dying state, for the pastor of
St. Anna's, the tiny parish church for the Vatican population
opposite the Swiss Guard barracks, reported that in the course
of one year he had conducted 15 funerals and performed no
baptisms. "Immigration" in the creation of new cardinals, the
recruiting of Swiss and the appointing of clergy and laymen, kept
the state alive, however.

The money of the Pope's kingdom was based on an agreement
with Italy. The Pope was authorized to put about $80,000 worth
of coins a year into circulation. They were identical with the
Italian lira except that they bore the pontiff's portrait. The Italian
and papal lire were interchangeable as legal currency in the two
countries. One of the papal coins showed up in change in Rome
about once every two weeks, I observed. In addition, the Pope
had the Italian-recognized right to coin in gold as often as he
wished. The Vatican issued 1,000 to 2,000 such pieces a year.
Their face value was 20¢ but real value was $8.

To see a pope's head on a Vatican coin always struck me as
odd, but the coins were far less colorful than those in the heyday
of the papal state two and three centuries earlier. At that time
it was Vatican custom to use appropriate mottoes warning the
holders of the coins not to set too much store by them. Some such
mottoes were: "It is better to give than to receive," "One should
lay up treasures in heaven," "The real pauper is one who is
miserly," "You won't find peace in this; the heart is where one's
treasures are," and "This is the root of all evil."

As a member of the International Postal Union the Vatican
issued postage stamps and drew a significant bit of income from
philatelists through the sale of the five or six annual sets. Although
the little state was shorter than most airports and did not see
its first helicopter until the late fifties, the Vatican post office
issued airmail stamps, too. Sometimes it decorated them with
angels. The Vatican was the only state in the world with a fourth
of its post offices on a roof top (St. Peter's, a surface so big it is

used also for a gift shop and a photographer's studio), and it was also probably the only state with no street addresses. The Vatican postman knew where everyone lived. The Vatican was happy to be in the Postal Union, one more recognition and reassurance of its freedom, and in 1949 issued two stamps to commemorate the union's seventy-fifth anniversary. The Vatican recalled, too, that the popes had their own stamps before 1870. In 1952 a series commemorated the 100th anniversary of the first pontifical postage stamp and reproduced it. It portrayed a top-hatted coachman setting off from St. Peter's with a carriage piled high with bundles—mail for the brigand-infested roads of the peninsula.

Among the most serious of the attributes of independence was the $3,000,000 Vatican radio station with its headquarters clustered around the 12-foot-thick walls of the tower which Pope Saint Leo IV built in the Vatican gardens in the middle years of the ninth century. The 1,000-year-old tower was filled with equipment for sending code radiograms to nuncios. A microwave radio bridge connected the radio offices with a 2-mile-square plot north of Rome where most of the rest of the transmitters were in place. The plot, 10 times the size of the Vatican State, was guarded by the papal troops. It was granted an extraterritorial status when Pius XII insisted that no adequate radio could be squeezed inside his tiny kingdom and that sovereignty demanded better than the primitive transmitter the Italian pioneer of wireless telegraphy, Guglielmo Marconi, had set up for Pius XI after the 1929 Vatican-Italian agreement. Using nearly 30 languages, the Vatican radio beamed Church orders behind the Iron Curtain and was paid the honor of such heavy jamming that reception was sometimes difficult even in Rome. But as one Iron Curtain Catholic wrote "the medicine is arriving." With no commercials it was always hand to mouth for the Vatican Radio, and its refugee priest announcers received Spartan pay.

Of all the papal kingdom's claims to independence the most important was reflected in my bombing expedition with Father Lynch. As Monsignor William Carew of the Secretariate of State told a group of newspapermen one day, what was important was that "it all started here." What gave Vatican Hill its power was the Christian tradition that Peter had lived and died there. What were the historic facts? Few Christian events of recent generations were so important as the story Rome correspondents covered piece by piece in the years just after World War II—the excavations at what was believed to be St. Peter's tomb. Several times I went down two stories beneath the floor of the great basilica to study the work. This was what was found:

Under the floor of the old basilica was a pagan cemetery of the second century after Christ. Constantine, the first Christian Emperor, had moved 40,000 cubic yards of earth to carve a platform for the first St. Peter's on the slant of Vatican Hill. Something must have drawn him to that especially difficult site, for good flat land was available nearby. The contention of Pius XII was that Peter's tomb was the reason. No sarcophagus was found and the few human bones discovered beneath the crossing of the great basilica could not, of course, be definitely attributed to any individual. Although as Father Kirschbaum, the great Jesuit archaeologist, commented, "No one would have doubted that they were the remains, let us say, of the Emperor Augustus, if similar evidence had pointed in that direction; it is only because these would be such important relics."

The work showed that Christian pilgrims had often worshiped at the site in the years just before Constantine erected the first St. Peter's. Cryptic wall scratchings were interpreted as devotional appeals to Peter. A simple shrine dated to about 150 A.D.

"Whatever it proves, for good or ill, we have here something that is fundamental," one Roman scholar commented.

Constantine had covered a holy place which had probably been associated with the birth of the world's greatest single religious force. With that spot beneath St. Peter's, the power of the Pope seemed sure of a life extending far into the earth's veiled future.

# 24. Vatican Reporter

Nothing is so intangible as man's relationship with God, and very little is so insistent and insatiable as a reporter's hunt for quick "hard" news. In that contrast lies much of the explanation of a side of the Vatican which concerned me immediately—its incredibly poor press relations.

The word "propaganda" was invented in Rome for it traces its origin to the Vatican's Sacred Congregation for the *Propaganda Fide*—the Propagation of the Faith. There is no doubt that through the centuries the congregation for foreign missions has worked marvels in spreading the Catholic religion, but it is also true that even at the start of the sixties the Vatican still failed to make use of the immense potentialities for "propaganda," that *Propaganda Fide* represented by the 200-man, 25-nation corps of Rome foreign correspondents.

The situation was reflected in a conversation between an American radio network correspondent and his newly arrived successor. The two had talked about the Italian Government and the Mediterranean and the frustrations of news coverage in a city with a midafternoon siesta. Everything seemed to have been touched upon, and then suddenly the new man raised a finger.

"Oh yes," he said, "what about the Vatican? How do I cover that?"

"Forget it," the veteran said. "It's impossible."

This was similar to what had happened twenty years earlier when a Chicago newsman was appalled to discover that the bulk of Vatican information came from an unofficial tipster—a monsignor who published a daily typewritten sheet of news and rumors. The monsignor, a former staff member of the Secretariate of State, who was on a *tu* basis with the Pope, seemed to know what was "going on," but no responsible newspaper correspondent felt sure of himself as he wrote articles based on Monsignor Pucci's handouts.

(It should be explained that a *tu* relationship in a Latin country is similar to an Anglo-Saxon's "first-name basis." Just as a Frenchman uses the plural *vous* in addressing all but his intimates, so does the Italian customarily employ the third person *lei* rather than the second person singular *tu*. It is roughly the way it would be in English if it were proper to call none but closest friends "you" and all the rest "Your Excellency.")

The American reporter determined to have nothing to do with dubious intermediaries. He would try the confident, direct approach used at home in Chicago. He went to the Vatican, managed to get through as far as the Secretariate of State (in itself an accomplishment), and asked to see Cardinal Pacelli, the reigning pontiff's "prime minister."

"What is it about?" he was asked.

"Nothing in particular," the reporter replied frankly. "I wanted to ask what is going on. It may or may not be news. I'd like to hear. If it's news I'll send it."

The reporter was assured that on that particular day the Secretary of State had nothing for him and that no interview would be necessary. The same exchange was repeated for a week. The following Monday the defeated reporter subscribed to Monsignor Pucci's service.

In my personal experience with Vatican coverage over two decades, I saw improvements that culminated in Pope John's decision to have a special commission on press, radio and television as part of the preparation for Catholicism's twenty-first ecumenical council. Significantly an American, Archbishop Martin O'Connor, was placed in charge. There was some closing of the gap separating journalists and churchmen. Thanks on that were due to American Cardinal Spellman and Bishop Thomas Gorman, a United States Catholic specialist in press relations. Fundamentally, though, conditions remained abysmally poor.

I recall one papal ceremony to which I had been given a ticket stamped CIRCULATE FREELY. I worked my way up among densely packed seminarians, nuns, ordinary laymen, diplomats and other dignitaries, until I was within twenty feet of a glimpse of the Pope. A brilliantly uniformed papal gendarme spotted me and blocked the way. The cold war between the Vatican police and the press showed in the young man's frosty expression.

"You can't stay here," he said. "Move on. Look it says: 'Circulate freely.' That means you must keep circulating!"

The frustrations of coverage were endless, perhaps most of all for photographers but certainly for writers, too. When I began as a Vatican reporter in the weeks just before World War II, journalists as such were excluded from papal audiences. A prince of one of Europe's old families received an invitation to a papal reception, and out of scruple sent word that he would accept with pleasure but that he felt it should be known that he was a newspaperman. The invitation was withdrawn. My own twenty-minute talk with Pius XII was arranged on a personal basis. It was specified that it was not for a "journalist seeking an interview." I had no authorization to repeat the contents of the conversation.

Far more serious, even at the start of the sixties there was still no authorized spokesman to whom news correspondents could go with their "queries": What is the Vatican attitude on the Catholic Kennedy as American President? What is the Vatican view on the morality of the atom bomb? What was the Holy See opinion on President Truman's dismissal of General MacArthur in Korea in the debate over MacArthur's desire to spread war to the endless Chinese mainland?

In the late fifties reporters were getting copies of the most important papal addresses in English, French and other languages as soon as the Pope started speaking or a little earlier, but correspondents were still groggy with the battle of years which they had waged before the Holy See would provide texts in good time. When I arrived in 1939 the custom in one American news agency was to have two Italian male stenographers glued to a radio set typing the Pope's words as they came over the Vatican transmitter.

An American staffer would snatch the bits as they came from the stenographers' typewriters and would have his story in thousands of newspaper and radio offices seconds later. Static was often bad.

"We'd get ten words out of twenty," an agency chief told me philosophically. "We'd put them in quotes and improvise the rest."

"We could never get any curvy quotes," another agency reporter lamented. "We'd just have to play it safe and dull."

By "curvy quotes" he meant the most colorful, dramatic and controversial comments of the pontiff—the ones most likely to make big and perhaps sensational headlines. Popes with a stern and ancient moral code often clashed with easier modern attitudes, and as reporters knew, the liveliest copy grew out of such conflicts. A "safe, dull" story risked being spiked altogether, so no one was contented.

When the Vatican finally began delivering quicker texts on the main addresses one agency man had a routine he followed faithfully.

"I'd just turn to the last two pages and start writing," he confided. "I knew the main point was generally there. But often I'd find the real story fifteen minutes later, somewhere else. Then I'd top with a new lead."

"Too late," a former managing editor of a major American daily interjected as the three of us compared notes. "By that time I would have had the first lead down with the printers and it would cost too much to reset."

Andrew Berding, later an American Assistant Secretary of State, and at the time head of the Associated Press Bureau in Rome, was one of many agency chiefs who visited the Vatican Secretariate of State in the years before World War II to beg for quick texts—preferably advances—and to urge the establishment of a press office. It was essential in view of split-second deadlines, he urged.

"But what's all the hurry?" was the answer.

Papal speeches were written for the years, even for the centuries. What difference did a few hours make?

The difference, an agency official said, was that if his opposition got into newspaper offices thirty seconds ahead of him the editors would start with that and stay with it even if the slower agency came through later with a better story.

The contrast in views between the eternity-minded and cautious Vatican and the news-hungry reporters with their emphasis on this day, and even this second, had appalling consequences. The Vatican knew that what sounded reasonable and necessary in one part of the world, such as in Latin Italy, might be badly out of step in another, such as the Anglo-Saxon United States. For that reason there was a probably invincible reluctance to provide correspondents with a counterpart of President Eisenhower's Jim Hagerty—an official spokesman. The Vatican, after insistence by American bishops, did set up a press office, but it was twice removed from the official source reporters wanted. It was called, not the Vatican News Bureau but "the Press Office of *L' Osservatore Romano*," the spokesman of a daily newspaper of only "semi-official" status. *L'Osservatore Romano* was so "unofficial" that it was omitted from the *Annuario Pontificio*, the Vatican yearbook which lists all Catholic bishops of the world and all official Church organs.

What the reporters wanted was an "infallible" Church source —someone who could commit the Pope and the Catholic Church on the main issues of the instant. That was just what the Vatican could never permit. In the first ninety years after the controversial proclamation of the Catholic doctrine of papal infallibility, the pontiff had invoked the awesome right rarely. Some said it had not been used more than a half-dozen times. All other papal statements, and even more so, those of Vatican subordinates, were debatable and therefore not necessarily binding on Catholics. Reporters knew that what made the big headlines were reliable pronouncements that compelled the adherence of all Catholics and for better or worse sometimes set them in conflict with local public opinion. The Holy See was determined, for reasons of doctrine, common sense and prudence, not to create such situations. The Church understandably prefers that its teachings be presented and interpreted to its communicants through the clergy rather than through the popular press. Consequently reporters found themselves up against goodwilled, good-natured but often uninformed Luciano Casimirri as head of the *L'Osservatore Romano* press office.

Very often if not always Signor Casimirri replied to correspondents that he did not know the answer to their questions. Sometimes he told them that their inquiries touched matters bordering on secrets of religion. The temptation to cover more and more with that reply was great, so newsmen were not surprised when, early in Pope John's pontificate, Signor Casimirri refused information on the shooting of Colonel Robert Nunlist, head of the Swiss Guards, on the ground that the matter was "too delicate." Ill and disgruntled, a guard who had been discharged had fired several shots at Nunlist, slightly wounding him. Within hours, however, despite Signor Casimirri's reticence, the story was out.

With the goodwill of various Church leaders, including Pius XII and some Americans, and with the drive of the newspapermen, the news stories of the Vatican became progressively better told. In the two-way approach the correspondents certainly did their share, but not always by methods "which we would like to have advertised," as one agency official confessed. "Tips," salaries, outright bribes and ingenious sales talks were put forward, and functionaries who received bitterly poor wages often succumbed. For all the loftiness of its ideals the Vatican is staffed by men, sinners all as one can see "if one peers into one's own conscience," in Pope John's words. One agency offered small sums to a printer in *L'Osservatore Romano* for the names of prelates named to be bishops. *L'Osservatore*'s composing room got such news first. The planting of a false name exposed the offender after awhile, according to the legend in the Rome press corps. Another Vatican employee, a layman who handled papal statements in the hours just before their release, was hired by several news organizations and provided them with many a "scoop" if only with the text of a speech already delivered and not yet distributed for general circulation. From the Pope's own point of view such premature release might have little importance, but as far as competitive news agencies were concerned it was a major breakdown in what correspondents considered a fair and proper equal access to the news.

I saw an example of how bad Vatican press relations could be on my first Roman assignment, just before the election of Pius XII in 1939. One agency had a series of mysterious exclusives on the health of the dying Pius XI. "The Pope has uremia; the Pope has had a heart attack." The agency had "tipped" an employee in the pharmacy of the Fatebene Fratelli and was getting copies of all prescriptions being sent up to the papal apartments. A medical student on the staff would study the medicines and tell his chief "That's for uremic poisoning" or "Adrenaline is used that way only for heart attacks, as far as I can figure here in my medical book." The agency would take a chance, publishing its informed guesses about the Pope's declining health as facts. "On average," the agency reported later, "we were right."

Newsmen got promises from the engineers on Vatican Radio to flash them the first word of the Pope's imminently expected death. One agency was sure that the Vatican's own news outlet would get the information quickest. Monsignor Pucci was briefed on how important the flash was. One news bureau induced international telephone operators to open wires for it to London as soon as any other agency asked for a similar line.

"I figured that as soon as they told me I had a line it would mean that something was up that I should know about," the bureau manager explained.

Aldo Forte of the United Press seems to have got the first flash. The night of Pius XI's death he told a friend, the man in charge of the Vatican firehouse, that he "had" to get back into the little state after other newspapermen had to leave at 11 P.M. The old man hesitated, but for friendship's sake reopened the bronze doors at 1 A.M. It was a long night as the old codger told of his unsuccessful attempts to learn English and the firemen played forty-card *scoppone*, an Italian card game. Looking down on the small group was a picture of Benedict XV bestowing a blessing and expressing the hope that "you will never have to prove what good firemen you are."

At 5 A.M. Cardinal Lorenzo Lauro hurried across the cobble-stoned Courtyard of St. Damasus toward the Palace of the Pope. He was the Pope's confessor. Forte dialed United Press and a line was readied to the news-distribution center in London. At the same moment, unknown to the U.P., an opposition agency was alerted by the telephone operator and the news-gathering machinery began to grind. At 5:31 A.M. the head fireman received a telephone call from Monsignor Giovanni Montini, the future cardinal who later became a strong possibility for election to the Papacy in 1958. The fireman's white walrus mustaches quivered and tears formed in his eyes. The monsignor had told him to push open the bronze doors to "let out the soul of the Pope." To do so would be to respect one of the strangest of the Vatican's ancient traditions.

"Is he dead?" Forte asked.

"*Morto, sì*"—"Yes, he is dead"—the fireman said.

Within a minute U.P.'s clients around the world had the flash: OFFICIAL, POPE DIED AT 5:31.

For his pains Forte was placed under a thirty-minute arrest in a corner an hour later. As soon as Monsignor Pucci arrived, excited and upset, he whispered indignantly to an officer of the papal guard, nodded significantly toward Forte, and presumably ordered the brief incarceration.

Days later, according to the story of another agency head, a priest signaled from a window of the conclave area giving one American news company a few seconds' beat on the election of Pius XII. To get that help the agency had pleaded that "Catholic news means an immense amount to us in New York, Chicago, San Francisco. You must help us. We always try to get our Catholic news straight." The beat was worth $5,000 but the priest refused any reward until finally he accepted the pair of binoculars the agency had used to catch the conclave signal.

The dismally poor Vatican press relationship could be traced back at least to the middle of the nineteenth century when the modern, democratic press, clamoring for the end of Church rule in central Italy, was temporarily suppressed in the Pope's fief of Rome. The press revived and *L'Osservatore Romano* was founded in 1861 to defend the Church against the liberals and to counter-attack. That mood of almost total warfare between the free press and the Vatican persisted throughout the nineteenth century.

The first press photographer at the Vatican was Giuseppe Felici. A poor farmer's son, he arrived in papal Rome from the hills of central Italy in 1863 not long after the invention of photography. He set up a camera shop and soon got permission to enter the Vatican to take the Pope's picture. There was no question of action shots such as news agencies would want later in the middle years of the twentieth century. There was no illustrated press to serve. Felici contented himself with stiff, formal photos. It was a rare year when he took more than twenty exposures, less than a day's shooting in the mid-nineteen hundreds. In those days Leo XIII had the reputation in Rome of being so astute that "with Bismarck and [Italian Premier] Crispi, he could run the world," but for Felici the problem was a hard one: how to make the wrinkled, not at all handsome old man, bent beneath his huge tiara, "look the Pope." That was Leo's wish and that was Signor Felici's task. Saint Pius X, remembered as a fatherly man, was next. By then Felici was "pontifical photographer" with a monopoly on all pictures inside the Vatican; a right which was to provide his family a bonanza a half century later. Pius X had to stand still for six seconds each time the aging Signor Felici took his portrait. Photographs of ceremonies did not begin until the time of Pius XI in the twenties. The first cracks in the Felici monopoly came in the thirties when *L'Osservatore Romano* demanded its own exclusive pictures taken by Francesco Giordani, a former member of the Papal Palatine Guard. Giordani was subsequently able to open a profitable store for photographs and religious articles.

After World War II more and more breaks in the Felici-Giordani joint monopoly occurred. Photographers arrived with letters of introduction from Cardinal Spellman. Well-financed American picture magazines tipped $12-a-week Vatican policemen. One United States magazine got the only good shooting angle at the funeral of Pius XII. As a rule, however, cameras were forbidden in the Vatican and young Signor Felici, member of his family's third generation, was the only one to be seen moving about in white tie and tails with a huge photographer's bag slung from his shoulder.

Friends of Signors Felici and Giordani assured Vatican officials that the two would never be obtrusive as they changed positions during papal ceremonies, or even more important, while taking a place on the very balcony of St. Peter's itself during the apostolic benediction. The reassurance was coupled with the warning that other photographers, notably the Americans, might at any time "move out in front of the Pope's throne for a close-up" or might in other ways disturb sacred rituals. There were two sides to it, but meanwhile the Felici and Giordani families acquired at least small fortunes, and the world press had poorer pictures than a system of freer competition would have provided.

The written coverage of the Vatican goes back to about the time of Giuseppe Seraiter, at the start of the present century. Signor Seraiter was a correspondent for an Ancona, Italy, Catholic paper, *Patria*—The Fatherland. He had the good fortune to make the acquaintance of a brilliant liberal priest in the Secretariate of State, Giacomo della Chiesa. The latter would talk over Church problems in the evenings in his rooms in the Capranica seminary. The priest became Benedict XV. At about that time, as the story was told in the Rome press corps, an American news-agency head fell to chatting with his local pastor, Father Pucci, who used to come seeking alms. The priest seemed to know the Vatican well, and some of the things he related were good for news stories. The reporter proposed a regular exchange and the Pucci News Service was born. Signor Seraiter joined it. Giulio Barteloni, one of Monsignor Pucci's young aides, was still carrying it on as the sixties began. Monsignor Pucci's nephew Filippo ran a rival service.

Monsignor Pucci's value was that he could semiofficially put out two types of stories—those the Vatican wanted published and those to which it had no special objection. The Monsignor could do it without involving the Church's full authority. The latter would have required much more caution. Monsignor Pucci could also be counted on to respect religious secrets.

A disadvantage, beyond the fact that correspondents felt frustrated in their effort to get to news at its source, was that the tipsters were tempted to scrape up news when there was little if any. One example was an eight-column headline in the fifties in a Denver newspaper: VATICAN BANS TV TO NUNS. One of the Vatican tipsters had found a story in an Italian priests' magazine expressing puritanical ideas on the subject of television, and had passed it off as the view of writers more or less "close" to the Holy See and to papal infallibility. The Rome bureau of the American National Catholic News Agency got a "rocket" from its Washington headquarters on another day asking why it had missed world Catholic statistics reportedly released by "competent sources." A tipster had found them as he browsed through a French Catholic magazine. They were at best unofficial.

One newspaper reporter asked his tipster whether Pius XII would go to Lourdes. "Impossible," he answered. "We started that rumor ourselves."

The story was half plausible but also at least half dubious. It made copy for a day and left the world readers of Roman news bewildered.

Who were the "high Vatican sources" quoted by the tipsters and their clients?

"Would you use it if I, for instance, told you that the Pope's secretary gave me the names of a few potential cardinals?" the editor of a responsible American Catholic publication asked a top Rome news correspondent.

"Coming from you, I certainly would," the journalist answered. "I'd use it one way or another."

The priest was known as one who weighed his words. He could be trusted. The Pope's secretary would have as much knowledge as anyone could have, even though popes are known to confide cardinals' appointments to few if any other persons. "One way or another" meant that the reporter would hedge by saying, "In addition to these, at least a hundred others could be named."

Most news came from *L'Osservatore Romano*. The Secretariate of State and the Supreme Sacred Congregation of the Holy Office planted articles there whenever they wished. Unfortunately for the news correspondents not all of *Osservatore* was so inspired.

"We know the broad limits inside which the Church can act and we write accordingly," an *Osservatore* editor said, "but we do it on our own authority and sometimes we're wrong. Then we hear about it."

Correspondents, given a bad steer, risked hearing from irate readers, too.

"No news is so closely scrutinized as that we send from Rome," an American agency correspondent commented. "It frightens me."

"What infuriates me," remarked another, a Catholic, "is that the lines I had to write in two minutes are criticized later in a Catholic paper by someone who has a whole month to think up what to say against me!"

As the sixties started there was still invincible opposition inside the Vatican to a staff proposal that a press officer be appointed inside each congregation. There was no action either on a suggestion that someone man the *Osservatore Romano* press office in the afternoons and evenings when reporters were at work on tips culled from that afternoon's edition of the Vatican paper. Signor Casimirri was still unable to get reporters good seats at functions. There were no press conferences to explain the background of carefully worded and sometimes all but incomprehensible encyclicals. There was even secrecy on the release date of important papal documents until minutes before newsmen were expected to interpret them to the world.

Part of the reason was lack of budget. Part, too, was the effect of an old mentality formed in the monarchical age before democracies existed. A change was slowly coming, however, and more and more the Vatican's spiritual message was reaching the readers of the secular world press.

# 25. The Pope Is Thousands

Popes change and sometimes differ as much as Pius XII and John XXIII, but the Vatican goes on through the tumultuous centuries. Part of the reason is that the Pope "is thousands of people," as one of the Vatican news specialists once pointed out to me. Encyclicals, for instance, were written by commissions. The Pope had final say, of course, but an idea of the share done by anonymous collaborators was provided by the experience of one team of encyclical writers which produced an encyclical of Pius XII. They had to visit the Vatican 350 times to get approval on various passages, and even had 5 conferences on one word alone. The Pope sat in on many of the talks.

Of the "thousands" who "are the Pope" an overwhelmingly large proportion is Italian, although the people of Italy make up less than 10 per cent of the world Catholic population, even counting the Marxist one-third as Church members. Nominally all but a fraction of one per cent of Italians are Catholic, but many high Holy See authorities consider only a third to two-thirds as being true adherents to the Faith. With that small share of the world Catholic population and with only 10 per cent of the Church's missionaries Italian, the people of the country held a fifth of the bishoprics, nearly half the cardinalates, 90 per cent of the positions in the all-powerful Secretariat of State, and a monopoly of the Papacy since 1523.

In the Secretariat of State at the start of the sixties, out of a staff of 150 there were only 4 whose native language was English. None of the 4 was in a position of prominence, nor was any member of the group likely to rise to a place of importance in the Vatican later. The most promising would probably return home as bishops just as Francis Spellman, a Secretariate of State aide in the twenties, did just before World War II. Monsignor Spellman not only became an eminent member of his nation's hierarchy, but cardinal. In 1946 when some of us asked the New York prelate about rumors that he might go to Rome as Cardinal Secretary of State, the first non-Italian in that post in many generations, the American seemed embarrassed. He answered shortly that he would never leave New York.

The same Italian dominance prevailed in the Vatican diplomatic corps. When the Church's academy for training priest-diplomats celebrated its 250th anniversary in 1951, journalists were given an unusual glimpse behind its usually closed doors. Eighty per cent of the enrollment, the school's officers said, was Italian. There had been one American among postwar graduates, Maximilian Gomez Macouzet of San Diego, California. The importance of the school in providing top leadership for the Church could not be overestimated. Of 1,247 graduates in 2½ centuries, 46 had become Vatican diplomatic chiefs of mission, 98 including 6 living at the time had become cardinals, 7 Vatican secretaries of state. The latter included Marquis Ercole Consalvi who is credited with saving French Catholicism from the depredations of Napoleon; Mariano Rampolla, who was vetoed for the Papacy in the sensational Austrian imperial intervention in the 1903 conclave; Raffaele Merry del Val, the courtly son of a Spanish ambassador, and one who is being considered for canonization as a saint; and Giovanni Battista Montini, Acting Secretary of State in the fifties, who was considered an eminent possibility for election to the Papacy in 1958.

The Italian and even the noble dominance in Church affairs would seem to be limitless and permanent, but a slow trend toward a more international and democratic leadership of the Church could be observed in a closer study of the men around the popes in mid-twentieth century. Half the graduates of the academy for diplomats have been noblemen. The school in fact was called the Noble Ecclesiastical Academy until Pope Pius XII, one of its former staff teachers, changed the name soon after his 1939 election to the "Pontifical Ecclesiastical Academy." Through the centuries the roll of alumni included 285 counts, 189 marquises, 63 barons, 17 princes, 6 dukes and several score who did not inherit family titles. But so many commoners had been admitted in recent decades that the name of the institution was a misnomer long before Pius XII changed it. Nobles may have been needed to set forth Church claims in the era when monarchies dominated Europe, but a devout and clever commoner is obviously at least as well adapted to that mission in the present revolutionary age of the ordinary man. At the anniversary the school said that commoners had outnumbered nobles 10 to 1 since 1900 and that only 2 noblemen had been graduated since Pius XII changed the school's name.

The same trend toward broadening was to be seen in the relative degree of Italianization in the College of Cardinals. In 1853, 44 of the 70 cardinals were Italian. Perhaps that was not so surprising. It was still the heyday of papal temporal control over central Italy, and the duties of the Pope as a spiritual leader were intermeshed with his function as an Italian king. The non-Italians were 6 French, 2 Austrians, 2 Spanish, 2 Portuguese and one each from Belgium, Germany, Hungary and England. Not one non-Caucasian or even non-European was included. From then the curve has run toward the non-Italians with non-Europeans and non-Caucasians also, winning a place in mid twentieth century. There were 18 non-Italians in 1859, 27 in 1889, 24 in 1896, 29 in 1939 and 42 after Pius XII's first consistory for cardinals in 1946. Similarly, foreigners have begun to take a larger share of the Curia posts. In the early sixties 8 of the 31 cardinals helping Pope John in the Church world government were non-Italians. Two were French and one each from the British Isles (a Scottish convert, son of a minister, William Heard), Spain, Germany (the brilliant former confessor of Pius XII and leader in the Christian reunion movement, Augustin Bea), an Armenian, an Argentine and an American (Aloisius Muench, of Milwaukee, the first United States citizen to take office as a curia cardinal).

Every cardinal in Curia was a potential pope, since it is considered desirable that any non-Italian chosen for the Papacy should have some understanding of the complex workings of the old Church administration. With so many non-Italian cardinals in Curia the possibility of the first non-Italian Pope in four centuries was greater but probably still small. In 1958 one Italian newspaper estimated that the chances for a "foreigner" on Peter's chair were 20 per cent. The same estimate of a fairly small chance remained valid as the sixties went on.

The university of the Jesuit order in Rome—the Gregorian—was a standing retort to the local cliché that "men of one nationality work together better." Scores of nationalities were gathered inside the four-centuries-old seminary, the world's foremost institution for the training of priests. "Foreigners" could collaborate effectively, the Gregorian proved, but other arguments for at least a temporary continuance of the traditional Italian dominance in the Papacy remained strong.

"I used to think that there should be occasional non-Italians," an Irish priest, an educator and theologian, commented. "But now after years here I am no longer so sure."

The less than usually nationalistic temperament of the Italians —steeped in centuries of Christian tradition and reflecting scores of events when adaptations had to be made to invading barbarians and to frontier savages—seemed adjusted to the uniquely difficult problem of governing a world church. The Romans themselves, however provincial they often were, believed in good faith that "Roman" meant "universal."

During the early postwar period and at the start of the sixties, a few non-Italians were prominent among "the thousands who are the Pope." Notable among them was Eugene Tisserant, son of a French veterinarian of Nancy, whose passion for foreign languages, priestly zeal, and forthright character carried him to Rome as a professor of Assyrian when he was younger than many of his students. This helped him to become a cardinal at fifty and dean of the Cardinals' College and second-ranking prelate of the Catholic world at sixty-seven, in 1951. He remained in that office into the sixties.

Cardinal Tisserant retained the mind of the French general-staff lieutenant which he had been. Already a priest in 1914 at the start of World War II, he immediately became an infantry private, was wounded within two months, was transferred as an interpreter and officer to the high command of the French Expeditionary Force in the Middle East, and had the amused satisfaction of hearing himself introduced fondly to one Pope (Benedict XV) by a future one (Pius XI) as "my military aide." Book-lovers both, the future cardinal and the future Pope worked together at the Vatican Library. A liberal who refused to take action against one suspected spy inside the post-World War II Russian Catholic community in Rome because there was no hard evidence to justify interference with the man's personal rights, the cardinal for more than a decade supervised Church relations with Eastern-rite Catholics and with the Orthodox who weighed reunion with Catholicism. A member of the small Curia which is available to advise the Pope, the cardinal—master of a dozen languages—salted his spiritual observations with military ones. When Russians threatened to sweep over Europe and the Vatican in the late forties, the ex-lieutenant made a cool appraisal of the Soviets as weak mountain fighters who could always be expected to give the Papacy a fortnight in which to decide whether or not to flee. In other areas along the Russian periphery softness in local troops never missed the eye of the stiff-backed bearded prelate.

Cardinal Tisserant was among the half-dozen foremost figures of the Curia. Others in a similar position in the early sixties were Cardinal Domenico Tardini, Secretary of State of Pope John and acknowledged "Number Two" of the Catholic Church organization of those years, and Cardinal Alfredo Ottaviani, head of the Holy Office, the Church's most important doctrinal center. As an indication of the extraordinary extent to which the relatively tiny city of Rome (Population: 2,000,000), had influence in Church affairs, both cardinals were Rome born. Both had been Rome seminary classmates. With Pope John the two held the greater share of Church authority.

Cardinal Tardini was known in the Roman figure of speech as "One with no fur on his tongue." Smooth phrases were not for him. He let visitors know what he felt, with sometimes painful clarity. One reporter who told the State Secretary that he understood from a Moslem envoy to the Holy See that there might be a Catholic-Mahometan link-up to fight the common foe of Communist atheism was invited to hurry back to the ambassador to straighten him out. The feelers which the *Times* of London put out just after World War II with regard to a Catholic-Anglican reunion were similarly rebuffed. The secretary's idea in both cases was that the fifteen nations which fought under American or British leadership in Italy during World War II never ceased being "Australians, South Africans, Poles" or citizens of a dozen other nationalities, and that no blurring of the lines between the Catholic religion and any other would be permitted however much the two might work in unison in behalf of limited objectives.

Cardinal Tardini's irony and skepticism irritated many, but there were innumerable occasions when governmental visitors received satisfaction. One involved an Axis diplomat. When he called, Monsignor Tardini was abrupt to the point of offense, but the envoy learned later to his gratification that the monsignor had turned in a faithful eight-page report on the conversation to Pius XII. No diplomat could have asked more.

The tart retorts of the papal "premier and foreign minister" spread as legends through the Holy See diplomatic corps. To one who complained about interference in politics by one small Catholic Action newspaper the cardinal demanded: "What do you read it for?" Behind the remark was common sense. The paper had a tiny circulation and was no real irritant in Church-State relations. The ambassador was from a country which had a concordat guaranteeing that the Catholic Church, the religion of the overwhelming majority, would stay out of politics.

Ambassadors often noticed that although Cardinal Tardini brushed them swiftly and unceremoniously aside in an effort to protect the Pope, the grievances they mentioned were often eliminated quietly and with no comment a few months later.

The cardinal, one may add, found himself the broadest target of his own irony. When he became ill with hardening of the arteries in the months before his death in 1961, he told 100 of us at a press conference that he had suffered a heart attack and that if it had been the least bit more severe "they would be wasting a hundred candles on me now when even one would be too many." One hundred candles burn around the coffin of a cardinal. I remembered the words of the doughty prelate as the Pope and 500 others—diplomats, journalists, Italian cabinet members and Vatican clergy—looked on and prayed at his funeral. There were 30 tall tapers in line on either side and 20 each at the head and foot of the coffin.

Ottaviani was the son of a baker whose family shop was still in service in the ancient and poor Trastevere quarter adjacent to the Vatican. The future cardinal and his classmate, Domenico Tardini, attracted attention at the time of World War I when the seminaries of Rome obtained state recognition by sending students to take the same examinations given to the graduates of public schools. To the pride of seminary directors, both Ottaviani and Tardini passed with high honors. In his years as a Secretary of State assistant, the future Cardinal Ottaviani had held a reputation for open thinking, but as the cardinal head of the Holy Office, guardian of the purity of the Catholic religious inheritance, he became known as a leader of the extreme Right Wing. He fought the tendency of Leftist Catholics to make common cause with Communists and also resisted pro-Socialist neutralist trends in Italy. He was credited with writing a controversial editorial in *L'Osservatore Romano*, insisting on Catholic lay obedience to bishops in certain limited and critical circumstances. The editorial was a sensation because of the embarrassment it caused to John F. Kennedy, then running for the United States Presidency on a platform guaranteeing that his own conscience and no American or foreign bishop would direct his White House comportment. The clamor died down when Vatican aides said that the editorial was aimed at Italian "Catholic Communists."

With the death of Cardinal Tardini there were no longer two Romans flanking Pope John in Catholicism's most influential positions. As his new State Secretary the pontiff summoned another native of his own North Italian countryside, Amleto (Hamlet) Cicognani. As in the case of John's succession to Pius, the new appointment emphasized how different can be the personalities who preach the same ancient message and strive to apply the same principles. As Cardinal Tardini was frank, so was his successor gently tactful. In twenty-five years as Vatican representative in Washington he had established a reputation for the very minimum of interference in the activities of the highly patriotic and independent American bishops. As he took office at the advanced age of seventy-eight, his most evident asset was that he—more than any other Papal Secretary of State in history—intimately knew the United States, the nation recognized by all in Rome as the main pillar of the West, and no doubt of the world.

Another in the Catholic forefront in Rome was one who was not a resident of the Eternal City in 1961. This was Cardinal Montini, archbishop of the huge North Italian diocese of Milan which is probably second only to Rome in its importance in the World Church. Its hundreds of thousands of nominal communicants, plus the fact that it has produced several popes, and hundreds of churches, automatically make its cardinal-archbishop a possible successor to the Papacy.

Cardinal Montini, along with Domenico Tardini, was one of the two monsignors Pius XII used for more than a decade as co-administrators of the Secretariate of State. As such the two churchmen, and especially Monsignor Montini, who was in charge of "ordinary affairs," gave instructions to bishops and even to patriarchs and cardinals. It was Monsignor Montini who broke the news to the future Pope John that he had been made cardinal and patriarch of Venice. In a reorganization in the early fifties, Domenico Tardini took over all State Secretariate functions, and the more experimental and studious Giovanni Montini went to relatively remote Milan. There, however, he acquired the pastoral experience which is considered another vital papal qualification. In the last years of the fifties and in the early sixties no one was mentioned as a potential pope as often as he was.

The Milan cardinal was the son and brother of Italian parliament members. A tireless reader, he carried ninety cases of books with him when he went to Milan. Many were sociological studies. A "late vocation," the humanistically educated future cardinal was in his twenties before he donned the ecclesiastical cassock. His encyclopedic, political mind was revealed to me one day in the late forties in his Vatican office as he ticked off the state of Catholic Church-State relations in every major nation. If he became Pope the Catholic Church would have a highly modern intellectual anxious to find the formulas of social betterment needed to restore faith to Europe's de-Christianized workers, and a man who would seek to find some way to nourish the Christian flame behind Soviet lines. Conservatives fearful of experiment, and perhaps some resentful of the years when a simple monsignor relayed the Pope's unexplained "yeses" and "noes," would oppose Montini's election, but many Church scholars would support him.

Apart from the most eminent there were scores of others: Cardinal Antonio Bacci, the Vatican's Latinist, who concocted 10,000 Latin words to supplement the ancient language's original 30,000 so that it might serve to cover all modern situations (he still had no "intercontinental ballistics missile" when I called on him in the late fifties but did have the ancient *missile, missilis*—neuter gender—as a starter); Father Jean-Baptiste Janssens, the "Black Pope," ailing ebony-clad leader of the 32,000 Jesuits of the world—a disciplined force at the Pope's instant service; Monsignor Thomas Ryan, Pope John's secretary, one of the non-Italian graduates of the academy for diplomats; Monsignor Loris Capovilla, another of Pope John's secretaries and a direct channel to the pontiff for many who knew the Vatican's inner workings; and Father Robert Leiber, the German Jesuit, who was Pius XII's secretary and assistant speech writer—one of the few who dared to speak bluntly to the pontiff of the forties and fifties, and one of Rome's valued experts on the meaning of the Pius pontificate.

The list could include dozens of other names but I would end with one whose story gives a particular point to any account of the men around the popes. He was Monsignor Patrick Carroll-Abbing, an Irish staff member in the Secretariate of State at the time of World War II. As a priest-diplomat he had an honored and pleasant place in society but as a clergyman he was sickened by the sight of 200,000 Italian orphan boys shining shoes, black-marketing, pimping, stealing, starving and freezing on the streets of the crushed ex-Axis nation in the wake of the liberation. It was no immediate responsibility of his, but then no one else assumed it. Too much else seemed to come first as Italy was picked up from her ruins. The monsignor induced a few of the aggressive, dirty, sometimes nearly naked boys to stay overnight in a cellar he found for them. He took note of the wads of money they had collected, "More than you and I usually see." He weaned them slowly into full-time residence inside the nominally self-run "boys' republics" which he set up. Each of them was paid in the "money" of the "republic" for schoolwork and for chores, and each "bought" his meals at the republic's "restaurants." A democratically elected boy mayor and boy judge handled discipline.

Two jobs were too much and the monsignor got permission to leave the Secretariate of State. By the early sixties the good man who believed that good could and should be done had raised $2,000,000 in the United States, had set up 50 "republics" in Italy for boys and one for girls, had several thousand children in his care and many thousands of decent and prospering young family men among his graduates. These combined properties, counting local land and utility grants, were worth $100,000,000.

Cardinal Roncalli, the future Pope John, had been among those quickest to say that he dreaded Rome's "papers" and longed for parish work, but to me Monsignor Carroll-Abbing, whose work I watched from a modest beginning to a glorious climax, remained the proof of how reassuringly short a step it is from the Vatican's splendid but impersonal Renaissance halls to the humblest human contacts and charity.

# 26. America, the Hope

The most important entry in the Vatican's annual list of accredited diplomats in the early sixties read:

*Stati Uniti d'America.* . . .

United States of America. . . .

Myron C. Taylor, personal representative of Presidents Franklin D. Roosevelt and Harry Truman, had left abruptly at the start of the 1950 Holy Year and had not been replaced except for one-day envoys on special occasions, but the Vatican held the door to a return patiently and hopefully ajar.

France, Spain, Britain, West Germany and two-score other nations had important missions to the Holy See, but few could challenge the fact that the nation represented by the dotted line loomed largest in Vatican minds. The reasons were numerous. The $4,000,000 seminary for American Catholic priests was the largest of the scores of similar national institutions in Rome. The contributions of American Catholics to foreign missions and to other world tasks of the Church often made up 50 per cent of all sums raised. The network of 20 universities and 260 colleges under Catholic Church auspices in the United States was without parallel in the rest of the Catholic world. Most of all, the role of the United States as the political mainstay of an imperiled Western world put the mere possibility of diplomatic ties with it higher in the regard of the Holy See than the reality of existing contacts with the nations which had once dominated the globe.

"The United States is the great hope," one of the most eminent Holy See diplomats told me one day. "Eire [with its many vocations] is another. So are the Netherlands [with a dedicated and growing Catholic minority]. And Africa."

Africa was on the list because of the millions of swift conversions in the years just before and after World War II. No other continent listened so readily to the Christian message. The Holy See diplomat made his estimate in the years just after the war before the explosion of independence movements and incipient anarchy, but even in the alarming period of the early sixties many of his fellows in the Vatican service still clung to the belief that Africa held promise.

Whatever the Dark Continent's potential role, it was the United States which drew most attention.

"You may be surprised," a French diplomat remarked in one conversation. "It is America, not France, that counts now for most. Take the Gregorian University [Rome's main seminary]. It is true that twenty per cent of the teaching staff is still French but only five per cent of the student body is from our language group. A third have English as their native tongue—far more than any other group and almost twice as many as those who are Italian-speaking. Some are from the British Commonwealth but it is the Americans who raise the proportion so high."

The remarkable relative decline of the French could be best appreciated only by realizing that it was France which, a century earlier, had provided the Catholic Church with three-fourths of her foreign missionaries.

Thanks, too, to the Americans, English was one of the most important languages among cardinals. Italian still dominated. In the early sixties two-fifths of the cardinals spoke Italian as their native tongue, but a sixth spoke English, half of them Americans. It was a change from the many years when Italian, French and Spanish had no serious rivals.

It was an immense advance for the United States and for the American Catholic Church from the early days of the twentieth century when Washington had been isolationist and the American Church seen as a mere missionary enterprise. Large changes came even in the course of the years during which I looked on. In 1939 I watched three Americans walk into the papal conclave.

They constituted a full 60 per cent of the United States citizens who had cast ballots for a new pope in all of Roman history. The only other two who had voted were Baltimore's Cardinal James Gibbons who had voyaged to Europe in 1903 on the correctly estimated chance that the ninety-three year old Leo XIII was about to die, and New York's Cardinal John Farley who managed to reach Rome in time for the election of Benedict XV in 1914.

In 1958 in Rome I covered the funeral of the first American appointed a Vatican diplomatic chief of mission, Cardinal Mooney, who was Holy See envoy to India and Japan from 1926 to 1933. I reported the arrival of the first American ever assigned to duty as a Curia cardinal, one of those active as the Pope's aides in the government of the world church. He was Samuel Stritch, retired archbishop of Chicago. A boy prodigy, he finished grade school at ten, took his Bachelor of Arts degree at sixteen, became a priest at twenty-two, America's youngest bishop at thirty-four, and finally an archbishop in Milwaukee at forty-three. His death before he could take office as director of World Catholic Missions deprived the United States of its first real chance at the Papacy. At least that was the conviction of one shrewd ambassador to the Holy See at the time.

Other American "firsts" were numerous at the Vatican. Cautious, soft-spoken Cardinal Aloisius Muench, of Milwaukee, who in 1951 had become the first American nuncio—a full-fledged Holy See ambassador—moved to Rome as the first American to actually take up Curia duties. What had been intended as Cardinal Stritch's privilege became his. By the early sixties several other Americans had key Vatican diplomatic missions. Gerald O'Hara represented the Holy See as Apostolic Delegate in England. Joseph McGeough, New York-born and a resident of Rome for most of his adult life, was in South Africa. Francesco Lardone, for thirty years a professor at the Catholic University in Washington, was a successor of Pope John in Turkey.

Perhaps the most spectacular of all the American clergymen with a background of Roman precedent-breaking was New York's Cardinal Francis Spellman, the first American—in the mid-twenties—to serve as a Vatican State Secretariate staff member. He was a symbol for the Catholic Church in the minds of many fellow Americans, and represented American Catholicism to many Romans. Not all of the comments about him were favorable in either Catholic or American milieux, but few individuals did more to bring the two worlds together.

Son of a Whitman, Massachusetts, grocer of Irish extraction, Cardinal Spellman was one of the promising seminarians to study at the so-called North American College, the United States seminary in Rome. He learned Italian, albeit with a flat Boston accent which he never overcame. He translated into English two devotional books of a rising Italian prelate, Monsignor Borgoncini-Duca. Father Spellman seemed a good candidate when the Holy See State Secretariate needed someone to handle English correspondence between the two World Wars. By the early thirties it was Father Spellman whom the Pope chose to smuggle two great anti-Fascist and anti-Nazi encyclical letters to the world press in Paris. By the late thirties, chosen by his Secretariate of State friend, the former Cardinal Pacelli, the priest was New York's archbishop. It was a post in which he was soon to have the services of ten assistant bishops—more such help than that enjoyed by any other prelate in the world other than the Pope himself.

Just as the cardinal risked unpopularity in the United States by demanding governmental aid for schools and the establishment of an embassy to the Holy See, so did he startle Romans by his Americanisms. One of his first acts in the Secretariate of State had been to hunt up a mimeograph machine to give reporters quick translations of papal speeches instead of making them wait for *L'Osservatore Romano*'s Italian version. Later as a newly-named cardinal in 1946, he held daily press conferences in the lobby of a central Rome hotel. Not until a decade later did Cardinal Domenico Tardini, the Secretary of State, timidly decide to permit three cautious press encounters of his own. In a city where no churchman except the Pope, or rarely the secretary of state, ever had anything to say, the New York cardinal's interviews were something from another world and not entirely approved.

The cardinal, it was evident, knew the value of the full and accurate reporting on which he could count. That fellow churchmen in Rome, fearful of a hostile "liberal press," would not risk or endorse such encounters did not daunt him.

Reporters covering the cardinal's activities grew used to the quips of a man who used to play infield for the Fordham College baseball nine in the Bronx, New York. When monks at the Church of St. John and Paul, his titular church in Rome, unveiled a bust of him which they had commissioned, his comment was typical: "I should have brought my horse; it would have been bigger, and certainly more handsome!"

When the dean of American cardinals mounted the bright red steps of the Pope's throne in installation ceremonies after John's election, his actions should have come as no surprise. He bowed deeply as required by ceremony, leaned forward for the kiss of peace, and then suddenly shook hands. Europeans were startled.

"The handshake," they explained, "is not liturgical."

Cardinal Spellman's alma mater in Rome, the North American College, was a key to the Vatican-American relationship. Pius IX had asked for its establishment in 1855 as an assurance that the Church on distant American soil should not drift from Rome. With the national Protestant churches in northern Europe as a warning, it is an eternal dread of the Vatican that there may be new schisms; the creation of separate national "Catholic" Churches. Distance can lend disenchantment. Put differently, there is a unique quality to living for a few years "near the cupola [of St. Peter's]," as rectors of the various national seminaries agree. Treading the streets where the first Christians bled binds ties of sentiment and conviction which help unite the universal church around the Pope.

Rome likes to choose bishops who know and are known by the Eternal City, so the North American College, 100 years old in the late fifties, was recognized on its centenary as "the West Point of the American clergy." Nearly a fourth of the American bishops at the time were North American graduates, even though the whole roster of graduates in the course of a century numbered only 1,500—little more than 2 per cent of the number of American Catholic priests of 1960. North American graduates had a private joke: "The three qualities needed to become an American bishop are to believe in God, to be loyal to the Pope, and to graduate from the North American College."

"And in case of absolute necessity," the story went on, "you can do without the first two!"

The college helped make American Church history and watched other parts of it unfold. Ulysses S. Grant visited the seminary after he left the White House. So did other Civil War Generals, William T. Sherman and Philip Sheridan. Defeated Presidential candidate James G. Blaine was a caller. So were Mark Twain and Buffalo Bill. Woodrow Wilson dropped by, the first American President to do so while in office. Dwight Eisenhower, the second, took off from the college grounds in an American Army helicopter. Seminarians, excited and thinking it a joke, were reprimanded gently by their rector, Archbishop Martin O'Connor, for laughing when Harry Truman, then an ex-President, was introduced as "Mr. President."

"It's still a very good honorary title," the Scranton-born former amateur boxer chided the embarrassed students.

Secretary of State John Foster Dulles permitted himself one of his few grins when the North American students cheered him as he arrived for lunch. As father of a Catholic convert and Jesuit priest, Avery Dulles, the Protestant chief of American diplomacy claimed a warm place in the seminarians' hearts. The butt of constant abuse in years of declining American power position in the world, the Secretary of State told the students after their applause: "I don't get that very often."

The election of the first American Catholic president, John Fitzgerald Kennedy in 1960, opened a new era of Vatican-American relations, but curiously an epoch of some pause. The Vatican had assurances from a top American diplomatic source in 1958 that "if Dulles lives another two years" there would be a resumption of the official American-Vatican relations which had existed after the American Civil War and until just before the 1870 overthrow of the papal states. The Vatican had made plain the fact that it did not want a Presidential mission such as Myron Taylor directed, but insisted on nothing less than a regular legation or embassy. Britain, with religious objections similar to those of the United States, had avoided diplomatic ties until World War I showed the desirability of establishing them. France, with similar hesitations, had restored interrupted relations just after the Versailles Treaty.

With a Catholic layman in the White House, the Holy See realized that hopes represented by the late John Foster Dulles were shelved for a while, perhaps for a decade. It is a Holy See axiom that Catholics in public office often lean over backward to avoid suspicion of undue favoritism to their Church. Kennedy, in any case, had made clear in his campaign that he felt that the debatable value of maintaining an embassy to the Pope was more than outweighed by the controversy and divisions such an appointment would mean inside the United States. The opposition of many American Protestants to such a tribute to the head of any one religion was clear.

To me as a Rome reporter it was equally plain, however, that the future was on the side of what was reported to be the Dulles, rather than what was known to be the Kennedy, position.

"The Vatican is too important to leave without our influence," a veteran American diplomat in Rome put it privately. "Why, they could even launch a holy war against the Communists before we were ready for it! And the Vatican is so important in Latin America."

According to that interpretation, it was less a question of what an American diplomat might learn at the Holy See "listening post" than of what he might be able to do to convince the Pope of the wisdom and virtue of American actions in the world. Certainly no single speech or encyclical of the popes could cause a quick change in world history, but its long, slow influence in many countries was a reality which needed to be appreciated.

Rome and Washington, with their common devotion to conservative and charitable values and their joint horror of Communism, edged closer to one another, however erratic the gradual approach might be. One eminent American politician remarked "not for attribution" that the large Catholic vote in his state was a reason for his occasional audiences with the Pope "although to my credit I never had my picture taken with him." There were some devices to which he would not stoop in order to curry electoral favor.

"I will say," he added, "that I had quite a few valuable talks with Pius XII." The American's wooing of the Catholic vote had paid an unexpected dividend.

Another eminent American announced that he had no top hat and tails with him so that he would have to call on the Pope in a business suit. Photographs of him in informal dress would be less likely to arouse anti-Catholic voters at home. An embassy diplomat seemed not to understand. He told the official that he could borrow his clothes if he wished. It was just at that point that a local paper printed a picture of the Washington representative in full dress at a reception earlier on the same trip. Without a further word the politician unpacked his formal clothes. In full sartorial pomp he paid his Vatican call.

American Catholic clergymen in Rome sometimes felt that Italian officials at the Vatican knew too little about the extraordinary Catholic parish organization in the United States, a system of schools and social activities that no other part of the Catholic world can match. Some wished that Italians at the Holy See would visit the United States more often. In my experience Italians rated the United States in general as a materialistic nation, but more and more began to recognize the American Catholic community as a fountainhead of faith, prayer, and religious vocations with few rivals in the world. The relatively scanty contribution of American Catholics to the intellectual and governmental life of the United States and of the Western world was recognized. Romans were aware of laments from Notre Dame's Father John Cavanaugh, Catholic University's Monsignor John Ellis, and *America* (Jesuit) magazine's Father Thurston Davis that there were few if any American Catholic "Salks, Oppenheimers and Einsteins," that only two American colleges (Cath-

AMERICA, THE HOPE 269

olic University in Washington, D.C. and St. Catherine's in St. Paul) rated Phi Beta Kappa chapters, and that there was what amounted to an American Catholic "cultural ghetto." All Romans understood that the brilliant and devout President Kennedy was an exception. Even so, as the sixties began, some in Rome mused that a largely de-Christianized Europe, weak from the ravages of hedonism and skepticism, might yet have the·Faith carried back to it by missionaries from a vigorous and confident America.

# 27. Teaching All Nations

The bewilderingly varied national situations in which Rome's missionaries exercised spiritual leadership were reflected in each day's heterogeneous flow of pilgrims into the Eternal City.

Failures as well as victories were represented. The former were reflected in 1949 in one strange press conference under the auspices of the Communist Czechoslovak legation. A suspended monsignor, Josef Plojhar, Minister of Health in the Soviet puppet cabinet, and a supporter of a Communist-organized pro-Moscow "Catholic Action" organization in Prague, tried to justify his position.

Perspiration formed at the temples of the government official in clerical dress as reporters grilled him on why the Catholic Church had barred him from saying Mass, on how he could take part in a government which had jailed Archbishop Josef Beran, Primate of Czechoslovakia's Catholics, and on whether he agreed with his Communist fellow cabinet members that "religion is the opium of the people."

The Communist "Catholic Action" was the subject of many questions, too. That very day the Vatican had announced the excommunication of all connected with it. The organization, the Holy See said, was a cynical contrivance of Kremlin atheists to get control of the Catholics who make up the majority of the Czechoslovakian population.

"I obey the Pope where I have to obey," the priest-minister said, "but nobody is going to tell me my politics."

The remark was almost but not quite orthodox. It is Church policy to leave politics in general to "Caesar," letting laymen, and usually priests, choose democracy or moderate dictatorship, republics or monarchies, conservatism or mild Socialism, but that day's decree against the Czechoslovak "Catholic Action" had touched on another doctrinal point. It was that what seems to be "Caesar's" is sometimes God's and that evil and antireligious Communism is a case in point.

He was not a Communist, the monsignor explained in a long, mimeographed comment distributed to the reporters. It was just that his own "Christian-Socialist" ideas ran "parallel" to those of the "Communist materialists." Foreign capitalists and liberals should not be allowed to use a frontier nation like Czechoslovakia as a barrier against "Socialist" reforms.

To many in the monsignor's Roman audience the words were fairly familiar. Scores of thousands of European Catholics, including even the saintly Cardinal Emanuel Suhard in postwar Paris, groped for a way to solve the same problems of wealth and poverty for which Communists offered their violent solutions. Many believed that "short stretches" could be traveled hand in hand with the Communists in opposition to tax-dodging, price-fixing and labor-exploiting capitalists.

"Obviously as a Catholic priest I cannot feel indifferent [about being denied the right to say Mass], but not even the greatest penalty [probably meaning excommunication] can change opinions which are the fruit of my life," Monsignor Plojhar said in answer to a question.

Being suspended from priestly functions was nothing new to him. Hitler, he added, had held him in a concentration camp for seven years.

"Do you put Hitler and Archbishop Beran on the same footing?" asked a reporter, attempting to find a hole in the tormented cleric's logic.

There was no answer.

Religion, the people's opium?

"Socialists," the priest said, "have different views on such subjects, just like Americans and Italians."

It was for history to say whether the "Christian Socialist" collaboration with the Communists would end in the suppression of the former. It would be for history also to say whether the faint postwar Americanization of free Italy could be compared with the Russification and Communization of captive Catholic Czechoslovakia.

The suspended monsignor represented one attitude among the unhappy 50,000,000 behind the Soviet Iron Curtain. Tall, taciturn, gray-haired Cardinal Stefan Wyszinski of Poland stood for another. In Rome in 1958 when the cardinals of the world assembled to elect Pope John, it was he who was usually singled out for the warmest applause in an appreciative and admiring Rome.

Listening to those cheers I was reminded of a ceremony a few months earlier in Poland just after the cardinal was freed from a Communist jail. A parish church was jammed to the walls as he mounted a pulpit to urge the Warsaw congregation to remain faithful.

"Try to know God," the straight-backed fifty-seven-year-old prelate told the crowd. "Get closer to Him. Be assured that He is with you. He is in each cradle rocked by a mother. His spirit will reach you through locked doors. His Church is the world's mightiest power. We have been celebrating the year of Christ the King. We should celebrate now a year of Christ the Worker. Christ was a plain man. His father was a mere artisan. He surely knew the troubles of everyday life. It's likely that he, too, had to pay taxes . . . Don't return evil for evil. Live in peace. God is always likely to triumph. With faith in Christ we shall always keep our Church and fatherland united . . . Thanks for the prayers you said for me when I could not be with you. And now let us pray for the good of our country. . . ."

The congregation burst into a nationalist anthem, against the old German invaders of the past, but evidently adaptable in anyone's mind to the Russian conquerors of the moment. It ran, as it was translated to me in whispers:

"We will never forsake our country. We will stay strong to ever fight anyone who comes to rule our homeland. We won't stand Germans spitting in our faces or foreign teachers making Germans of our children."

The emotion was intense. It was the emotion of a prisoner in chains; strong and struggling but still enchained. Along with the case of Monsignor Plojhar it summarized the state of Catholics all through Communist lands; in Lithuania, Hungary, Yugoslavia, Mainland China, North Vietnam, North Korea. Catholicism had been dealt a hard blow—virtually an obliterating one in the case of the 3,000,000 Chinese Catholics—but one that might yet provoke new progress.

The Church thrives on adversity, a top official of the Congregation for the Propagation of the Faith told me in the early sixties. "Yugoslavia," he said, "is an example. It [the Church] was quite comfortable and middle class and soft before the war. Now after the Tito persecution it is vital and flourishing again."

Spain offered a similar case. After the killing of 7,000 clergy in the Civil War of the middle thirties, the seminaries of the country were among Europe's most crowded in the early sixties. Three thousand prospective seminarians were being turned away each year for lack of school space.

Those, who like Monsignor Plojhar, said they believed that Catholics and Communists could collaborate for social reform, were not limited to members of the throng already captured by the Soviets. Streams of articulate Leftist Catholic pilgrims to Rome made that clear during the fifties, the Abbé Pierre, a leader of the French Catholic radicals, reflected it as he told me his story one day. An underground fighter against the Germans, he had been elected to parliament, and then appalled by the plight of bums who sleep under the bridges of the Seine had gone to live with the outcasts. A man of quick wit, he discovered that ragpicking rather than starvation was an available alternative. He organized a ragpickers' union, made a dramatic midwinter radio appeal for shelter for others who were freezing outdoors, and momentarily found himself at the head of what looked like a march to political power. Parisians by the thousands emptied their attics of junk to help him. I talked to "the new St. Francis" after he had called on the prime minister, Joseph Laniel.

"It's grotesque," the leather-jacketed abbé said. "Cabinet members run to get their pictures taken with me to prop up their own small popularity! The Premier received me as if I were an ambassador. I reassured him that my ragpickers and I had no other ambition than to be the fleas that hop on cabinet members to warn them by our bites!"

The France of the time, the middle fifties, was in the hands of "moderates," pro-Americans steering a middle course between the archconservative policies of a Rightist police state on the one hand, and the extremes of near-Communist radicalism on the other.

"Moderates," the ragpicker clergyman said, "are politically idiotic. They are no longer in touch with the people. A man with no house for his children does not understand 'liberty and justice.' Why build so many cannon [as part of Western defense programs] if men won't fire them when the time comes? I don't say to throw them all into the sea. I say build eight or five instead of ten, let's say, and use the rest for homes and bread."

I asked how the Premier had answered.

"He replied with moderate things."

Was the priest more confident after the talk?

"I have hope," was the noncommittal answer.

Just as swiftly as he had soared to the headlines the abbé vanished, but the anguish of the many Continental Catholic intellectuals he represented continued long afterward as one of the salient facts of a Communist-challenged Western world.

Along with Cardinal Wyszinski, another member of the Sacred College who was applauded in Rome—even amid the solemnity of a papal ceremony in St. Peter's—was a Negro who did not abandon paganism until he was eight; less than forty years earlier. He was Laurian Rugambwa of Tanganyika, the first Negro cardinal.

Tall, slim Cardinal Rugambwa, master of a half-dozen languages including English, Italian and German, was an example of the achievements but also of the limitations of the Christian effort in the last continent to emerge onto the world stage. A natural dignity failed to conceal his bewilderment as he spoke to a group of us just after his 1960 appointment.

"Will you speak now for all Africa?" we asked him.

"I might feel that was my task," was the cautious reply, "but

I do not yet know what others think—Father Robinson, here, or the Congregation for the Propagation of the Faith."

Father John Robinson at the cardinal's elbow was an Englishman who along with other members of the missionary order of the White Fathers had taught the pagan boy his catechism, drilled him in Latin, and then helped him step by step as he prepared for doctoral studies in Rome; a bishopric at forty and finally the cardinalate at forty-eight. Only one other member of the Sacred College was younger.

At fourteen the future cardinal had applied for training as a priest at a seminary at Rubya, near Lake Victoria, in his banana-growing home area in central Africa. He was only the 477th pupil in the seminary's history. The school had been organized in 1904, a mere 34 years after Stanley, Livingstone and other explorers had opened the area. In the span of a single lifetime a child of mid-African savagery had achieved membership in a body that symbolized much of the loftiest idealism of the old and sophisticated West.

Some thinkers in Rome did not exclude the possibility that seeds planted in primitive Africa might reap a harvest of rich spiritual fruits for Europe, with missionaries coming from the Dark Continent one day to rekindle the faded European fervor. Those who thought so had statistics to support them. A government tax survey in Catholic Austria in 1959, for instance, showed that only one-third attended Sunday Mass while in 90 per cent Catholic Portugal at least half ignored the weekly Mass obligation. In France some priests looked after as many as 12 churches and ecclesiastical sociologists lamented that much of the country was "de-Christianized." In Catholic Belgium the Socialist Marxists had a chance for full power.

Africa, on the other hard, had seen prodigies of conversions. By the early sixties a third of the Dark Continent's bishops were native Negroes. There were more than 30 of them. Church membership was 20,000,000. There were 2,000 native priests. Twenty-five years earlier there had been only 5,000,000 African Catholics. As late as 1939 there had been no African bishops. At the time of World War I there were only 90 native African priests.

Africa was a hope of the Church, but the Vatican looked south without illusions. However earnest young converts might be, the stern Catholic law of celibacy for priests of the Latin rite was something with no counterpart in African experience. A substantial number of seminarians and priests took wives and turned away. Bishops were called upon to organize their priests and dioceses in the Western and ancient Roman manner and found it hard to do so. Vague tribal ways were all that race memories suggested to them. Men like Cardinal Rugambwa could be expected to play far less forceful roles than such assured Westerners as New York's forceful Cardinal Spellman, but the accolade at St. Peter's for Cardinal Rugambwa reflected Rome's joy that at least one more hurdle on the way to "teaching all nations" had been cleared.

The world of Asia was reflected in Rome in the fifties in the Holy Year Mission Exhibition. How far could the tiny minority of Christians go in good conscience—amid the multitudes of the world's greatest continent—toward "baptizing" Confucianism, Buddhism, Hinduism and the other great philosophies? One missioner begged Rome's permission to portray Christ as a cross-legged figure such as Buddha. His argument was that folded limbs were an Oriental symbol of teaching. One Hindu inscription put up at the Missionary Exhibition was hastily taken down again when the future Cardinal Celso Costantini, the acting "Red Pope," decided that it went too far in "baptizing" the alien and irreconcilable. In general, Confucianism was accepted on the grounds that veneration of ancestors was equally a Catholic idea and that Catholicism added something that Confucianism lacked: a belief in an immortal soul and a knowable hereafter. Buddhism, however, was generally treated diffidently as a pantheistic doctrine too full of repudiations of the Christian concept.

Latin America, with a third of the world's Catholics, was a constant Vatican preoccupation. The way Protestantism had grown from 17,000 members to 4,600,000 in 40 years did not escape the eye of the Secretariate of State. The advance of Communism caused even more concern. As a sign of the way the Vatican felt the young could and should take the place of the old, the Holy See begged for United States missionaries for a nominally all-Catholic Latin America where there was only one priest for every 5,000 of the faithful. The number was only a fifth of what was considered normal and necessary. Archbishops in the United States who showed an awareness of the Latin American crisis, John O'Hara in Philadelphia, Richard Cushing in Boston, and Joseph Ritter in St. Louis, were those whom popes favored in promotions to the College of Cardinals.

# 28. Changeless and Changing

My first worry as a reporter at the Vatican was that there would be too little news. If reporting is the recording of change what could be more nearly changeless than a Church dedicated to conserving the old Christian message?

To my pleasant journalistic surprise I found a ferment of adaptation. Church scholars and officials were at work in dozens of fields of doctrine and administration grappling with problems of reinterpretation and readjustment in the face of scientific discoveries in a rapidly evolving world.

The problems seemed to succeed one another without limit: if the worker-priest idea of the French was to be condemned as too full of moral and intellectual temptations for newly ordained youths, was there any other way to close the gap between labor and the altar in the Latin countries? To what extent did experimental science, including modern historical research, call for modification of traditional ideas including the very interpretation of the Bible? How far should married laymen be permitted to advance inside the Church in view of the shortage of clergy in Latin America and in many other areas including parts of the United States? What was the role of modern art in Church worship? What was the answer to the global "population explosion" and to demands for contraceptive birth control?

On all these questions and on many more, clergymen—often under bond of deepest secrecy—were at work inside the quiet buildings around St. Peter's Basilica and in chancery offices throughout the world. With no specific, apparent change on any one day—as Renaissance-costumed Swiss Guards and Napoleonically garbed police stood protectively beside long-cassocked priests all through the Vatican—a cautious, meditated evolution, at least of surface forms, was under way.

A few of us saw it in the early sixties when we were invited to a housing project on a hill above the Vatican Basilica. Six plump, soft-skinned young men in overalls were at work swinging picks and pushing wheel barrows with the best will in the world, toiling to make the foundations for a five-story hostel for servant girls. Priests had noted that many peasant women seeking work in Rome as housemaids had drifted into prostitution and crime. With little or no cash in hand, the clergymen had set to work building a wholesome home for such immigrants. The youths on the job were newly appointed priests or seminarians. Their superiors had agreed that a half day of manual labor each week plus full-time toil during annual three- and four-week vacations would serve many good purposes: healthy exercise; a small but direct and constructive contribution to the mountain of social work needed in a European world of harsh class divisions; and at least a small bond of solidarity with the Continent's de-Christianized proletariat.

How did this differ from the abandoned worker-priest idea? Well, clergy in charge explained, the "brutalization" which un-varied physical labor tends to bring with it would not threaten youths nine-tenths of whose year would still be spent on books and things of the spirit. Would that be enough to convince cynical Continental laborers that the clergy was not parasitic? The answer was suggested in an exchange between our Vatican guide and a $3-a-day Roman laborer handling one of the technically more complicated parts of the job.

"Why do they work here like us laborers?" the man asked of the gentlemen-clergy.

"Well," Luciano Casimirri responded, "we hear all the time about selfishness. They are trying to do something for others."

The thought had not occurred to the worker but he accepted it.

To what extent should art and science take their places in the company of the tenets of the old faith? Decisions on that, I discovered, were the work of every day. I found evidence of that as I wandered into St. Peter's one morning to find Count Enrico Galeazzi, Governor of the Vatican State and an architect and engineer, in lively conversation with Monsignor Ludwig Kass, who had been head of the German Catholic "Center" Party in the thirties. Monsignor Kass was the last to hold out officially against Hitler as the latter rose to total power. The Vatican had called him to the safety of Rome where he had been given charge of administering St. Peter's. The count and the monsignor were discussing a $3,500 thousand-pound electronic organ which Cardinal Dennis Dougherty of Philadelphia had just sent as a gift after hearing a modest harmonium at a solemn Vatican ceremony. In Dougherty's mind a harmonium was fit only for a humble church and certainly not for the Holy See. To Monsignor Kass, on the other hand, the American-developed baby organ was a "revelation," and if Church liturgists approved, might possibly replace the noisy, acoustically ill-adapted German pipe organ in use at St. Peter's for 50 years. Could electronics replace the familiar pipes? It was a question for ceremonial specialists, but as the little machine poured sound into a basilica which had always smothered the old organ's best efforts it was apparent that one more change was on its way.

St. Peter's encountered modern technology on many subsequent occasions in my experience. One such was in the early sixties when Mario Salmi, a seventy-year-old Roman art historian, asked permission to test the bronze in the famous seated statue of St. Peter in the nave. The toe of the statue has been caressed by so many millions of the faithful that it has been worn down and shines like silver. No one knew how old it was but some thought it might even be pre-Christian—perhaps a statue of a pagan emperor which had been converted to Christian uses. Salmi, on the contrary, was sure that it was the work of Arnaldo di Cambio, a sculptor and architect of 1232 to 1310. His test seemed to prove his point. Instead of the proportion of 10 per cent lead used by ancient Romans there was only a trace of that metal. Four-fifths copper and a fifth tin, the composition of the statue was typical of the bell metal of the thirteenth and fourteenth centuries.

One of the more spectacular corrections imposed by historical research was the change in the list of popes. It was the work of Monsignor Angelo Mercati, prefect of the Vatican archives. He convinced the Vatican's highest authorities to revise the numbering of the popes in the yearbook. In that list Pius XII was the 261st successor of St. Peter, but Monsignor Mercati said that current studies, including his own labors in the archives, indicated that Pius might be only the 255th. St. Cletus, the Roman, and St. Anacletus, the Athenian, who had been considered for many years as the third and fifth popes were really the same person, Monsignor Mercati believed. Felix II in the fourth century, Christopher in the tenth, Alexander and John XXIII in the fifteenth, should also be dropped from the papal line, and Gregory VI in the eleventh century and Clement II in the thirteenth may or may not have been true heirs of Peter's powers. On the other hand, Boniface VI had been added as one who had served as a legitimate pope for a few days in April, 896, and it was conceded possible that 2 others were pontiffs—Dioscorus for 22 days in September and October 533, and Leo VIII from 963 to 965.

The old list had been largely the work of Giovanni Marangoni, supervisor of the catacombs during the eighteenth Century. Marangoni had leaned heavily on portraits of the popes in the basilica of St. Paul Outside the Walls. The St. Paul list was started in the fifth century but had not been kept up systematically until the ninth.

Monsignor Mercati's work attracted scrutiny, for much of the position of the Catholic Church rests on the belief that there has been an unbroken chain linking the present pontiffs to Peter and through him to Christ. The monsignor carefully insisted, however, that none of his changes "weakened the continuous, uninterrupted descent of the Holy Pontiff as successor of St. Peter and as Vicar of Christ."

The same re-examination in the light of new knowledge was going on in the delicate field of Biblical studies. With Pius XII's counsel of prudence but also with his encouragement, scholars concluded that substantial sections were "poetry" or even myth rather than literal history. How much was "parable" and how much an accurate report remained a subject for patient investigation.

As science made its demands and gave its contribution, so did art. The gingerly *rapprochement* of the two, with the Church insisting on art as an instrument leading onward to prayer, and artists defending the rights of self-expression and inspiration, was symbolized in a papal audience in 1947 for Giacomo Manzu. The sculptor, son of a Catholic sacristan, and a man of religious instincts, had incurred the disapproval of the Church by showing Christ totally naked on the cross and even by depicting an unclad Mary Magdalene embracing him.

He had no irreverent intentions, the artist told me. He wished merely to "show Christ close to humanity." Historically the crucified Christ had been stripped, and it fitted better aesthetically for adjacent figures to be similarly uncovered, the sculptor said. With his wife, his sister and his seven-year-old son the artist had a twelve-minute audience. He told me that the Pope, "put his hand on my shoulder and said I had this great gift and should put it to the service of the soul of man and of Christianity," Manzu said afterward. "He said I should try to avoid nudes for nudes' sake. I believe he meant by that that I should avoid exposing the sexual parts and that I should cover them."

Church officials said that Manzu would be considered again for liturgical art assignments. Manzu in turn said that if ecclesiastical limitations clashed with his artist's conscience on any project he would withdraw from it.

Cubism, abstract art, statues suspended in midair like birds in flight, the taking advantage of new effects permitted by modern materials—and even men in modern clothes mixed in with traditional Church figures as a symbol of the relevance of ancient truths to current times—began to appear in such churches as Rome's Sant' Eugenio (built in Pius XII's honor), but the reconciliation of Church and art was still only partly accomplished as the sixties began.

Change affected the clergy and the traditional Church organization even more directly. The questions were many. Should the cloisters with their severe remoteness from the world and their frequent deep poverty be modified? Would it be better for the cloistered to do "practical" work like teaching and nursing rather than concentrate so heavily on prayer? Rules were revised to let the shut-aways do more lucrative labor but the Vatican insisted that the importance and value of prayer should not be treated lightly.

Were any other modifications desirable among the clergy? The Vatican saw the wisdom of some but resisted others. Nuns were encouraged to modernize their costumes, some of which were a danger to sisters who drove automobiles, and many of which set these women so far apart from the world that their value as teachers and workers in other fields of social service was diminished. Nuns, as one slangy young American priest summed up the trend with typical male lack of consideration for feminine style, should "take those bird cages out of their hats!"

Should the changes go so far as to permit a married clergy? Some in the Church echoed Protestant ministers in arguing that man needs woman for emotional and psychological completion. Even St. Peter was a married man, to judge from Scriptural reference to his in-laws, others maintained. Celibacy for the Catholic clergy of the Latin West had not been introduced until many generations after the time of Christ. The idea of letting married men serve as deacons, preaching sermons and distributing Communion but not hearing Confessions gained ground, but in the early sixties resistance was strong against too-rapid alterations in such a sensitive field.

Liturgy, too, underwent change. Evening masses, once unthinkable, became common, and there was powerful pressure inside the Church for the use of English and other modern languages in the early part of the Mass. The Vatican showed willingness to set Latin aside in ever-larger parts of the Church cult, but few if any of the clergy believed it wise to abandon Latin for all of the Mass. The memory of how the adoption of local languages went hand in hand with nationalism and a rejection of central Church doctrines at the time of the Protestant Reformation was too vivid to permit casual tampering with one of the notable bonds that held the world Church together.

In all this re-examination the controversial "Index of Forbidden Books" was not ignored. Six thousand titles were on the proscribed list in the early sixties, 90 per cent of them obsolete, by the word of the head of the Holy Office himself—the sternly traditional Cardinal Alfredo Ottaviani. Why some of the books had been banned no one now knew, he conceded. Some were once sensational volumes now nearly forgotten. The "Index" might well be revamped drastically but no one ought to object to the fundamental idea that man needs "road signs" in intellectual and spiritual life as well as on highways, the cardinal argued. Some system for warning the faithful away from pernicious literature seemed likely to be maintained.

Of all the problems clamoring for attention and change perhaps the most dramatic was contraceptive birth control. I accompanied seminarians of ninety-two countries to the United Nations' Food and Agricultural Organization in Rome. It was agreed that they should co-operate back home with F.A.O. efforts to improve food production. More to eat, more social welfare measures, more generosity on the part of Anglo-Saxons in underpopulated areas like Australia and New Zealand and in rich countries like the United States rather than immoral population-control measures were obviously the Vatican's answer to the disturbing expansion of population and misery, at least for the present.

Would the Vatican modify its views on contraception? Would it ever reverse its stand that it is unnatural and immoral to interfere artificially with what it called the obvious purpose of the sex act—the procreation of children? One bishop confided that "If I had a hundred thousand dollars I would endow the search for a legitimate method of birth control"; for some way to limit the frequency of conception without committing and encouraging what the Church has condemned as immoral for centuries. All that could be said at the start of the sixties was that the issue of contraception haunted Vatican theologians as a capital problem of the times, but that no grounds for reversing traditional convictions were in sight.

# 29. Heaven and Earth

The real Vatican is not the colorful, paradoxical, and often anachronistic papal state recorded on the motion-picture film of tourists. It is not the diplomacy of the Secretariate of State where, as one ambassador told me, embarrassing notes go unanswered "as if you were probing at a pillow." The essential Vatican is more intangible and less visible. It is reflected in the prayerful efforts of Pope and cardinals, monsignors and simple priests, to reach out toward the sacred and eternal, toward the true and the divine.

In a sense, a Viennese priest saying his Mass, or a woman in the rear pew of a New York church, telling her rosary, achieve what Holy See officers may manage in their most elevated moments—communication with God—but even during the routine of office hours (because of the nature of the Catholic Church) Holy See functionaries are often called on to deal with what is virtually unknowable in man's relation with his Creator. Therein lies the real Vatican.

Of the many churchmen who bear such responsibilities, one whom I visited often and with pleasure was the smiling, cherubic Monsignor Salvatore Natucci, the "Devil's advocate." It was his task to screen the many appeals which streamed in from all over the world for the glorification of persons believed to be present in Heaven with God as "Blesseds" or as saints. In 1950, 741 applications were in the monsignor's files. He alone had approved the introduction of 50. Even if no more were added it would take 200 years to act on all of them. Everything written by the prospective saint had to be studied for hints to his character. Every person who had known him had to be interviewed. Hundreds of pages of testimony about his life had to be collected at a cost of thousands of dollars for travel and other expenses. Generally, unless the Pope waived the requirement, proof of the person's miracles worked through prayer had to be given.

Much about Monsignor Natucci was the opposite of what I had expected. His little office was in a modern, marble-floored building in the ancient Rome slum of Trastevere. An elevator whisked visitors up to it. The office itself was astonishingly understaffed. The monsignor did much of his own secretarial work, although an eight-foot shelf of applications for beatification and canonization sat facing him as a perpetual reminder of the years, even decades, of work which remained to be done.

Through Monsignor Natucci's small room, during the years I knew him, passed the cases of: the first "man with a tie" to be beatified, Contardo Ferrini; the first American citizen saint, Frances Xavier Cabrini, an Italian immigrant nun who died in Chicago in 1917; the first native of American soil likely to reach the Catholic altars, Venerable Katherine Tekakwitha, an Iroquois Indian native of what is now Auriesville, N.Y.; and probably the first native-born American citizen saint, Elizabeth Seton, an early nineteenth-century convert from Episcopalianism.

Each of the stories was a triumph of virtue. Ferrini, an Italian lawyer, who died in 1902, had been harassed as a child by classmates who used to sketch him with a halo, teasing him for being so "saintly." He shared a room for awhile at Messina University, Sicily, with Victor Emanuel Orlando who entered history after World War I as one of the four writers of the Versailles Peace Treaty (the others being Woodrow Wilson, George Clemenceau and David Lloyd George).

Mother Cabrini was a founder of hospitals and asylums and was chosen by Pius XII to be the Catholic Church's patron saint for emigrants—the first United States' citizen to be enrolled along with St. Patrick (patron of the Irish), St. George (of the English), St. Anthony (for those seeking lost articles), and St. Barbara (of artillerymen) as a heavenly intercessor with God.

For three centuries since her death the Canadian grave of

Katherine Tekakwitha had been the goal of pilgrimages by Catholic Indians who never forgot the way the twenty-four-year-old maiden, a convert to Christianity at eighteen, had tormented herself with penances and had fled from her Mohawk Valley tribe rather than marry and give up her treasured virginity.

Mother Seton, founder of the American Sisters of Charity, had been baptized a Protestant at fashionable Trinity Church, Wall Street, in her native New York, two years before the Revolutionary War. Converted to Catholicism on a visit to Italy, she founded an order which had 50 nun members at her death and 9,000 by mid-twentieth century.

Besides cases in Monsignor Natucci's files which reached fruition in the grandiose St. Peter's canonization ceremony, there were others which languished. Accuracy rather than haste was what mattered. The oldest pending potential beatification was that of Alberto de Albertis, a Franciscan who died in the high Middle Ages, in 1239. His case was still considered and might yet win out in the unbelievably slow grinding of Church machinery. Proof that de Albertis' cause might succeed was provided in a similar inquiry. Pope Innocent XI, the former Benedetto Odescalchi, who died in 1689, was beatified in the middle fifties with two miracles of 1690 serving as proof. Sister Maria Maddalena Cantarini had been cured of cancer of the left breast, and Ignazio Diamanti of Rome of an ulcerous condition of the tibia, according to 250-year-old documents of the Congregation of Rites. The real barrier in the path of the beatification had been political. The French Government had long blocked the case successfully because of Innocent's many battles with King Louis XIV over the latter's intrusion in Church affairs. Pius XII, centuries belatedly, overrode the Gallican resistance.

Others such as Christopher Columbus remained further from the honors of the altars. For a century churchmen, including Pius IX in the mid-eighteen hundreds, had urged the beatification of the discoverer of America on the grounds that he was a devoted layman who had explored the Western Ocean more in the interests of Christianity than in those of the Spanish throne.

But the belief that Columbus's son Fernando had been born out of wedlock stood in the way.

Perhaps an injustice had been done to the navigator by not opening a formal trial "to see what would come out," Monsignor Natucci confided to me, but the cost of financing the historical inquiry would have been prohibitive.

The idea of having a saint "with a tie" was Pius XI's. He and others felt that the mid-twentieth century needed saints closer to its own day as evidence that holiness was no phenomenon of Biblical times but a natural part of modern life as well. Accordingly, when the portrait of Blessed Ferrini was hoisted high on the gilt walls of St. Peter's for the beatification ceremony all of us in the congregation stared up at a costume that was very different from the customary ancient toga. The new blessed was portrayed as present in Heaven in the wing collar, modern trousers and elegant cutaway which he had worn as a lay professor.

Both Pius XI and Pius XII set records in raising dozens of new blesseds and saints to the altars beside revered apostles of an earlier generation. Soon everyone in and out of Rome had contact in one way or another with a person proclaimed a saint or considered for canonization. Leading the delegation of nuns to the canonization of Mother Cabrini was the sister in whose arms the saint had expired in Chicago. Now head of the order, the nun modestly begged reporters not to identify her.

At about the same time, in the months just after World War II, Bishop Clement von Galen, a six-and-one-half-foot-tall giant, a famous opponent of Hitler, was applauded as he walked past our press box in St. Peter's with New York's Archbishop Spellman and thirty other clergymen to receive the red hat of cardinal in history's largest such ceremony. By the fifties the late Cardinal von Galen was under Church investigation for beatification, and within another decade the late Pius XII himself was under such study.

Popes were curiously little favored for beatification, Monsignor Natucci commented. Founders of orders such as Mother Cabrini or Mother Seton had the support of followers who were willing to incur large expenses. Laymen such as Blessed Ferrini were known by only a small circle of acquaintances and could be studied as thoroughly as possible in relatively little time. Popes, on the other hand, with their mountains of writings and their minutely recorded dealings with so many clergymen and nations, presented a dauntingly large field of inquiry, and generally after their deaths had few advocates who cared to finance the effort.

It was Pius XII who told Monsignor Natucci that he would like to see "us do something for popes," and it was at his authoritative suggestion that the Congregation of Rites' own resources went into the beatification of Innocent XI and the canonization of Pius X—the first two popes raised to Catholicism's altars since the seventeenth century. Several other popes were under study for similar recognition: Benedict XIII, of 1724–1730; Innocent X of 1644–1655; Pius V whose death in France as Napoleon's prisoner probably marked the lowest point of Catholic prestige since the Middle Ages; Pius IX, the ill-fated last ruler of the Central Italian pontifical kingdom; and Pius XI, the blunt-talking opponent of Hitler, Mussolini and Stalin during the 1930's.

The logic of the Catholic cult had some strange consequences as many beatifications and canonizations occurred. Faith in the immortality of the soul and in the final resurrection of the dead implies reverence for the physical remains of those declared blesseds and saints. The bones of Blessed Innocent XI were exhumed by a small group of Vatican workers, were clothed in vestments of the reigning pontiff, Pius XII, and placed on exhibition inside crystal caskets under altars on either side of the nave of St. Peter's Basilica along with Saint Pius X. Lifelike silver masks covered the faces and hands.

Even less familiar to the psychology of the Anglo-Saxon world were two other events which took place in the first months of the reign of Pope John; the transfers of the bodies of two newly canonized Italian saints half the length of Italy and back again. They were Saint Pius X who was returned to his old diocese of Venice for a few weeks to fulfill the promise he had made casually before the papal election to go back alive or dead, and Saint Don John Bosco, a priest famous for his work among boys. I watched Pope John bid his farewell to the freshly repainted glass-walled funeral car carrying Pius X as the train pulled out of the Vatican railway station, and I looked on from the Venice canal banks next day as a 100-gondola procession accompanied the ballasted funerary boat to St. Mark's Cathedral for prayers and veneration. Members of Don Bosco's century-old order asked papal permission to take the saint's body to Rome for dedication of a great new "church of St. John Bosco." When the saint had visited Rome a century earlier to ask papal approval for his work among youths (whom he taught to "pray, study, do manual labor and play") he had been so little known that he was introduced to the pontiff as "Don Bosser." This time as tens of thousands of us looked on, John XXIII visited the priest's casket at the new church to pray for his Heavenly help. In the audience were scores of members of Don Bosco's order. With its 20,000 members it was already greater in numbers than the 700-year-old Dominicans or the fifteen-century-old Benedictines, and was exceeded only by the Jesuits and Franciscans, each of whom counted about 30,000.

Gathering of evidence of miracles and judging the sanctity of lives of candidates for sainthood were not the only Vatican tasks that touched on the mysteries of another world. An example was provided in connection with the huge new Catholic shrine of Fatima in Portugal. Three unschooled shepherd children had reported a series of visions of the Virgin Mary in 1917. The Madonna, they said, had called on the world to reform and repent and had warned of catastrophes if there were no spiritual improvement. Two of the three children soon died and the survivor, Lucia, became a cloistered nun. Between the two World Wars the bleak plain of Fatima became a center of intense Catholic devotion. Dozens of religious institutions were built there and hundreds of thousands visited the spot as pilgrims. Fatima became a word revered in Catholic devotion, and parishes were named for it. Lucia, a generation after the events of World War II, wrote a letter "to be opened by 1960" giving what was said to be the last of the Virgin's message. It was then, apparently, that the Vatican silently intervened. An alarming rumor had spread among many Catholics that the Virgin, through Lucia, had forecast the world's end in 1960 as a punishment for the nonconversion of Communist Russia. The Church, an intimately informed cardinal tartly told me at the time, is "run by the hierarchy, not by letters or by private visions." Nineteen-sixty went by without the nun's document being published. Caution and prudence, but not invincible skepticism, are the marks of the official Catholic approach to the occult.

On of the great Church events of recent years offered evidence of a capacity for belief—the proclamation of Catholicism's third new dogma in four centuries. Pius XII, replying to a century-long series of petitions from Catholics in Spain and other countries, sent a confidential letter to more than 1,000 bishops of the world asking whether he should proclaim as an article of faith the fact that Mary was raised up bodily as well as spiritually into Heaven after her death. Replies came promptly from all but 86. All but 22 assented and only 6 of the latter said they doubted the doctrine should be defined as a divinely revealed truth. The other 16 questioned whether the proclamation would be "opportune." Orthodox churches agree with Catholicism on all Christian dogmas published prior to 787 but do not accept more recent ones, such as that of papal infallibility, set forth in 1870, and Mary's Immaculate Conception, enunciated in 1854.

Noting the virtual "mathematical unanimity" among the bishops, Pius XII proceeded with the solemn bull advising each Catholic that if he denied or willingly put in doubt the truth of Mary's assumption "he should understand that he has fallen short in the Divine and Catholic faith." Just as Christians in 381 had proclaimed the dogma that the Holy Spirit was divine, in 432 that Mary was the Mother of God, and in 451 that Christ was both Man and God, so had the half million of us that day in 1950, exactly in mid-twentieth century, beheld another added to the 2,000-year-old list of 100 Catholic dogmas. A faith that was set and formal in so many ways had shown its vital capacity to evolve toward beliefs clearly and firmly held.

# 30.  Ecumenical Council

When the 774 theologians and bishops of the Roman Catholic Church's Twentieth Ecumenical Council met at the Vatican in 1869 for the first such assembly in three centuries, Giuseppe Mazzini, the apostle of a modern, united, democratic Italy and the foe of the theocratic central Italian papal states, wrote jeeringly: "You have come to Rome for the latest and last of the councils. The first," Mazzini added, "was at Nicea in 325, a solemn veritable baptism of the success and orderly unity of the religion which that age desired. This final council in which you will take part will prove, regardless of what you wish, that we face now the impressive fact of a religion in decline and the inevitable imminent rise of another one."

Mazzini was wrong, as Pope John could not refrain from pointing out exultantly when he addressed 500 members of commissions of preparation for the Twenty-first Ecumenical Council in November, 1960. The out-moded papal states had been swept into discard within months of the democrat's dark predictions, but the Roman church had been purified and strengthened in the process. By the time of the twenty-first council, the low ebb of mid-nineteenth century Catholic fortunes had been succeeded by such great new prestige that men of scores of religions, non-Christian and Christian alike, could talk seriously for the first time in centuries of the possibility of a common world faith or at least of a union of believers in defense of values threatened by atheism.

All such talk implied some understanding with Catholicism,

for no other religion—Christian or non-Christian—had so large a membership or such organization. To what extent would the Catholics co-operate in fashioning a common code, a joint devotion? To what degree could the Catholic Church provide leadership in that direction? It was obvious in the early sixties that the ecumenical council would give the main answers to both questions.

Even in the council's early stages of organization some of the replies were already apparent. For one thing the council, unlike the seven held during the first eight Christian centuries, was not a meeting of all Christendom. Orthodox and Protestants were excluded because of their separation from the Catholic Church. It would be an internal Catholic affair but nevertheless a religious event of no small significance. The council of 1869–70 had shown how great the interconfessional repercussions could be when it was interrupted midway by the fall of the papal kingdom. The council fathers had decreed the controversial dogma that the Pope is infallible when speaking, with full authority, on faith and morals. They had been unable to get to another proposed dogma to follow it—the rights of bishops as heirs of their own part of Apostolic and Divine authority. The shock among Orthodox, Protestants and even the "Old Catholics" who quit Rome and formed their own church at the time might have been attenuated by subsequent decisions if the council had gone on as planned. Belatedly, after a nine-decade interruption, there was a strong likelihood that council fathers would return to the bishops' rights issue. German Catholics, it was known, were pressing for such a discussion. At long last one obstacle to Christian mutual comprehension might be lowered if not removed.

Any statement by the council emphasizing the rights of churchmen outside Rome would make it easier to reach an agreement on reunion with Orthodox, Lutherans, Anglicans and others.

In the early months of the sixties the work of 700 members of council preparatory commissions was surrounded by secrecy, but one archbishop privy to part of the effort was convinced that the Catholic Church would come out of the great meeting "rejuvenated." Because of the premature end of the 1870 meeting no general review of Church custom and thought had occurred since the previous ecumenical council at Trent, Italy, in the middle of the sixteenth century. That one had been summoned at the height of the shock of the Protestant secession. Many felt it had put Catholicism inside certain rigid bonds which persisted to the present.

"The world has changed more in the past one hundred years than in ten thousand before," the archbishop commented. The council would have to face all the modifications of liturgy and attitude, "but not of basic principle" which a new era of quick travel and instant communication implied.

What could those changes be?

In the forefront was the issue of a general religious reconciliation. Hopes were limited, as Pope John, Cardinal Augustine Bea, the Jesuit Father Charles Boyer and other leaders in the reunion effort confessed, but at least some progress toward interconfessional amity was made even in the course of council preparations. A little was a great deal after centuries of interfaith warfare in which there had been both moral and physical violence.

The Catholic position on the eve of the council, as spelled out in dozens of more or less authoritative statements, was that much Christian truth and virtue existed in the Orthodox and Protestant churches, while many human failings and many "unessentials" went under the name of Catholic. If Orthodox and Protestants would agree to certain Catholic "essentials" reunion could be worked out, preserving the "good" in the ritual and characteristic virtues and ideas of the various sects.

What were the Catholic "unessentials?" Council fathers might be called upon to draw a sharp line between the two, but Catholic scholars in conferences on the margins of the preparation listed some: the Mass precisely as Latin Catholics celebrated it was only one of several possible divine services; the Orthodox cult, for one example, was rich in beauties stemming from Apostolic times and unquestionably as valid as Latin ceremonies (Pope John emphasized that in the early sixties by taking part in several ceremonies almost identical with those of the Orthodox); the heavy Catholic emphasis on Latin could be attenuated even more than it had been in recent years, with more use of English and other local languages; and there was no reason, as Jesuit Father Thomas Corbishley said with humor in London in January, 1960, why non-Catholics uniting with Rome should approve everything that passes for art in various Catholic parish churches or "the academic standards in all Catholic educational institutions."

The "good" among non-Catholics?

Many a Catholic had a lot to learn from Calvinists on how to savor the treasures of the Bible, from Anglicans on how to conduct divine services with austerity, from Lutherans on comprehending how free a gift is the grace of God, and from the Orthodox on how deeply a Christian can plunge into the mystic side of his cult, Father Boyer, the eminent Roman authority on reunion, expressed it.

At that point, however, the "essentials" of Catholicism came to the fore. Father Boyer said firmly that Catholics could admit that many members of their Church might find better examples of various virtues among certain Calvinists, Lutherans, Anglicans or Orthodox neighbors than inside their own immediate Church circle, but they could not concede that the Catholic Church would be incomplete and not the true religion of Christ until a Catholic-Calvinist, Catholic-Lutheran, Catholic-Anglican or Catholic-Orthodox reunification took place. All aspects of full Christian worship and virtue already existed somewhere inside the multifarious Catholic world, he insisted. To say less would be to deny that the Catholic religion is the true one of Christ, and no Catholic could do that without surrendering his faith.

In his first encyclical Pope John summed up tersely what he held to be the essence of Catholic unity: a single faith, one direction for the Church, the same worship, the same Holy Sacrifice (of the Mass) and the Seven Sacraments. Among the seven key sacred rites was matrimony with all that implied about the holiness of the marriage bond and the Church's objections to divorce.

Each phrase in the papal definition was subject to definition and interpretation, but it was clear that the Church insisted on much that separated Catholics and non-Catholics. The first peril in all interfaith discussions was the danger of "indifferentism" from which Pope John felt that the dogmatic and united Catholic Church, as the "one true" religion, would be the first to suffer. By indifferentism he meant the idea that one religion is as good as another and that the relative validity of rival creeds is unknowable. Having erected his bulwark against indifferentism, Pope John was cordially willing to go further in concert with the ecumenical council fathers in exploring how and whether Catholic and non-Catholic essentials could be brought together in the desired greater Christian unity.

For many Church authorities there was little immediate hope of anything but small-scale conversions. In 1,000 years of separation between Western and Eastern Christianity about 10,000,000 Orientals had returned to communion with Rome, accepting papal supremacy while retaining non-Latin rituals. Various other Easterners, worried by Communism and hungering for a wider Christian brotherhood, might re-establish bonds with Rome. Several tens of thousands of Copts in India rejoined Catholicism after World War II, and many more in a group of 500,000 Jacobite and Monophysite Christians—members of fifteen-century-old sects—convinced Rome authorities that they were ready to join the Catholic communion if various financial problems could be overcome. Schools, churches and cemeteries in India were the property of various ancient Christian communities. To accept allegiance to Rome would entail the need to build new ones. Rome lacked the funds to help.

Of 1,000,000 Coptic Christians in Egypt, Vatican officials were convinced that at least 100,000 were prepared to reunite if enough priests could be sent to the Nile delta to establish contact. No such small army of clergy was available, however.

Other Easterners whom the Vatican believed to be on the threshold of union were 4,000,000 Copts in Ethiopia, 2,000,000 to 3,000,000 Armenians, 100,000 Jacobites of Syria, 600,000 Malabar Jacobites, and 100,000 Nestorians in Persia, Turkestan and Malabar. The Nestorian Christians recognize only the first two ecumenical councils—of 325 and 381. They left the world Christian communion when they denied that Mary, whom they otherwise honored highly, was "Mother of God." The Monophysites denied that Christ had the double nature of God and man. Both the Jacobites and the Copts are Monophysites.

As the new ecumenical council approached, the Catholic Church accepted almost everything about the clergy, hierarchy, cult and sacraments of the 165,000,000 Orthodox, but the traditional offer of many Orthodox to accept the Pope as "first among equals" was rejected as insufficient by such spokesmen as Father Boyer. Some authoritative voices in Rome sought to placate the Orthodox by emphasizing that in the Catholic view Jesus Christ was head of the Church with the Pope merely his "vicar," and that infallible knowledge was attributed to the pontiff only in limited circumstances and only as head of the whole Church. However, *Kathimerini* of Athens, the conservative Greek paper, surely expressed the view of many Easterners when it commented dryly on December 30, 1958, that the "separated brothers," as Pope John called non-Catholic Christians, might better stay—at least in the Orthodox case—merely "good cousins."

Why *Kathimerini* and other responsible and goodwilled groups were dubious was all too easy to understand. Professor Amilcare Alivatos, one of the best canonists of the Greek Orthodox Church, remarked, for instance, on February 1, 1959, that his church would not accept the three Catholic dogmas added since the middle of the nineteenth century: Mary's conception without original sin, papal infallibility and Mary's bodily assumption into Heaven. In 1953 in a widely circulated booklet—"Infallible Fallacies"—a group of priests of the Church of England had underlined Anglican stands against certain "doctrinal errors of the Roman church": the papal infallibility, the Immaculate Conception of Mary, and also indulgences, the helping of sufferers in Purgatory through the merits of the members of the Christian church of all time in this world and in the other, and finally, the Catholic system of "spiritual dictatorship."

Just as doctrinal lines were drawn tightly on one side, so were they on the other. Some Catholic churchmen wanted to see the twenty-first council add another of the disputed dogmas of Mary, that the Madonna was the "Mediatrix of all Graces," the exclusive channel through which Jesus worked among men. "Not rarely,"

*L'Osservatore Romano* reported, theologians in heavily Catholic countries wanted the cult of the Virgin emphasized to a maximum, while those seeking peace with neighbors in areas of small Catholic minorities discouraged any wave of new Marian dogmas. Many who were in a position to observe doubted that the "Mediatrix" dogma was "mature."

If that tribute to Christ's Mother was not ready to be proclaimed, John, the Pope of the early sixties, was in the forefront of those honoring the Virgin. In his apartment was an old painting of the Madonna with six angels on either side chanting her praises. Mary, John told an audience, was Daughter, Mother and Wife of the Trinity. But that did not mean, as many Protestants felt, that the Virgin replaced or blocked the way to Christ and to God. "Here's the great teaching," as John told an audience in August, 1959, "we love Jesus and we love Mary. We pray that all including the separated brethren and those far off [presumably meaning Jews and other non-Christians] may revere the Holy Virgin and turn to her."

The debates were often the same ones which had gone on from the time of Luther, from those of the unsuccessful fifteenth-century ecumenical council of reunion with the Orthodox, from the fifteen-century-old quarrel which launched the Monophysite tradition, from even earlier in the very first years of the Church. With Protestantism split into 500 factions in the United States alone, the possibility that the ecumenical council or any other group could find a common denominator reconciling the "essentials" of so many rival traditions and conflicting sectarian interests was nil.

Even so, hope remained. On the eve of the council aged Pope John trusted that the spectacle of a majority of Christianity cordially united in a single faith would draw others toward Rome in the search for the fellowship which has always been a Christian aspiration. That would raise the question of the theological victors and vanquished. Should peace come through a general reconciliation with Rome, though the prospect was slight indeed, Roman theologians promised that travelers to the Eternal City would find affection and humility, an attitude replete with recognition of wrongs and errors throughout history by a multitude of the faithful, if not by the Church as such.

Was there any possibility of a general religious or even Christian accord? Talking to the Metropolitan Nikolai at the Russian Orthodox Church headquarters in Moscow in 1958, I thought as a reporter that there might be, at least eventually.

Unity? "We pray for it," the blue-eyed white-bearded churchman answered gently, "all the time."

The state of the Church under Soviet Communism? Numbers of faithful after four generations of official atheism? I thought the prelate's sighs were more significant than the answers he gave through two Communist interpreters. His church, he said, was free to work for "peace." Church attendance had fallen but there were still more applicants for the seminaries than there were places in the limited number of small Church schools allowed by the government. The Russian church, he said—in the traditional Christian affirmation—would "survive until the end of time." Deep, sad breathing punctuated his words. One cannot conclude too much from the impression of a single interview—or even after dozens of them—but my years of conversations and study as a journalist had convinced me that the hunger for religious unity was a reality of the mid-twentieth century which this Catholic Ecumenical Council, by its size, unity and leadership, could surely stimulate and at least partially satisfy.

# 31. The Pope's Divisions

The then Secretary of State Cardinal Tardini chuckled during one of his few press conferences as he discussed the Holy See's never very opulent finances.

"Oh yes," he said, "we have one other expense: the defense budget!"

The cardinal took the military potentialities of the 100 Swiss, the few dozen gendarmes, and the several score volunteer Palatine and Noble Guardsmen no more seriously than Stalin had when he reportedly asked derisively: "How many divisions has the Pope?"

Counting all the middle-aged, round-waisted dentists and salesmen in the Palatine Guard and all the "Black" aristocrats in the nobles' platoon the Pope had little better than a company, let alone a division. Yet the Church led by the pontiff was a worthy and tested opponent of the ideology which was Stalin's own great military auxiliary. In many parts of the world Catholicism was the decisive factor in resisting Communism. In Poland it was the rallying point for resistance to Russia. In Western Europe its political movement—Christian Democracy—provided many of the great postwar governmental figures: West Germany's Konrad Adenauer; France's Robert Schuman and Georges Bidault and to some extent the piously Catholic Charles de Gaulle, Italy's Alcide De Gasperi and Amintore Fanfani. Portugal's António de Oliveira Salazar, and Spain's Generalissimo Francisco Franco were also Catholic political leaders. In Latin America and Africa, too, the Church was an effective intellectual and political rival of Communism.

How many divisions did the Pope have? Certainly the equivalent of many armies. An eminent member of the postwar American ambassadorial corps once criticized one of his colleagues to me on the grounds that "he assesses everything else well—economic positions, military and so forth—but he always leaves out what I consider a major factor, moral influence." The things men consider important enough to fight and perish for certainly belonged in the diplomatic balance, the ambassador said.

Were the Pope's "divisions" ready to die for their faith?

Not all, to be sure. Father John Considine, director of the Latin American Bureau for the United States Catholic hierarchy, counted the ardent members of the Rome communion south of the Rio Grande at only 10 per cent. Among the United States' own Catholics he put the figure at a notably high 50 per cent. Pius XII, it is known, never accepted the estimate that the planet's Catholic population was half a billion, about 55 per cent of the world Christian total. In many Latin areas less than half the baptized Catholics attended Sunday Mass even though most preferred to "die in the Church," receiving the final sacraments.

"The day is over when Europe could see religious wars," one of the main Curia archbishops remarked to me. "Europe's Catholics would not fight another of them."

One reason for this was the low ebb of religious feeling in countries like France where there were only two-thirds as many priests in relation to the population as there had been eighty years before. Another reason, the prelate said, was on the positive side; the happy fact that most men now recognize that the sword is no means of carrying religious conviction to others.

The Pope's "armies" were not of one mind on all matters, and in that lay both weakness and strength. Even the very question of whether the "sword," or governmental power, should be used to help the faith was one on which some disagreed. No one, of course, believed that the tragedy of Europe's old Catholic-Protestant wars should be repeated, but states like Franco's Spain and Salazar's Portugal felt, for example, that the freedom of the press should be cut to what Pius XII implicitly condemned as a scandalous minimum. In Spain, Catholics were of a divided conscience under Franco in the early sixties, many elderly bishops seeing the dictatorship as a lesser evil compared to a return of the Communist terror of the thirties, while numbers of the younger priests, seminarians and Vatican officials argued quietly thàt there was need for far more democratic freedom and social justice of the liberal Christian Democratic type.

The weakness of the papal "armies" lay in the scandal, confusion and wasted strength of internal quarrels over what appeared to be fundamentals. Their strength was rooted in the very ferment of speculation and the earnestness which gave rise to the discord. That there was variety under the cover of world Catholic unity was indubitable. For me it was summed up on the one hand by the nuns of Father Foucauld, a new order of bandannaed, lumber-jacketed sisters "married to poverty" after the fashion of the heroic former French army officer of the early nineteenth century who died a mute and unprotesting martyr among the Mahometan nomads of the central Sahara. On the other hand there was the contrast, in my memory, of the eighty-year-old Bishop Louis Marmottin of Rheims, France, who told me why he had permitted champagne bottles to be depicted in the fifties in the restored stained-glass windows of his medieval cathedral. Catholicism had always stayed close in spirit to the workers, depicting in her churches their shovels, axes, saws, oxen and all the other labor paraphernalia and products, the bishop of the champagne vineyards told me. A frown shadowed his face, however, as he talked. What was behind my interest?

"Ah, the champagne!" the octogenarian finally had it. "You're not sure abôut it! That's Methodist, isn't it? You have many Methodists in America, don't you?"

It set him reminiscing.

"You know I had a Methodist general from the United States here just after the War. He edified me. Whenever I said grace he bowed his head reverently."

It was not the reaction the bishop of nominally Catholic but anticlerical Frenchmen had been accustomed to encountering.

"When the first anniversary of the United States troops here occurred, the general invited me to his mess. There was a cake with one candle. The general sliced it with his saber and speared me the first piece. You know we French would consider that very droll but he intended it as an honor!"

Different people, different customs, the bishop was gently advising me. A glass of champagne, so long as it was not followed by too many others, had nothing wrong with it either from the view of the drinker or from that of the producer and seller, the bishop was sure. He took an occasional champagne with pleasure himself. What was all right in life was acceptable, in a sense, in church. However far the champagne-bottle windows seemed from the be-sandalled sisters of Father Foucauld, all Catholics worshiped the same God.

One who was hard at work tying the Catholic world together in the early sixties was the Archbishop of Milan, Giovanni Battista Montini. Sixty-three years old in 1960, he was the first cardinal appointed by John XXIII and the likeliest to succeed to the Papacy. How feasible and how desirable was religious unity in a world of many views; a world of sincerely held and often contradictory opinions? In a sense it was a question not only for Catholics concerned about the impact of their faith but also for all men seeking a peaceful life together. In a 1960 pastoral letter to his huge and industrious North Italian diocese, "Italy's Brain," the possible future Pope gave his answer:

Men must be permitted to live side by side in freedom and in calm but that does not mean that they should consider all religions equally good or that they should give themselves up to skepticism with regard to the various faiths. They should not feel that "a religion which is positive, exclusive and organized such as the Catholic" is by that fact a foe of religious unity. The truth is that the world's inability to achieve a unity of thought and to end spiritual divisions is the real reason society is "so deeply unhappy, so poor in ideas and enthusiasm, and so lacking in the shared spiritual concepts which are its own inner joy, nobility and strength."

The cardinal balanced his affirmation of man's right to live in freedom and peace with an assertion of the Church's privilege to woo men to its view of Christ without coercion, and of a united community.

The story of the Church's efforts to win the world would con-tinue far into the future; few churchmen foresaw an end to it. Among the few were the critics and opponents of the Church in Rome who said, in 1869 when Pope Pius IX and his Curia fell through a rotted floor at the more than 1,000-year-old Church of St. Agnes, that it was symbolic of collapse. Ninety years later, almost to the day, John XXIII recalled the episode and empha-sized the fact that, on the contrary, the Church's prospects were even more promising nearly half a century later.

How bright was the outlook? Father Calogero Gliozzo rated it brilliant in the Jesuit *Civilta Cattolica* in November 1958. The Roman pontificate, he said, could be sure—as it looked out over 500,000,000 faithful organized inside a united church and directed by a hierarchy professing full fealty to the Papacy—that its posi-tion was one of social importance and of "extraordinary moral power."

Certainly the Vatican had a unique place in the economy of the planet. It directed the oldest of human institutions. It har-bored the oldest court. The Catholic Church remains, as H. P. R. Finberg said at Oxford in February, 1960, "the most wonderful institution our world has known."

The future? Surely it would be no smooth path, or would it be all victories. It is a paradoxical law of the Church that good times are bad and vice versa, an archbishop-diplomat told me. Yugoslavia's Catholics were lukewarm, in Rome's view, until Marshal Josip Broz Tito's Communist persecution infused new fervor in the forties and fifties. Spain's vocations flourished after the Civil War slaughter of 7,000 clergy. The eradication of the 3,000,000-member Catholic Church in Communist China, in the view of some of the most eminent Vatican officials, might prove to be merely "a burning off of the fields as a prelude to a success-ful resowing." Quietly during the decades of Communist power in Russia, priests trained at the "Russicum" college in Rome ready to go into a de-Communized Soviet bloc to fan the Christian re-ligious fires known to be still alight in a third or so of Soviet hearts.

Hopes for the future rested in good part on the emergence of

one world. With communications and transportation nearly in-
stantaneous and common ideas capturing men's minds, some
Vatican observers felt that for the first time since the Roman
Empire there was a possibility of one world religion.

In glimpsing that possibility they did not lose sight of the
obstacles. The bitterness which separates Christians was reflected
in the early sixties when a top-level delegation of an important
non-Catholic Western nation called on the Pope. The Vatican
offered limousines to carry the visitors to the Holy See. The
driver of one of the cars went back to his churchman superior
later, his face troubled. He held a religious medal the pontiff
had given one of the secondary members of the mission as a
souvenir.

"He left it on the seat," he said. "He told me to sell it!"

As for the political importance of the Catholic Church, it has
none and will have none until there is a religious revival among
its members, in the opinion of one Catholic envoy of a major
Western power. Catholicism in France and in the rest of Europe
is at its lowest level in centuries, and even in Africa—continent
of quick conversions and high Vatican hopes—Islam is winning
adherents more rapidly, other students of the Church commented.

There was much truth in all that, but there was another side.
I called on Cardinal Maurice Feltin in his unobtrusive villa headquarters in Paris and found him content and confident. The days
of devout Saint King Louis were far in the past, but the first
years of the twentieth century when clergymen had been in-
sulted on French streets were also vanishing from memory.
There was a Catholic elite present everywhere in France—in the
universities, in government, in literature, and on the stage.

"A man working with tar in the streets sprayed my white
cassock and ruined it a few days ago," a Dominican in Rome
told me. "But that happens very rarely now."

If the era of Catholic willingness to use force to get converts
was slipping into the past so was the ferocity of non-Communist
anticlericalism.

Some in Rome sadly conceded many misdeeds and misjudg-
ments of the past. I knew one priest who suffered at the memory

of the Church condemnation of the genius, Galileo. While some regretted past wrongs, still others stepped forward in the hope of doing future good. Year after year the ancient Beda College gave a score of "late vocations" to the Church: Anglican ministers who wished to become Catholic priests; a jet pilot who felt the call of the altar; a man of seventy-eight who died of a heart attack a few months after his ordination; the vice-president of the famous American Cavanagh Hat Company, Father Garvan Cavanagh, who decided at forty-nine, after successful careers as a capitalist, army lieutenant colonel, Connecticut State legislator and park commissioner, that "Life is more than piling dollars on dollars."

Month after month the thousands came to the papal audiences "seeking," as a prelate who arranged invitations for tens of thousands, commented. Aging papal courtiers conserved their memories of the most notable of those encounters; of the American Protestant admiral who just before a private audience, told his flibbertigibbet wife not to "goof now, honey"; or of the Kennedys who swarmed all over the Papal Library in 1939. One young Kennedy toyed with Pius XII's pectoral cross, others combed his book collection, while the father of the future President of the United States lamented: "I want to be known here as 'Ambassador Kennedy' not as 'the father of those nine children.' "

Underlying the fundamental serenity with which the Vatican regarded the future in the early sixties was the same confidence, based on Christ's biblical promises, which the Orthodox Metropolitan Nikolai had expressed to me in 1958 in Moscow. It might one day be necessary, in the event of a Communist advance, to move the Church's headquarters temporarily out of Rome to Spain or some other area, a cardinal of the Curia remarked in the early postwar years, but even if that should happen he believed that the Church's future was assured. Nothing I ever learned as a reporter made me doubt it.

With the Bible and tradition and reservoirs of study represented by the Church's hundreds of colleges and universities, the Vatican faced the challenge of the new era of space travel. Genesis would seem to be inadequate and out of date with its message to man to "subdue the earth," but Church followers had Pius XII's words to an astronomical congress on September 20, 1956 to point the way to the adaptation of ancient religious thought to the reality of a whole new scientific generation. "The Lord God," he affirmed, "meant to set no limits to man's efforts at conquest." All creation was man's province and if he were no longer "imprisoned on this earth" space travel would provide new occasions to observe "the things which God has spread in such profusion through the world."

With Communism a major problem at mid-century it was clear that the Kremlin had a formidable foe in the Vatican and in religion. "A concept worked out in twenty-five free post-Athenian centuries is certainly, one must believe, better adapted to human nature than is one which has been experimented with for only four decades behind the Curtain," one of the topmost American policy-planners told me as I described my experiences as a reporter in Budapest during the 1956 Hungarian Revolution. The church and its message of brotherhood and peace would survive.

For the Vatican reporter there was, finally, the rarest of satisfactions. The plight of most of his journalistic colleagues was to live with the ephemeral. He, instead, touched the eternal.

# Index